Cultivating Minds

Cultivating Minds is a ground-breaking unification of the ideas of Simmel and contemporary perspectives in cultural psychology. The theoretical framework proposed is based on an integration of core philosophical, sociological, and psychological ideas from the intellectual traditions of pragmatism, socioculturalism, constructivism, and transactionalism.

The primary focus of this work is on cultivation as a metaphor for identity formation. According to this idea, each and every human agent is an active producer of its own development and identity. The cultivation model expands existing sociocultural perspectives by elaborating further how an individual's cultivation of the sociocultural environment is mediated through artifacts and objects. A concept exemplified by the identity processes demonstrated by graffiti artists. The idea of the cultured mind has profound implications not only for cultural psychology but also for theories of identity and, of course, development. It affects the way we understand the formation of the self and, in the end, the growth of the person. The result is a theory which captures the convergence between identity, culture and development in new and far-reaching ways.

Urs Fuhrer is Professor and Chair for Developmental Psychology and Educational Psychology at the Otto-van-Guericke-University, Magdeburg (Germany). His major research interest is in the role of culture in human development, specifically the relation between family education and child development, identity formation and violence within the family.

Cultivating Minds

Identity as meaning-making practice

Urs Fuhrer

LONDON AND NEW YORK

First published 2004
by Routledge
27 Church Road, Hove, East Sussex BN3 2FA

Simultaneously published in the USA and Canada
by Routledge
29 West 35th Street, New York, NY 10001

Routledge is an imprint of the Taylor & Francis Group

Typeset in Times by
Keystroke, Jacaranda Lodge, Wolverhampton
Printed and bound in Great Britain by
MPG Books Ltd, Bodmin
Cover design by Jim Wilkie

This publication has been produced with paper manufactured to strict environmental standards and with pulp derived from sustainable forests.

British Library Cataloguing in Publication Data
A catalogue record for this book is available from the British Library

Library of Congress Cataloging in Publication Data
Fuhrer, Urs, 1950–
Cultivating minds: identity as meaning-making practice/Urs Fuhrer.—1st ed.
p. cm.
Includes bibliographical references and index.
ISBN 0–415–30713–9
1. Identity (Psychology)—Social aspects. 2. Culture—Psychological aspects.
3. Meaning (Psychology) I. Title.
BF697.5.S65F84 2003
155.2′5—dc21 2003010850

ISBN 0–415–30713–9 (hbk)

Contents

Figures and table

Foreword

Jaan Valsiner

Social scientists and their gardens of delicious ideas:
the making of new knowledge

Urs Fuhrer's book brings to our contemporary psychology an example of careful nurturing of sophisticated scientific ideas. These ideas have been known in the history of the social sciences—yet they have neither been appreciated, nor advanced further. Fuhrer succeeds in the latter. Through his cultivating mind, historically known ideas become tools for further scientific understanding.

Scientific ideas have complicated fates. It is often the case that an idea becomes famous—is reiterated in textbooks and glorified in the talk of scientists—and through all that attention – becomes futile. It may become a consensually accepted "black box" explanation—easy to use, but lacking actual explanatory value. Notions such as "evolution," "rationality," "dualism" and the like are widely used, fiercely disputed—and yet not overcome by new ways of thinking on the classic themes. Likewise, hero myths about scientists of the past have often been built by historians of science—without a focus on the scientific thought as a tool for further discoveries.

Fuhrer creates no myths. Starting from reintroducing the classic system of ideas developed by Georg Simmel a century ago, and linking these ideas with the semiotic ecology tradition developed within contemporary cultural psychology, Fuhrer provides a unique theoretical synthesis that is likely to be a new cornerstone for our basic knowledge about human *psyche.* Contrary to the brutality of post-modernist thought, which has broken knowledge in the social sciences into many tiny fragments, Fuhrer builds a general perspective that is both universalistic in its theoretical realm and context-specific in its empirical elaborations. Cultivating minds operate within behavior settings, and cultivate those settings. Whether the latter entail adolescents playing basketball at midnight, or the thrill of writing graffiti, the construction of personal identity out of its opposite state (described as "nothingness" by Jean-Paul Sartre) is at stake. It happens as human beings live their lives. Cultivating a mind is not an option, it is a human-species-specific characteristic.

Probably the most critical breakthrough in our thinking about the human *psyche* that is fostered by the cultivating-minds perspective is the necessity to change the axiomatic mindset of the social sciences from one version of an evolutionary perspective to another. Instead of assuming the prevalence of *natural* selection—without intentional or teleological concepts—social sciences need to consider the primacy of *artificial* selection of directions for *further* development of persons and societies. Cultivating a garden—a real one rich in pear trees, or a knowledge one that is rich in complex idea systems—requires the presence of a forward-thinking and strategic gardener, whose actions make it possible for the garden to bear the desired harvest. "Natural" selection of theoretical ideas in the social sciences would amount to the dominance of the common-sense fashions (or socio-moral ideologies) of the given time and society. Surely some of these ideas "win" over others—but no novelty becomes constructed that way. In contrast, "artificial" selection of the theoretical ideas for further cultivation opens the door for new fruits to be harvested in our garden of knowledge. Yet some thinker has to select the seeds for cultivation. Fuhrer's careful use of the ideas from the past of our social sciences to construct new understanding of the issues of identity is an excellent example of how history of a science can innovate—or cultivate—its future. In measured and intellectually sophisticated ways, the author leads the reader through the basics of developmental science. The notion of probabilistic epigenesis (developed by Gilbert Gottlieb) is creatively integrated into the texture of cultivation.

In sum, *Cultivating Minds* lives up to its promising title—the theoretical knowledge tree of the reader is prepared to bear new and delicious fruits in future seasons. Perhaps that is the best that can be expected from any good book.

Jaan Valsiner
Clark University

Preface

This is a humanist book about human development. It is also a book about culture and identity. This book is also the result of a developmental psychologist's long-term fascination with continuity and change and with the link between culture and mind, especially in its relationship to identity issues. The multitude of approaches that are united behind the label identity are in need of a comprehensive theory. Such a theory has not emerged in recent decades, and thus its seekers often end up turning to theoretical systems of the past that are built around the idea that the self, identity, and personality are products of sociocultural life. Thus, this book signals a new appreciation of the value and relevance of cultural psychology to identity developmental studies.

Throughout this book, the terms identity and self are used interchangeably. Identity is the understanding of the self as generally outlined by William James (1890) and his followers (see Lapsley & Powers 1988). He presents the subjective self (the "I") as a coordinated, fourfold experience of agency, continuity, distinctness, and reflection. In addition, it includes an objective self (the "me") and that forms the basis for the subjective self (the "I"). Of course, I take note of many overlaps between James's vision and more recent philosophical analysis, but my cultivation research on identity issues is guided more by the broader sweep of the former.

As it is emphasized repeatedly in this book, cultural developmental psychology is process-focused. It treats human psychological phenomena such as identity or the self not as entities, but as processes. These processes include culture (as action opportunities) in the form of functioning mediating possibilities through which individuals experience themselves as agents of their own meaning-making activities or practices to cultivate their selves. That is, identity or the self are constantly constructed, reconstructed, or socially co-constructed through culture. And cultural mediation always occurs as part of a larger unit of social-cultural structuration referred to as context, setting, situation, activity, action, or practice. In this sense, culture places limits on individual behavior while at the same time offering opportunities. If we generalize this point of view, then cultural psychology deals with the analysis of those mediational processes through which subject and world mutually create each other. Person and culture are seen to coevolve or transact, and this approach implies, of course, a strong orientation towards development (cf. Cole 1996, Lang 1988, Valsiner 1997).

Many major theorists who have become recognized as proponents of that view are frequently mentioned in the contemporary literature—the American pragmatists William James, John Dewey, and George Herbert Mead, the Russian work in the Vygotskyan tradition, William Stern's personalistic approach, and, most important for the present book, and hardly known in the psychological literature, Georg Simmel's work on culture and individuality.

All these authors have some common origins in their theorizing about the person–culture relationships. Most of these authors also have their philosophical roots going back, among others, to Vico, Hegel, Marx, Herder, Kant, and von Humboldt, though some of them have largely remained hidden in the more recent debate about what identity is all about. Quite well-represented these days within cultural psychology are the four intellectual traditions and frameworks that go under the labels pragmatism, socioculturalism, constructivism, and transactionalism. A reconsideration of the possibilities for a cultural psychology of identity formation, however, is an integrative form of engagement and struggle with the judgements of all four frameworks.

The aim of this book is thus to analyze both the historical and the conceptual connection between these lines of theorizing. I will also show how contemporary theorizing on identity formation in developmental psychology could benefit from the core ideas shared by these authors. The problem, however, is: in what way does culture transform into a person's identity? And in what way does personal identity transform into culture? To capture this problem we do not—as cultural psychologists—have to search for the order as found in cultural facts. Rather, by arguing along with Jerome Bruner, we have to study "order imposed by human beings" under developmental issues so "that the central concept of a human psychology is meaning and the processes and transactions involved in the construction of meanings" (Bruner 1990: 33).

In this line of reasoning, the idea of identity as a meaning-making practice towards the expansion or creation of action possibilities for the growth of the self will be the leitmotif of *Cultivating Minds*. From here, human beings transact through their cultural opportunities as media, thereby cultivating the world as well as their identity in structuring their I–world relationship with regard to their developmental possibilities.

For meanings, to use Bradd Shore's (1996) challenging expression, are always "twice born." They are instituted in culture, the canonical or sociocultural meaning *of* some thing or act, and the idiosyncratic meaning *for* some individual on some occasion. The challenge for cultural psychology is to understand how these two aspects of meaning processes transact to ensure both a communal life and, at the same time, to permit the idiosyncratic play of individual imagination, personal projects, or personal identity. Still, however, little attention is given to the complexities of these meaning transactions with respect to identity issues.

This insistence in cultural developmental psychology that contexts and meanings are to be theoretically represented as part and parcel of the psychological system and not simply as influences, factors, or conditions external to the psychological system distinguishes cultural developmental psychology from other forms of developmental psychology that also think of themselves as contextual (or situated). The aim of cultural developmental psychology is not first to separate the psychological system from its nonpsychological context and then to invoke some type of external setting effect or outside situational influence on psychological functioning. The aim and the challenge are rather to recast or soften the contrast between person and context so that the very idea of a context effect will take on new meaning because our theoretical language for psychological description will be contextual or rather "culture-inclusive" from the start (see Valsiner & Winegar 1992).

The distinction between cultural developmental psychology and other contextualistic approaches in developmental psychology (see Bronfenbrenner 1979 or Lerner 1989) is subtle, important, and easy to overlook because all approaches to developmental psychology that emphasize "context" share much in common. Cultural developmental psychology shares with all forms of developmental contextualism the assumption that the mind of human beings can only be realized through some situated process of person–environment transaction or dynamic interaction. For example, one of the aims of a cultural developmental psychology has been to move toward concepts of interdependence, described in terms of persons and contexts as "creating each other" (Briggs 1992), as "making each other up" (Shweder 1991), as "shaping each other" (Cole 1996), or a "co-constructing each other" (Valsiner 1997). Beyond that general point of similarity, however, cultural developmental psychology should be understood as a rather special type of contextual approach.

In the concept developed in this book, the relevant contexts for the realization of mind are meaning-making acts or practices. The primary emphasis is on contexts thought to be relevant for the realization of the self in the sense that such contexts are the means or the medium for transforming the self into a distinctively functioning identity, the distinctive way that people think, act, and make meaning in the light of particular goals, intentions, motives, values, and practices. The notion that the psychological self, or identity, is guided by meaning and that meaning is largely socially constructed attracted increasing attention in the second half of the twentieth century (see Bruner 1990, Kegan 1982). However, despite admissions that meaning lies in self as much as in culture, mainstream developmental psychology shows little evidence today that carries a deep commitment to understanding identity or the self as primarily a developmental problem of meaning making (see Josephs 1998 for a notable exception).

Rather than focusing on the psychological development in terms of the emergence of the self as a meaning maker (Kegan 1982) and semiotic subject (Shweder & Sullivan 1990) or on the social construction of meaning (Gergen 1991), the present book tries instead to develop a concept of identity where identity as a meaning-making practice refers to people's use of a range of cultural artifacts as opportunities towards structuring I–world relationships. According to the view presented here, which bears a close affinity to the ideas of Georg Simmel, and John Dewey, and also traces its genealogy back to Hegel, an artifact is an aspect of the material world that has been modified over the history of its incorporation into goal-directed human action. By virtue of the changes wrought in the process of their creation and use, artifacts are simultaneoulsy ideal (conceptual) and material. They are ideal in that their material form has been shaped by their participation in the interactions of which they were previously a part and which they mediate in the present (see Cole 1996 for a more elaborated discussion of the material-conceptual nature of artifacts).

Along these lines of reasoning, Georg Simmel's cultivation principle expands interactional, dialectical or dialogical attempts of the self in that individuals together with their artifacts create a landscape of action possibilities through which individuals experience themselves as agents of their own meaning-making activities or practices to cultivate their selves. I will use Simmel's view of culture as a platform for the conception of a new paradigm, called *Cultivating Minds*, which goes beyond the well-known triadic or triangular models of cultural mediation of the mind as they are, for example, rooted in both the Peirceian pragmatic and the Vygotskyan tradition.

The *first chapter* focuses on identity formation through semiotic mediation. Here, I want to show that Vygotskyan theorizing opens specific ways of thinking about how sociocultural processes enter into identity formation. From Lev Vygotsky, I want to go on from Charles Sanders Peirce's famous dictum that I–world relations are of triadic semiosis, to William James' classic analysis of the self, and to George Herbert Mead's important modification of the Jamesian position.

The *second chapter* describes the many parallels between today's cultural developmental psychology and thoughts on this topic at the beginning of the twentieth century. Here John Dewey's insights into the larger question of meaning still remain among the most penetrating to date. I then outline William Stern's systemic personalism with its theorizing on the developing personality, which brings me even closer to a culture-inclusive conception of identity formation. In a similar vein, Ernst Boesch translates culture into action-theoretical terms. Finally, the chapter turns to Mihalyi Csikszentmihalyi and Eugene Rochberg-Halton's application of philosophical pragmatism to a theory of culture and self. However, all of these approaches share some limitations with regard to a truly cultural developmental model of identity formation.

Before introducing Simmel's cultivation model, however, the *third chapter* outlines the origins of his work on culture. The chapter reconstructs the scientific developmental line from Herder's conception of culture as a medium for reflective thought, to Hegel's idea of the embodiment of mind in culture, to *Völkerpsychologie* with Moritz Lazarus' famous metaphor that man is both the creator and the creation of culture. Finally, the chapter describes Simmel's outstanding work on culture and individuality.

The *fourth chapter* captures the concept of cultivation. In Simmelian terms, cultivation means increasing the total value beyond that of the natural mechanism. For Simmel, the essence of culture is that subjective mental energies—Simmel called them the "individual law"—obtain objective cultural forms which are independent of creative life-processes, but which are re-subjectified into the subjective cultural forms and so bring the bearer to a more subjective development of his/her identity. Cultivation is thus a value-increasing process which works both on the cultural mind outside of us and on the mental mind inside of us.

The *fifth chapter* treats the concept of identity as the psychological dimension of I–world relationships. From the view of cultural developmental psychology, identity can be described in terms of meaning-making actions or practices associated with being an "I" in a particular cultural community. To outline this idea, I refer to the transactional (pragmatic) world view in which action becomes the link between individual and environment. A transactional approach assumes that the aspects of a system, that is, a person and context, coexist and jointly or co-constructively define one another and contribute to the meaning and the nature of the holistic event.

The *sixth chapter* captures the problem of how identity depends for its continued existence on a process of cultivating the external as well as the internal, one that can and should transcend the individual's growth of his/her self. While the perspectives mentioned above were mainly concerned with guided structure formation, they gave little notice to this second aspect: man's self-referenced creative activity, where meaning transaction means that people themselves experience their identity as meaning processes, and they—as agents—actively create it through culture. Identity formation is always "twice born." It is constituted through culture, the sociocultural meaning *of* some thing or act, and the idiosyncratic meaning *for* some individual on some occasion. Thus, identity as meaning-making practice always works simultaneously on two minds—it is a process of cultivating minds.

In the *seventh* and *eighth* chapters, I present some empirical material to illustrate how the cultivation model can be used in framing the phenomenon of identity formation on the boundary of person and culture. The attempt to rethink development as cultivation or meaning-making practice leads to the question of what makes artifacts such as behavior settings (*sensu* Barker 1968) attractive media for the study of children's cultivation.

In the *seventh chapter* I tackle this question by using data from diaries of 184 children aged 10, 12, and 14 years who lived in a rural Swiss town. The data show that the cultivation approach is useful in demonstrating that children's developmental opportunities within a more or less stable environment are limited. In fact, the qualities of both the physical milieu and the social rules are important aspects of behavior settings in terms of opportunities for cultivation to children's self-specific needs.

The *eighth chapter* focuses on graffiti, which, I argue, creates as a media for the self an aura of exclusivity. From graffiti a person's inner character can be read as by their handwriting. This is to say that letters, words, and symbols could be the building blocks to define character and a graffiti artist's rebellious need to express him/herself. Interview data for graffiti artists show that graffiti is, at least in part, a strong quest for identity formation. The case-study analyses make clear that the great challenge of graffiti is to create a design framework for the letters in one's name which is so personally tailored that it allows for the expression of one's identity. Since the set of letters in the name that one paints does not change, the way they are painted is what conveys meaning. And this is what it means fully to cultivate one's self. In contrast to the traditional concept of socialization, in the cultivation model, nonconformity can also be positive and stimulating for developmental growth.

Taken together, *Cultivating Minds* captures the convergences between identity, culture, and development in new ways. That is, the components of culture themselves become—or do not become—parts of individuality, and so on. Thus, one cannot theorize about identity as a psychological quality of the I–world relationship without reflecting on culture and development as well as on cognition and motivation. Indeed, it is precisely the fact of both culture and development that provokes the question of identity as an act of structuring I–world relationship by creating self-related developmental possibilities through meaning-making practice. These action possibilities, then, serve two functions: first, they are a medium for identity formation, and they are the motive force in re-formation of one's identity; while, second, they are the motive force in the sense that when a new identity has been achieved, as in the combination of the old I–world relationships, they open up new action possibilities. This is another way of saying that two systems, the internal mind and the external mind, each with discrete properties, when meaningfully combined, create a new system with emergent properties. This is at the heart of the *Cultivating Minds* paradigm.

In fact, the idea of a "cultured mind" has some far-reaching implications not only for how psychologists need to think about culture but also for how psychologists need to think about identity and, of course, about development (see Valsiner, 2001). This is not simply the problem of thinking about culture and mind but specifically the challenge of conceptualizing "culture in mind" and—mostly overlooked by developmental psychologists—"mind in culture." This is a developmental conception of the mind—both the internal and the external mind—and of identity as well, with far-reaching consequences for understanding the formation of the self, and, in the end, the growth of the person.

Acknowledgements

The inspiration for this book began in the late 1980s when I prepared the lecture *Introduction to Cultural Psychology* at the University of Berne in Switzerland. During this work I discovered the forerunners of modern cultural psychology, among them was the German philosopher Georg Simmel. He explored in an imaginative manner the interface between human beings and the cultural forms with which they are surrounded. When I read Simmel, I had to recognize that personal development, although it pertains to the individual, can be reached only through the mediation of culture. Simmel regards this reciprocal process of cultivation as emerging out of the use of purposively formed objects in such a way that human beings create forms of culture that take the process of the development of individuality into real and ideal spheres beyond the individual.

These ideas around the formation of individuality were later elaborated at the University of Magdeburg in Germany during the late 1990s. Here I found the intellectual space for a dialogue between philosophy, sociology, and psychology on the work of Georg Simmel. In this enterprise and in the ideas that grew from it, the contributions of Georg Lohmann and Jürgen Wittpoth were invaluable. The book, then, was conceived as such in 1998–99, during my sabbatical at the Laboratory of Comparative Human Cognition (LCHC) at the University of California, San Diego. The happy mix of intellectual stimulation and leisure that the laboratory afforded made it possible for me to begin to transform numerous strands of my research and thinking into a coherent form that eventually (and slowly) became this book.

Early versions of most chapters were presented at workshops, conferences, and planning groups at various institutions in Germany and the United States. Those include the seminar *Culture and Development* at the University of Magdeburg, the graduate seminar *Advanced Developmental Psychology* at the University of California, San Diego, and several interdisciplinary workshops on *Cultivation Research* at the University of Magdeburg. However, I particularly want to thank the participants of the LCHC's Monday lab meeting at the University of California, San Diego for their thoughtful reflections on an early manuscript of the book.

The book has also benefited from many comments and suggestions from numerous colleagues and students over the years, among them were Ernst E.

Boesch, Eugene Halton, Ingrid E. Josephs, Florian G. Kaiser, Henning Breuer, and Peter Tulviste. The final version, much altered and somewhat trimmed, has benefited greatly from many comments and suggestions. Michael Cole, Yriö Engeström, Eugene Subbotsky, and David H. Feldman read through the final version of the book in its entirety. Comments by four anonymous reviewers and by Jaan Valsiner of an earlier version of the manuscript were helpful in turning it into this final form. I am also grateful to Katie Vann for her assistance in revising the English text of this book.

A very special note of thanks goes to Michael Cole at the Laboratory of Comparative Human Cognition at the University of California, San Diego, who allowed me to spend my sabbatical at the LCHC to complete my manuscript. His faith in the book project and encouragement over the half year period at La Jolla was a critical factor in the book's completion. Thanks to his enthusiasm, encouragement, and criticism.

U F
Magdeburg, Germany
December 2002

Part I

Identity and the significance of meaning

Chapter 1

The semiotic mediation of the self

Neither Vygotsky nor post-Vygotskian lines of research offer a complex account of the role of sociocultural processes in identity formation. However, at first, I want to consider how sign-mediated action can be transformed into mental action or the self. Second, sociogenetic theorizing, in attempting to state rigorously the conditions of those mediations, includes many of the issues for the *Cultivating Minds*. Beginning with Peirce's powerful criticism of the "spirit of Cartesianism," to James' classic analysis of the self, and to Mead's important modification of the Jamesian position, the pragmatists consistently sought to undercut the "dichotomy" of subject and object.

Vygotskian and post-Vygotskian view of the self

For Lev Vygotsky, development is defined as a "true" sociocultural process (cf. Cole 1996, Daniels 1996, Van der Veer & Valsiner 1991). Children participate in collaborative activities in which shared thinking provides the opportunity to be involved with experts in joint cognitive processes, which the child may internalize for later use. Along these lines of reasoning, Vygotsky (1981) emphasized the significance of psychological tools and their place in his theory of internalization, which has recently received a great deal of attention (e.g., Rogoff 1993, Wertsch 1991). This mechanism helps us to grasp the intimate connection between the social nature of higher-order psychological functions which are, at the same time, semiotic. Intellectual abilities are assumed to develop with cultural means through the joint participation with more skilled partners.

Although Vygotsky never developed a theory of identity, his approach provides the foundation for such a theory through its linking of the social dimension with the development of the higher mental functions. I thus assume that the close genetic relationship that he saw among the forms and functions of social, egocentric, and inner speech might also be reflected in the process of identity formation. Speech, as a multi-functional and self-reflexive means in social interaction, shapes consciousness by creating new functional connections among psychological processes, among them, processes of identity formation. Since language is both a social institution as well as a communicative system, its development socializes thought at two levels: the child joins a sociocultural system and a world of others to whom he/she speaks. This point is critical for any truly social theory of identity. In an early paper on consciousness, Vygotsky (1978) makes the point: "We are aware of ourselves in that we are of others; and in an analogous manner, we are aware of others, because in our relationship to ourselves we are the same as others in their relationships" (Vygotsky 1978: 29). If the personal pronouns are the origins of the self, they owe their uniqueness to their determination by the system of language and discourse. That is, consciousness of self is only possible if it is experienced by contrast. We use "I" when we are speaking to someone who will be "me" in my address. It is this condition of dialogue that is constitutive of person, for it implies reciprocality "I" becomes "me" in the address of the one who in his/her turn designates him/herself as "I."

If I take this point seriously, Vygotsky's position about the social origins of psychological processes take a renewed force. Language sets the opportunity of a dialectic between the individuality of every act of discourse and the linguistic system, and this dialectic is constitutive of the development of subjectivity. This, in turn, implies that our consciousness of self and other emerges as the product of the use of language in concrete situations of interpersonal communications.

Consequently, the self is social in two senses: first, it is one pole of a dyadic relation constituted repeatedly in the ongoing praxis of discourse; while, second, the dyad itself is structured by its position within a social system which has a structure that systematically links social indexicality and grammatical structure in an ongoing sociocultural dialectic. Thus, all the higher mental functions take on a basically social, communicative, and dialectical, or even dialogical cast. Mediational means, or cultural tools, are resources for individuals that shape, empower, constrain, and have the potential to transform action. Such means, in turn, facilitate and make possible both a relationship to oneself and to others, serving the function of communication and social contact. It is, however, still an open question of how to think of mediated action as the unit of analysis for a sociocultural approach to identity formation.

In a similar vein, the post-Vygotskian tradition alters the very essence of how a psychological inquiry itself is conceived and realized in its practical and epistemological functions. The very formulation of the traditional question of what the psychological processes such as self, identity, personality, and cognition are like has been changed into the question of how these processes are possible. In this sense the psychological inquiry can be viewed as the context in which the psychological phenomena can be co-constructed and reconstructed.

In the framework of Gal'perin's (1967) theory the concept of internalization bears the very important meaning not just of developing something new, but of creating a specific realm of action that yields additional possibilities for adaptation in humans. By characterizing an action through object-related parameters and by demonstrating the identity of the objective operational content of action in the course of its transformation into mental form, Gal'perin emphasized the objective status of mental actions. This perspective of internalization in no way implied that meaning is "within the individual." However, the main concern here is to clarify the conditions under which the child cooperating with an adult within the zone of his/her proximal development comes to be able to perform a new action on the internal plane. The function of the "social other," however, has been explicated mostly with regard to its cognitive aspects. Moreover, the role of the social dimension in the co-construction of meaning and self remained in the background of this research line.

In contrast, the concept of the co-construction of meaning—shared understanding—is central to the post-Vygotskian research line in the US (cf. Cole 1996, Rogoff 1993, Wertsch 1998). For example, Rogoff's idea is that children's cognitive development occurs in the context of guided participation in social activity with more experienced partners who support and enhance children's understanding and skills in using cultural tools. Although Rogoff's elaboration is consistent with the Russian line of post-Vygotskian theorizing, it places more emphasis on the role of children as active participants in shared activities. In contrast to Gal'perin or Davidov, Rogoff is also quite critical of the concept of internalization and employs instead the concept of appropriation through participation. Thus, the concept of shared social activity is used here as the explanatory mechanism for children's growth. However, it is only one pole of the gradual process of subjectification of a new activity by the child. As a consequence, neither the operational content of new activity forms that must be mastered by the child nor the transformations of this activity's psychological structure are analyzed in this approach; the psychological mechanism of the formation of new cognitive processes, which then regulate the child's action, remains unspecified (see Stetsenko & Arievitch 1997). The focus on intersubjectivity, although highlighting the important dimension of the co-construction of the self, stops short of explaining how the self or identity really emerge in shared activities.

From this brief exposition of the two research lines in the post-Vygotskyian psychology, one can conclude that, though they have many common standpoints, each of these research lines focused mainly on only one of the two indispensable aspects of development within self-processes—namely, either on social interaction or on internalization—while somehow neglecting the other aspect. However, I believe that the efforts of both approaches still need to be synthesized—and to be elaborated to the externalization side—to produce a fully fledged account of identity or the self.

With this as the conceptual background, however, I would like to turn to the zone of proximal development (ZPD) metaphor, which has become a most popular construct in research bearing on human development (see Cole 1996, Valsiner 1997). It is a theoretically grounded construct understood generally as a person's readiness to learn and develop in a particular area or zone. Yet, the significance of this simple allusion to a person's bandwidth for potential growth may ultimately lie in that it requires us to study humans in the very process of discontinuity, of change, and synthesis. It requires attention as to how social forces help to constitute the zones through which individuals may possibly develop, and as to how these become part of a menu of action opportunities. Vygotsky (1978) notes an aspect of all developmental phenomena that is generally overlooked in identity research and which is of equal if not greater importance than identity status or styles. This is the ZPD, defined by those [mental]

> functions that have not yet matured but are in the process of maturation, functions that will mature tomorrow but are currently in an embryonic state. These functions could be termed the "buds" or "flowers" of development rather than the "fruits" of development. The actual developmental level characterizes mental development retrospectively, while the zone of proximal development characterizes development prospectively.
>
> (Vygotsky 1978: 86–7)

As Valsiner (1997) notes, in order to understand the process of internal development more clearly, Vygotsky provided an operationally defined example that is often confused with the definition of the ZPD. In fact, it is the distance between the actual developmental level as determined by individual problem solving and the level of potential development as determined by problem solving under adult guidance or in collaboration with more capable peers. When now the ZPD is considered in the context of identity formation, as a higher psychological function, the original definition makes most sense. It may have primacy or be latent at the individual level. On the social plane, however, certain conditions or zones must be encountered before personal identity emerges. That is, identity formation through social interaction occurs mostly through different means and activities available in a person's immediate culture. In the context of identity development, two children may be identical twins yet one may develop a particular personal identity and not another one when development occurs in different contexts. What the latter observation illustrates is that many of the characteristics of development are context-dependent or situated. Moreover, activity settings mediate personal identity through routine activities embedded in everyday life that are linked with action opportunities. These include formal and informal "curricula" for both personal and cultural identity development. Some settings have significant others and patterns of social interaction relevant to modeling and the acquisition of mediational tools. As active ingredients of culture, it is not difficult to see how these vary by group composition, ethnicity, class or gender. From here, it follows that activity settings have their own ZPD. Personal identity is an individual cognition, whereas cultural identity is a socially shared cognition. Both identities change during a person's lifetime through social participations in various activity settings that mediate change.

One implication of the ZPD concept, then, is that at the sociocultural level the interactions among groups cast certain models for identity formation at the individual level. Depending on the context, certain zones for identity development are either structured for individuals to enter into or shaped by individuals themselves when they entered them, on the basis, for example, of the salience of affinity of group/cultural aspects. Some groups, like individuals, may explore and undergo crises while others may simply conform to ascriptive norms with respect to forging a cultural sense of self. A sociocultural view of development must account for both, social-to-individual as well as individual-to-social processes in explaining the development of any type and process of identity formation.

In this sense, identity research must examine contexts in which identity is under transforming shifts (see Penuel & Wertsch 1995). For example, studying identity within social-movement organization meetings or communities of learners provides insight into the way that individuals and groups can struggle against dominant discourses of their identity to co-construct a different way of speaking about themselves and develop new forms of action (see Lave & Wenger 1991). Taking mediated action as the unit of analysis, however, allows me to ask a different set of questions about the way individuals use cultural tools to create their identities. The sociocultural framework to identity formation asks us to focus on specific questions about the mediational means or cultural tools that people employ to construct their identities in the process of different activities and how they are put to use in particular actions. When identity formation is seen in the sociocultural framework as shaped by mediational means or cultural tools, then questions arise as to the nature of the diversity of cultural tools and why one, as opposed to another, is employed in carrying out a particular form of action. In this regard, Vygotsky provided little guidance on how to examine these processes in identity formation. Although Penuel and Wertsch (1995) have offered a Vygotskian view to identity formation, their sociocultural approach to identity is not sufficiently elaborated.

George Herbert Mead's contribution to the social origin of the self

With the concept of the "looking-glass self," Charles Horton Cooley (1902) described his view that the self recognizes itself via a process of self-reflection of the reactions of others, which function as a mirror. This conception was developed further by George Herbert Mead (1934), who stressed the role of "the generalized other." In Meadian terms, people gain a sense of identity through seeing themselves through the eyes of others. Via their judgements, one's identity is formed. Because the person takes on the attitudes of others, he becomes conscious of the self as an object or individual and thus develops identity. For the generalized other is that sign dialogue that constitutes reflective thought, consisting in the dialogue between social self and social environment and internally between the interpretive spontaneity of the "I" and the internalized others comprising the "me." Many psychological approaches to identity development are grounded in the basic assumption that identity develops in "I–me" dialogues (cf. Bruner 1990, Damon & Hart 1988, Kegan, 1982).

In terms of the framework I have advanced so far, individuals can take the perspective of the objects they own to gain a view of themselves through the symbolic meanings of their possessions. But what has been argued so far also indicated that people can understand and evaluate others in terms of their artifacts. In this way the identity of other people becomes visible in objectified form too. Mead argued that there is more to significance than purely conventional meaning. Mead's "conversation of gestures" (derived from Willhelm Wundt), although retaining the idea of signification as a communicative dialogue, holds that the generality of gestural communication is found in the gestures themselves. Mead's concept of the "generalized other" derives from his attempt to develop a broad theory of sociality that could include reflective intelligence as an emergent property of nature. Along the pragmatic lines of theorizing, Mead attempted to undercut the modern dichotomies of thought and action, individual and social, by viewing mind as a social, communicative act. In a similar vein, structure is not dichotomized from its manifestations but includes its "instances" and embodiments. For Mead, these relations constitute the individual but do not appear as other things in its experience; the world constitutes the thing but does not appear in the thing. In our experience the thing is there as much as we are there—our experience is in the thing as much as it is in us.

Coming back to Mead's theory of the self, for the generalized other it is the sign dialogue that constitutes reflective thought, consisting in the dialogue between social self and social environment, and, internally, between the interpretive spontaneity of the "I" and the organized and internalized others comprising the "me." Thought itself is an internal dialogue for Mead, as it is in James' (1890) theory of the self that Mead inherited, and in Peirce's semiotic. Thus he could say, "our experience is in the thing as much it is in us" (Mead 1934: 613), for it is in the communicative act as a whole, and not solely in an individual or social subject, that meaning is located. Unfortunately, the original understanding of Mead's (1934) concept of the role model has been narrowed, so that psychologists today tend to call the behavioral patterns of another person the "role model" (Damon & Hart 1988). This view overlooks the fact that, according to Mead, any object—on the basis of its "symbolic significance"—can exercise this effect.

He expressed this idea in *Mind, Self and Society*, where he wrote that inanimate objects can serve as elements of the "generalized other" or as role models. Thus, the ability to be, at one and the same time, I-myself and the other, whereby the other may be a person or also an artifact, gives the other meaning as a symbol. At the same time, Mead emphasized the dialectic of differentiation and integration that can be regulated via role models. Thus, the origins of personal identity in early childhood are seen in the child's developing notion that he/she is distinct from his proximal environment (see Kegan 1982).

Like James, but unlike many other self theorists, Mead argued that not only persons but also physical objects could act as true elements of the generalized other, and that culture, instead of being reducible to an underlying elementary form or structure, acts as the means for a dialogue between social group and its environment:

> Any thing—any object or set of objects, whether animate nor inanimate, human or animal, or merely physical—toward which he acts, or to which he

> responds, socially, is an element in what for him is the generalized other . . . Thus, for example, the cult, in its primitive form, is merely the social embodiment of the relation between the given social group or community and its physical environment—an organized social means, adopted by the individual members of that group or community, of entering into social relations with that environment, or (in a sense) of carrying on conversations with it; and in this way that environment becomes part of the total generalized other for each of the individual members of the given social group or community.
>
> (Mead 1934: 154)

The general other of a child, said Mead, is variable and "answers to the changing play of impulse," yet even this level of the generalized other is universal in form. The generalized other asserts increasingly universal standards as it grows. Standards that impart objectivity to the given situation, and whose realization it is the task of the situation to achieve. This is not the colorless, bland, unmediated objectivity proclaimed by positivism and denounced by many structuralists and symbolic interactionists, but an objectivity whose elements (the individuals and their indications) form perspectives within it and give it the character of a mediated unity.

However, identity is more than simply a passively internalized set of societal attitudes and prescriptions. That is, the individual reality is a social product, but not a passive replica of beliefs and attitudes transmitted by socialization agents. Rather, it consists of a unique intersection of perspectives which are integrated and transformed during social interaction, but which nevertheless reflect "the unity and structure of the social process as a whole" (Mead 1934: 144). Early on, a child can only adopt the perspective of a specific person with whom he/she interacts directly, and thus internalize the attitudes of that individual. Subsequently, the child is able to adopt the perspective of several specific others simultaneously and thus comes to see him- or herself from the viewpoint of, for example, his/her whole family or group of playmates all at once. But Mead speaks of a fully developed self only when particular attitudes are generalized into an internalized set of representations of larger social units and society as a whole.

I propose that this kind of process can equally be applied to the link between artifacts and identity. Initially, young children learn the range of meanings of material possessions through observing and imaginatively taking part in others' interactions with their possessions. They do not only learn their instrumental uses, but also observe people acting toward others in terms of material symbols. Through social interaction and communication, such as in the family and in peer groups, children may soon develop a more integrated and complex representation of their material objects as part of their identity.

To give a simple example, as the little girl comes to understand what it means to be a mother through enacting this role with her dolls, the dolls become embodiments of the cultural meanings of motherhood: the social role of mother and the personal attributes of a mother. This, in fact, is the primary meaning of the term "role model" for Mead (1934), a representation of the community that becomes internalized as the generalized other. Moreover, by simultaneously taking the perspective of self and those of others, individuals come to understand the meanings of their own possessions as parts of their identity.

During an individual's development of identity, this *triadic* nature of the identity–possession link—self, other, artifact—is gradually extended beyond the reflected appraisals of specific others. With the evolving identity, reflexive evaluation in terms of possessions derives from a generalized set of internalized sociocultural meanings, transmitted not only in direct social interaction but also through social institutions, such as schools or the media. Identity is thus significantly affected by an evaluation of the total symbolic significance of one's own possessions. They form a sign-complex—a symbolic *Gestalt*—of identity. Even dwellings and houses are vital sources of memories, places of get-togethers and traditions, a shelter for those persons and objects which define the self. Overall, identity is seen as a social self-dialogue.

However, neither symbolic interactionism nor sociogenesis can provide a comprehensive theory of meaning that seems to be the goal of the ongoing restructuring of identity theories. Along these lines of criticism, a new set of canons about the nature of identity began to emerge, rather more "transactional" concerns. Through interacting with, and reflecting upon, our material possessions, we evaluate ourselves on the basis of their symbolic meanings without requiring the physical presence of others. In other words, transactions with cherished possessions are communicative dialogues with ourselves. This means that, in part, our sense of identity is established, maintained, reproduced and transformed in our relations with our possessions.

Charles Sanders Peirce's semiotic of the self

More recently, those interested in semiotics have become increasingly aware of the contemporary relevance of Charles Sanders Peirce (1931–1935), who not only founded pragmatism but also founded modern sign theory. Peirce defined the sign as a triadic process rather than a dyadic structure and viewed meaning as essentially relational:

> A sign . . . is something which stands to somebody for something in some respect of capacity. It addresses somebody, that is, creates in the mind of that person an equivalent sign, or perhaps a more developed sign. That sign which it creates I call the interpretant of the first sign. The sign stands for something, its object. It stands for that object, not in all respects but in reference to a sort of idea, which I have sometimes called the ground of the representamen.
>
> (Peirce 1931–1935: 2.228)

Peirce thus argues that a sign only has meaning in the context of a continuing process of interpretation. Thus, a symbol, in his view, is given its meaning by its interpretation as a law, general rule, or convention. Because each sign is part of a continuous temporal process of interpretation, his theory is intrinsically process-oriented—and therefore incompatible with structuralistic definitions of sign and meaning *à la* de Saussure or Lévi-Strauss.

In this chapter, I will describe, in a step-by-step manner, a synthesis. The synthesis, it may be recalled, takes off from the seeming discrepancy between Peirce's and Mead's internal conversations, i.e. their theories of how thought works. For Mead it was I to me and present to past. For Peirce it was I to you and present to future. To describe the discepancy in this way, however, rests on some prior assumptions. I will discuss three major ones. First, I am assuming that, for Peirce, thought is always an I–you conversation. But he also sometimes described thought in ways that seem incompatible with the conversational metaphor. The pragmatic maxim, for example, seems to make the thinker into a logic-machine, examining events like a scientist looking for empirical invariants. The notion that thought is dialogical and comparable in any way to a chat between friends or neighbours, is simply too imprecise and loose to fit the (early version of the) pragmatic maxim. Even the sign–object–interpretant, semiotic definition of thought, which is quite different from the pragmatic maxim approach, is not particularly open to the conversational model. For one thing, neither sign, object, nor interpretant are, for Peirce, persons. The communicating persons are tacked on to two ends of the semiotic triad, making it a pentad. The internal triads themselves are structures of meaning, not human agents. The sign does not talk to the interpretant, nor is it at all clear how the interpretant could talk back or respond to the sign.

Although the semiotic theory of thought is not as incompatible with the dialogical metaphor as the pragmatic maxim is, it is not particularly open to either. However, I somehow personalized and conversationalized the semiotic triad by equating it with the temporal phases of the self, the sign–interpretant–object becoming the I–you–me. In other words, I took Peirce's three, somewhat different definitions of the self—those associated with the pragmatic maxim, the semiotic triad, and the I–you conversation—and showed how the conversational definition could include the other two.

Second, Peirce did not explicitly use the word "I." He simply used "self" or the pronoun "he." When the self talks with the upcoming self, Peirce described the conversation as being between the present self and future self or "you." But there are good arguments that Peirce's present self was about the same as Mead's "I." In the context of discussing Descartes' "cogito" Peirce (1931–1935) referred to the "I" as the power of voluntary action and the idea of an unconstrained cause of some future events.

Since this associates the I so intimately with freedom, and since, for Mead, the present and the I are the locus of freedom, it does not seem unreasonable to refer to Peirce's self of the present as the "I." However, for the Peirce–Mead convergence it is not necessary that Peirce's "I" be exactly the same as Mead's. All I need to show here is that they both use the I as the semiotic sign, i.e. as one element of the semiotic triad.

Third, in the internal conversation only the present self or I can speak. That is, action can go on only in the present, not in the future or past. Since speech is action, speech too can go on only in the present. And since the present of the self is the I, only the I can speak. The me and the you can only listen and be spoken to. If they were to speak, they would have to do so in some way that transformed them into the present, thereby allowing them, indirectly, to use the communicative powers of the I.

Having laid out the framework surrounding the Peirce–Mead synthesis, I can now turn to its substance. As I explained above, the semiotic interpretation of the I–you–me triad is the core of the synthesis. Along this line of reasoning, I am using the word "structure" to refer to the general relationship among present, future, and past aspects of the self. These temporal phases can be called the I, you, and me, and they can be semiotically mapped as sign, interpretant, and objects. This gives the structure of the self three parts which I will refer to as agencies: the past–me–object; the present–I–sign; and the future–you–interpretant. From here, the pure semiotic triad of sign–interpretant–object is abstract and general. It does not include, or necessarily imply, an addressor–addressee or utterer–interpreter. This additional pair is present only in concrete situations, i.e. when the triadic meaning is actually communicated. In these cases we have the communicator, the semiotic triad by and in which the communication goes on, and the communicatee. This adds up to five places, i.e. a pentad (see Chapter 6 for the tetradic conception).

This is still not quite complete, however, because there is no reason to view the pentad as a hexad. To explain the move from a five-place pentadic to a six-place hexadic scheme the concept of reflexivity is needed. Most communication is linear, between addressor and addressee, but it is also, in part, reflexive, i.e. between the addressor and him- or herself. In other words, the semiotic stream of communication not only goes out to the listener, it also goes back, reflexively, to the speaker.

That is, the speaker communicates (1) in semiotic triads (2, 3, and 4) to the listener (5) but in addition the speaker communicates reflexively with him- or herself (6). Figure 1.1 shows, albeit in quite inadequate spatial terms, what the six-place relation looks like. The speaker communicates to the listener, via semiotic triads, in a linear manner. But at the same time the speaker, using the listener as a kind of mirror, communicates back to him/herself. Thus, the speaker in the hexad is counted twice, once as communicator and once as reflexive communicatee.

The hexad "contains" the triad in the same way that the overal structure of the self contains its contents. The containment is functional rather than spatial or physical. It is a triad within a triad, the inner being subordinate to the outer. More generally, the I–you–me triad emerges from the primates, defines our lines of primates, contains the other semiotic structures and processes, and is the common denominator, and therefore the democratizer, of all the self agencies. Along this line of theorizing, the concept of structure is used in three ways: (1) it mediates between variants and invariants of democracy; (2) it decenters the Cartesian self without eliminating it; and (3) it unifies Peirce's theory of the semiotic self.

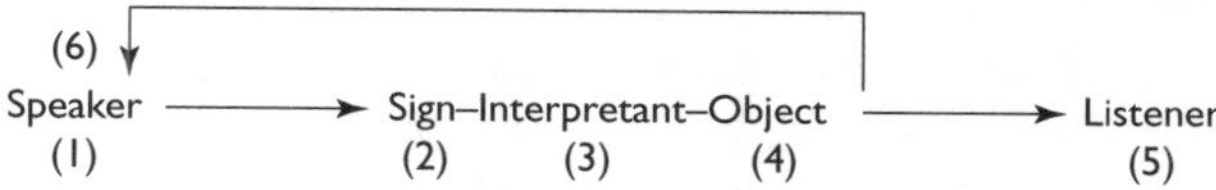

Figure 1.1 The communicative hexad

That is, "decentering" suggests that the self is still there, after the decentering process, but more spread out, dispersed or in some way decentralized. If the self is decentered externally, from its environment, as Copernicus did to our planet and Darwin to our biological species, the self becomes less important and its environment more so. If the self is decentered internally, as Freud did with the unconscious, there is still a self, albeit a more dispersed, after the decentering.

Here, the pragmatists had a form of decentering that combined the external and internal modes of semiotic mediation. Externally the self will be made less isolated by being partially incorporated into the social. Much of this decentering will be covered in Chapter 2. Internally, the pragmatists decentered by dispersing the self among the three agencies: I, you, and me. Descartes' monological, unitary self was spread into three communicating parts. Thus, the I–you–me structure offers an intermediary position between the over-centered Cartesian ego and the effaced or eliminated post-structural one. It is neither unrealistically centered nor unnecessarily reductionistic. It is neither socially isolated nor socially absorbed. Rather it is in a balanced, interpenetrating relation with society. It disperses agency throughout the semiotic triad, but nevertheless recognizes human agency.

Thus, the notion of structure is the missing key to Peirce's semiotics of the self. He never mapped the self onto the semiotic triad, i.e. he never explained what part of the self was the sign, what part interpretant and what part object. In fact, if the self consisted solely of a word or words, he did not explain how the self is *sui generis* and irreducible to language. If pragmatism is America's greatest contribution to philosophy and Peirce is the greatest pragmatist, then the problem of Peirce's semiotics of the self is an important piece of unfinished business in America's cultural history.

Concrete objects and the "me:" William James' selves

Another issue that should be considered here is the relation between concrete semiotic objects and the rather abstract notion of the "me" as a continuous and underlying semiotic object. William James (1890) used the term "the empirical self" to refer to all of the various ways people think about themselves. And it was James who had the idea that things one owned were part of the self. He went on to group the various components of the empirical self into three subcategories: the material self, the social self, and the spiritual self. For James, the social self refers to how we are regarded and recognized by others, whereas the spiritual self is our inner self or our psychological self. It is comprised of everything we call *my* or *mine* that is not a tangible object, person, or place, or a social role. Our perceived abilities, attitudes, emotions, interests, motives, opinions, and wishes are all part of the spiritual self. In short, the spiritual self refers to our perceived inner psychological qualities.

Finally, James' material self refers to tangible objects, people, or places that carry the designation of *my* or *mine*. It is epitomized by the well-known and often quoted passage on the material self in William James' *Principles of Psychology* (1890):

> The *Empirical Self* of each of us is all that is tempted to call . . . *me*. But it is clear that between what man calls *me* and what he simply calls *mine* the line is difficult to draw. We feel and act about certain things that are ours very much as we feel and act about ourselves . . . In its widest possible sense, however, a man's Self is the sum total of what he can call his, not only his body and his psychic powers, but his clothes and his house . . . his reputation and works, his lands and horses, and yacht and bank account . . . If they wax and prosper, he feels triumphant; if they dwindle and die away, he feels cast down.
>
> (James 1890: 279–80)

A good deal of research supports James's intuitions regarding the close connection between possessions and the self (cf. Belk 1992, Csikszentmihaly & Rochberg-Halton 1981, Dittmar 1992, Habermas 1996), social-psychological (Hormuth 1990), and developmental issues (Fuhrer & Josephs 1999). People spontaneously mention their possessions when asked to describe themselves. Already Gordon Allport (1949) argues that the process of gaining identity progresses from infancy to adulthood by extending the self through an expanding set of things regarded as one's own. These "things" can include memories, skills and relationships with other people, but, by implication, subsume material possessions.

Hall (1898) discusses the role of clothes in children's early sense of self as important extensions of their awareness of their physical self. But infants appear to establish a special relationship with just one or two physical objects during the first two years of their lives, usually a cuddly toy which is used for comfort and reassurance. Winnicott (1953), in particular, focuses on the peculiar status of this treasured object as the first "not-me possession," for which he coins the term transitional object. He isolates two main processes which account for the immense importance of this object. First, children establish an affective relationship with their cuddly toy because it symbolizes the nurturing person in the sense that it provides comfort and security. And, second, transitional objects play a significant role in the beginning development of a self–other distinction: the cuddly toy is perceived partly as self and partly as belonging to the environment. More recent contributions on transitional phenomena propose explicitly that early possessions play a significant role in the successful individuation and construction of a sense of personal identity in very young children (e.g. Mitscherlich 1984). Essentially, because children learn to treat their transitional objects as a substitute for the absent nurturing person, they gradually come to discover themselves as entities separate from their nurturers, and as persons who interact with an external physical environment.

However, even this very early development of a self–other distinction and the meaning of treasured possessions are subject to social influences. For example, Furby and Wilke (1982) found that the type of preferred object and the way infants interact with it reflect gender stereotypes. As early as the end of the first year of life, girls tended to prefer soft arousal-reducing objects and boys solid, arousal-stimulating possessions. However, Stanjek's (1980) cross-cultural investigation on transitional possessions in West Germany, rural India and East Gabon indicates that the special importance of the first treasured possession for self-development may well be a Western cultural developmental phenomenon. He found that neither Indian nor Gabonese children had any special objects at all, but had almost continous body contact with the nurturer. In contrast, over 70 per cent of West German children needed at least one such object to be able to go to sleep. This finding implies that transitional objects may serve culture-specific functions for self-development (Gulerce 1991).

The particular aspect of the role of early possessions in self-development becomes even clearer when the patterns of children's interactions with respect to objects are scrutinized. Numerous investigations document the frequency and predominance of quarrels over toys during play activities up until the age of about four or five years (cf. Ramsey 1987). Thereby the possessiveness in preschool children often is interpreted as an expression of individuality and self-awareness, rather than as a manifestation of acquisitiveness. This progressive developmental step means children's concern with defining the boundary of self as distinct from others, which is expressed by claiming possessions as "mine" and by commenting on the possessions of others: "your." The notion of a developmental phase finds support in investigations which discovered that the use of possessions as a predominant category of self-definition declines somewhat after about four to five years of age (cf. Damon & Hart 1988).

There seem to be several reasons for this. First, possessions serve a symbolic function; they help people to define themselves. The clothes we wear, the cars we drive, and the manner in which we adorn our homes and offices signal to ourselves (and others) who we think we are and how we wish to be regarded. People may be particularly prone to acquire and exhibit such signs and symbols when their identities are tenuously held or threatened (see Wicklund & Gollwitzer 1982). These functions support Sartre's (1956) claim that people accumulate possessions to enlarge their sense of self.

Second, possessions also extend the self in time. Most people take steps to ensure that their possessions and mementos are distributed to others at the time of their death. Although some of this distribution reflects a desire to allow others to enjoy the utilitarian value of these artifacts, Belk (1992) has argued that this dispersal also has a symbolic function. People seek immortality by passing their possessions on to the next generation.

Third, people's emotional responses to their possessions also attest to their importance to the self. A person who loses a wallet often feels greater anguish over a lost photograph than over any money that is missing. Similarly, many car owners react with extreme anger when their cars are damaged, even when the damage is only slight in physical terms. Likewise, many people who lose possessions in a natural disaster go through a grieving process similar to the process people go through when they lose a person they love (see Belk 1992).

Finally, the tendency to value self-relevant objects and entities even extends to letters of the alphabet. When asked to judge the pleasantness of various letters, people show enhanced liking for the letters that make up their own name, particularly their own initials (Nuttin 1987). This "name letter effect" provides further support for James' assertion that our sense of self extends far beyond our bodies to include those objects and entities that we call *ours*.

Indeed, the self begins to use possessions to symbolize the self. The problem is that the more the self becomes identified with symbols outside the self the more vulnerable it becomes. At this point, James goes on to write that the sudden loss of one's possessions results in a "shrinkage of our personality, a partial conversion of ourselves to nothingness" (James 1890: 124). To prevent its annihilation, then self forces us to be constantly on the watch for anything that might threaten the symbols on which it relies. The constituents that become central components of the self are those in which a person invests the most psychic energy (see Rochberg-Halton 1986). And currently the symbols of the self tend to be more of the material kind. If psychic energy is invested in a home, furniture, a retirement plan, or stocks and shares, then these will be the objects that must be protected in order to ensure the safety of the self. The advantage of identifying the self with possessions are obvious (see Csikszentmihalyi & Rochberg-Halton 1981, Dittmar 1992). For example, the man who drives a Rolls-Royce is immediately recognized by everyone as someone successful and important. Objects give concrete evidence of their owner's power, and the self can increase its boundaries almost indefinitely by claiming control over greater quantities of material possessions. Objects are, however, not the only external symbols by which the self mediates itself. Kinship and other human relationships are also very important. We invest a great deal of attention in those who are close to us, and thus they become indispensable to our sense of who we are. Especially in societies where fewer material possessions are available, ties with others are the central, defining components of the self (cf. Markus & Kitayama 1991).

Thus, each person's goals are to a great extent similar to those of everyone else. After these goals are reasonably satisfied—or blocked beyond hope—we then turn our energies to developing our own unique potential, to achieve what the psychologist Abraham Maslow (1968) has called "self-actualization." It is also at this point that, more often than not, the images of the self that people create are not intended to represent the self as it is, but rather as it *ought to be*. Such discrepancies are, of course, entirely functional, in that they potentially serve the purpose of propelling the individual toward more desirable states of being (see Boesch 1991 and Josephs 1998 for a more detailed view on this point).

Overall, I have now shown that Peirce, Mead, and James all had concepts that linked the me to nonpersonal objects, i.e. to the it-as-object. The structure of the self as an I–you–me system, i.e. as a three-point reflexive self-awareness, is the basic source of semiotic power. The reason we think about concrete objects, such as the french horn, the mountain bike, the Rolls-Royce, or the inline skates, is that we can thereby think about ourselves. The reflexive structure of the self originates and generates semiotic power in somewhat the same way as the heart pumps blood. All semiotic energy is a more specific form of energy that flows through the life of the self. Perhaps the word "life" is not a bad metaphor for the power of the structure. Because the self is alive, i.e. because it is a self-aware, I–you–me system, it can engage in the processes of the psychologically living. Without this semiotic life or self-awareness we could not think at all.

Chapter 2

The self as act

John Dewey's insights into the question of meaning still remain among the most penetrating to date. Both the study of change and the inseparability of aspects of psychological systems are firm transactional underpinnings of this approach. William Stern's systemic personalism brings me even closer to a culture-inclusive conception of identity formation. In a similar vein, Ernst E. Boesch builds his cultural-action theory upon a model of a human who is a meaning-making subject. And, finally, synthesizing Peirceian, Jamesian, and Deweyan pragmatic theorizing, for Csikzentmihalyi and Rochberg-Halton meaning is transaction.

Meaning as "trans-action:" John Dewey's pragmatic theory of meaning

In the spirit of the neo-Hegelian idealism, Dewey—like pragmatists Charles Sanders Peirce or Josiah Royce—proposed that the purposive act is the starting point for understanding how people make meaning. In his seminal 1896 essay, *The Reflex Arc Concept in Psychology*, Dewey criticized the concept of the reflex arc on the grounds that it had failed to take into account the situatedness of the organism. He argued for the, then, novel thesis that the interests and habits of the organism, its active situations, influence how its stimuli are chosen. That is, a response in one context can serve as a stimulus in another, and all stimuli are contextualized within the act. Dewey proposed that the reflex arc concept should be reconceived as organic coordination, in which the purposive concrete act is the starting point. One of the implications of Dewey's argument, which grew into his mature formulations of pragmatism, is that "psychic behavior," that which forms the self, is an organized coordination that includes the external object, representation, and resultant conduct as interdependent phases of itself, thus linking self and world.

After 1905, Dewey increasingly turned his attention to the construction of a "philosophy of culture" (see Hickman 1998). Most importantly for the present book, *Knowing and the Known* (1949), written in collaboration with Bentley, represents Dewey's attempt to move beyond the models of "self-action" utilized in classical philosophy and the "interactional" models of modern mechanistic physics in order to develop a "transactional" way of thinking that honors the dynamic features of human behavior. Thoughts and feelings emerge simultaneously through our efforts to coordinate our behavior within the soil and sunshine of our physical and social environments—we live *through* the environment. It is therefore essential, Dewey insisted, that we recognize the initial unity of transaction between human nature and the rest of nature. Experience for Dewey is simply what occurs when we carry out transactions with our environment. Dewey worked to develop the implications of this crucial insight throughout his long career.

Consequently, the focus of his interest is to conceive the individual mind as a function of social life. For Dewey, the mind—broadly conceived to mean the embodied human self or the growing person or the social individual—is developed in an environment which is social as well as physical. The mention of "development" of the individual mind introduces Dewey's belief that we do not start as selves—we *become* selves in the process of social living. Individuality, in his terms, is not originally given but is created under the influences of associated life. His point here is not just that what was potential becomes actual when provided with the proper conditions, as, for example, the growth of a seed into a plant is sometimes understood. His point is rather that persons are incomplete without a social component and develop into what they are—individual members of groups, socially grounded selves—in the ongoing process of living in a social environment. We need to recognize, he states, that as part of this social environment, our various institutions are both means and agencies of human progress and means of *creating* individuals.

In this developmental process, Dewey maintains that there is an intimate and reciprocal relationship between the ability to use language and the ability to develop a self. Through social intercourse, for example, through sharing in the activities embodying beliefs, the individual gradually acquires a mind of his/her own. That is, the growing child becomes a person by means of developing a sense of his/her self in the process of interaction with others, and his social self then structures and colors the child's subsequent experience. Because the development of the self is through social processes, Dewey maintains that we become familiar with our developing selves indirectly.

Apart from the social medium, the individual would never know himself; he would never become acquainted with his or her own needs and capacities. We understand ourselves as part of larger processes; we adopt others' aspirations and spurnings; we judge success and failure relative to some social context. Dewey points out that we understand ourselves in the light of our understanding of our social context; and this means that we understand ourselves, in part, in the light of others' evaluations of us. For Dewey, these others are the large circle of intimates, acquaintances, and passers-by with whom we interact. As we are first developing, our role is largely passive, we accept the evaluations that we receive. As we develop, however, we become more able to select those whose evaluations are to matter to us. One of the implications of his argument is that "psychic behavior," which forms the self, is an organized coordination that includes the external object, representation, and resultant conduct as interdependent phases of itself, thus linking self and world. From the Deweyan perspective, therefore, it is more accurate to give the psychic component of energy its full due and to see it arising in the context of the environmentally situated interpretive act—what Dewey (1896) called "organic coordination" and, much later in his philosophy, "transactions" (Dewey & Bentley 1949), what Peirce (1933) termed "sign," what Mead (1934) characterized as "the act," and what Rochberg-Halton (1984) has designated as "cultivation."

By "transaction" Dewey meant that the elements of any act of intelligence are not determined as independent entities, but only gain their status as elements in and through the act itself. In the words of Richard Bernstein:

> From a transactional perspective, an "element" is a functional unit that gains its specific character from the role that it plays in the transaction. From this perspective, it is the transaction that is primary. A transaction does not occur with an aggregate or combination of elements that have an independent existence. On the contrary, what counts as an "element" is dependent on its function within a transaction.
>
> (Bernstein 1966: 83)

When experience is so defined as a process of transaction, it is conceived of as doing or acting, but it also has a passive aspect. On the one hand, the human being acts upon or does something with and to other things and persons. Such activity is characteristic of the relation of all organisms to their environment, and the higher the life-form the more extensive and important is the activity. On the other hand, experience involves undergoing the consequences of such active responses to things and persons. In reaction to the child's activities, things and people do something to him/her, furthering in a cooperative fashion some activities and resisting and blocking others. This twofold process of transaction is experience. Rephrasing the reflex arc problem in a broader context, we have the basic Cartesian problem of how to bring together an independent mental subject and a physical object. Against the Cartesian assumption of a mental subject and an external object needing to be brought together or mediated, the pragmatists began with the process of sign-mediation, from which could be prescinded a subject or object. "Environment," however, is not something around and about human activities in an external sense; it is their medium, or milieu, in the sense in which medium is *inter*mediate in the execution or carrying out of human activities, as well as being the channel through which they move and the vehicle by which they go on (see Dewey & Bentley 1949).

Thus, for Dewey (1934), an object is expressive; it says something to us. The object, by its concrete properties, can stimulate new insights, new understandings. It seems important, then, to allow for the inherent character of the thing to have some influence in the interpretive process of meaning. In *Art as Experience*, Dewey (1934) introduced a distinction between perception and recognition as a way of dealing with the role of an object's own qualities. Recognition is when we experience an artifact and interpret it only as something we already know. The act of recognition may be conscious or unconscious, may or may not cause pleasure, or may or may not restore balance to a disturbed psyche. In any case, it does not produce a new organization of feeling, attention, or intentions. Many people relate to objects through recognition simply because of habituation, or because they are unable to give their full attention to all the information received from the environment. Perception, on the other hand, occurs when we experience a thing and realize its own inherent character. It might be very ordinary, such as one's own diary or the battered, straw-bottomed chair painted by Van Gogh, and so eloquently analyzed by Heidegger. The point is that the object imposes certain qualities on the viewer that create new insights, which is what makes any experience aesthetic in Dewey's perspective.

In the following paragraphs, I will use the term "transaction" in Dewey's purely formal sense, according to which the object of every cognitive act attains its meaning only within trans-actions. Dewey's transactional theory of meaning takes something into account that many theories of meaning unfortunately neglect: the generative way that the genuinely new is created or co-created in experience by means of transaction. What Dewey and Bentley (1949) in *Knowing and the Known* call "transaction," and what I wish to show as appearing more and more prominently in the recent growth of contextualistic approaches in developmental theorizing, is, therefore, in technical expression, neither to be understood as if it "existed" apart from any observation, nor as if it were a manner of observing "existing in a man's head" in presumed independence of what is observed (Dewey & Bentley 1949: 104). The transaction, as an object among and along with other objects, is to be understood as unfractured observation—just as it stands, at this era of the world's history, with respect to the observer, the observing, and the observed—and as it is affected by whatever merits or defects it may prove to have when it is judged, as it surely will be in later times. Thus, "trans-action" (*sensu* Dewey & Bentley 1949: 108) is where systems of descriptions are employed to deal with aspects and phases of action, without final attribution to "elements" or other presumptively detachable or independent "entities," and without isolation of presumptively detachable "relations" from such detachable elements.

Consequently, it was important to Dewey that an object also has an influence upon the way it is experienced, on the basis of its own, intrinsic or "expressive" features. This interplay between individual experience and objective "effect," that in transactions has an influence upon itself, is the way in which meaning transactions and development take place. Meaning transaction, in this sense, implies primarily the intention of the actor and only secondarily the characteristic of an object (Dewey & Bentley 1949). All components of a situation are linked together through transaction. Such simultaneity of finality and effectiveness is not possible in objects as objective, physical things. Therefore, characteristics of things appear only in the present, but they function in consciousness as purposive, future-oriented, generative "signs," or "symbols," and are the basis of individual development. Symbols are neither exclusively mental nor physical, neither subjective nor objective in nature, but rather form transactions by including person and culture. Consequently, objects appear to make a more active contribution to the meaning process. And it follows from here, that meaning is an "act" or, under the Deweyan transactional issue: meaning is "trans-action." At this point, it is interesting to note that Dewey and Bentley (1949) refer to Georg Simmel's (1908a; see Simmel 1950) *Sociology* when they say that the world is full of illustrations of transactional phenomena like those Simmel is describing so realistically in his work.

William Stern's purposive self as unitas multiplex

The Hamburg professor William Stern—in collaboration with his wife, Clara Stern—strongly influenced the course of psychology in Germany during the first three decades of this century, when the German scene had an impact on the international development of this science (see Ash 1995, Kreppner 1992). His philosophy of personalism as an overarching concept grew out of Stern's intention to overcome the either-or thinking of his time and to lay the ground for a new mainstream psychology which should be able not only to reconcile the old controversy between mind and matter, but also to bring some new holistic ideas into psychology. By emphasizing the person as a fundamental unit in psychological theorizing, Stern turned against the elementarists in psychology who were dominant at the end of the nineteenth century.

Stern's critique, expressed most fully in his own writings from 1928 onwards, was summarized crudely but effectively in the slogan, "No Gestalt without a Gestalter." The claim was that the perceiving subject was relatively unimportant for Gestalt theory. Stern maintained that continuing references to the dependence of perception on the state of the organism at a given time were not sufficient to account for the specifically human aspects of experience, especially for people's intentions giving meaning to their actions. That is, Stern conceived the person as a "goal-directed whole," the psychophysically neutral "point of convergence" of the inner and the outer worlds. The linking of genetic disposition with environment led to the rich conceptualization of personality as a *unitas multiplex*.

His personalistic perspective on the person can be summarized by at least three points (see Stern 1938): First, every person is markedly active. The active nature of a person contains three components: an acting person requires the intensive expenditure of energy, with which the person holds concentration for a limited time (i.e., the dynamic factor). Second, a person's actions are purposive. Each action possesses its own temporal patterns, the culmination of which occurs in the last part of the process, the outcome of the acting. Everything else focuses upon this teleological (or subjective) factor. An action operates as the driving motive; for the goal, which lies still in the future, has a causative effect upon the action process, determining the choice of support, promoting the rejection of unsuitable elements, preventing relapses into psychical processes alien to thought. Thinking and acting are governed by an arrangement specified to the goal. That is, human beings are teleological beings. Thus, causality and teleology collapse; the person is *causa finalis*. Third, in every act the person assumes a position as a center of action with respect to his/her world (i.e. the positional factor).

Along this line of theorizing, for Stern, the aim of human life involves the affirmation by the individual, in his/her being and acting, both of his/her own intrinsic significance and of the objective significance of the world, so that he/she acquires reality as a person through the coalescence of the world of objective values with his/her own substance. This coalescence or incorporation the personalistic theory designates as *introception*; it denotes the activity that gives direction and form to all genuinely human life. The process of introception leads to the person's inner representation of cultural norms, values, and rules. This process has been described by Stern as a permanent fight between the individual's own vital needs and wishes and culture and society's formats. The process of introception causes tensions and frictions, promoting developmental shifts as it contributes to the awakening and differentiation of conscience. In turn, values and norms are incorporated into the person's value system. Tensions are seen as starting points for increased activities pushing the individual through a sequence of metamorphoses, which may occur in synchrony or asynchrony with other developmental processes.

The unitary and meaningful pattern of life that introception endeavors to establish is called personality. Although the concept of "person" in the sense given above may be applied to any individual organism, personality, for Stern, is a uniquely human category. The person is a totality, that is a *unitas multiplex*. This must be taken literally. All the multiplicity included in the person, the hegemony of elements, events, phases, strata, is integral to the totality and not just superficially cemented to it or supported and conditioned by it; it is the consonance of multiplicity with the personal whole and of the person with the world, that makes human life possible. However, this consonance is not merely a perpetuated harmony. The more amply a living totality is articulated and the more various the multiplicity integral to it, the less self-evident is its life.

The closeness of this general perspective to, for example, Heinz Werner's "orthogenetic principle" is obvious. He postulates that developmental psychology has one general regulative principle. This principle, which he terms the orthogenetic principle, states that "whenever development occurs it proceeds from a state of relative globality and lack of differentiation to a state of increasing differentiation, articulation, and hierarchic integration" (Werner 1957: 126). Thus, whenever development occurs, the changes that characterize it follow a specified sequence. Consider, for example, a relatively young child. We spend a day with the child and decide to take a short walk. While doing so we see a dog. The child points and says, "Doggie." We smile, perhaps, and say, "Yes, that's a doggie." But soon we see a cat, and the child also points and says, "Doggie." Similarly, when the child sees a picture of a raccoon in a magazine, he/she also says, "Doggie." We might conclude, then, that the child has a relatively global (undifferentiated) concept of animals. Now suppose that we visited this same child about a year later. On the basis of Werner's orthogenetic principle we would expect that if the child's animal concepts had developed, they would be relatively less global—they would be more differentiated. Thus the child might now say "dog" only when a dog was in fact in view, and "cat," "raccoon," "horse," and so on, when appropriate. On another, still-later, visit we might notice some other things. The child might notice some other things. The child might now show evidence of knowing that all dogs, cats, horses, and so on are animals and, in turn, that animals are different from trees. In fact, we would see that the child's animal concepts had not only become more differentiated but had also formed into a hierarchy—that is cats, dogs, and horses had all become instances of the class "animals." Still later, perhaps, we would see that increasing differentiation and hierarchical organization had occured. The child would have developed a concept not only of dog but also of different breeds of dogs and, in addition, might be able to show evidence of knowing that within each breed there are puppies and adults and/or males and females of that breed. Moreover, the child might be able to differentiate types of plants and might know that both plants and animals are in a similar, higher-order class (living things) and are different from nonliving things. What we would see with the development of a child's animal concepts is a change from having relatively global, undifferentiated concepts to having concepts organized into hierarchical structure. Thus, Werner's orthogenetic principle holds that all developmental changes should proceed from globality to differentiation and hierarchical organization.

Coming back to William Stern's concept of the person, the objects of the world are not present solely in relation to "me" as the center, but have their own significance and their own proper quality. This fact results in a personified recentralizing of all dimensions. The object has its before and behind, its past and future. Nonetheless, it is insufficient for the person to attribute dimensions to objects and persons outside him/herself; he/she must also come to terms with the dimensions of the world, and adapt him/herself to them.

This is the occasion for a development in two directions; certain extensions proper to the person must be made manifest as proper only in the person, and are therewith subjectified; others become recognized as having community with others and therewith objectified (cf. Stern 1938). Thus, the categorical imperative for a person must be: Introcept! That is, shape your self towards personality by introcepting objectified components into the subjectified self. Human development, then, means to find one's own "form" through intensive introception. Thus, a person permanently represents his/her own product (the analogy to the claim that individuals are producers of their own development is obvious; see Lerner & Busch-Rossnagel 1981).

In all these introceptions there dwells an intention, whose goal may be an object, a relation, a total meaning. The apprehension of an independently existing single object requires its identification by referring images to something which remains constant in time. In infants thought of individual objects may be observed as soon as recognition of identification evolves from the bare feeling of familiarity on seeing the face of the mother or of a doll. The progressive "objectifying" of individual objects is a very slow process which is never entirely concluded; it is never more than a small fraction of the personal world of an individual within which those realizations, deliminations, oppositions and identifications are sought and won. How greatly the thought of identity in reference to an object exceeds bare concrete imagery is best seen in the difference between inanimate and animate objects. Many images correspond to an inanimate object, such as a certain "mountain" or a "toy." The difference between them is not ascribed to the object, however, but simply to the momentarily shifting relation of the subject to it; here the thought of remaining unchanged constitutes the thought of identity (Stern 1938).

This thought of identity, however, does not appear without concrete aids belonging in part to external perception and in part to the perception of the self. The course of time in which objects change their quality is experienced as continous. At the same time the subject is experienced as identical with his/her previous being. "I" have recollections of former states as "mine." "I" have the consciousness that the line of my life is never broken; consequently the most varied states at different times in past and future belong to the same "me." Here, for Stern, identity is supported by the immediate environment of the person; by analogy to this true self other objects thus take on a kind of personal identity. The process of identification as the ability to perceive similarity as well as difference or otherness thus signifies a quality under a personal aspect; exchangeability and substitution, nonrelevance of differences, in the service of personal aims. It seems as if Stern very closely touches systemic thinking when he states that the course of development is regulated by two different features: the tendency to maintain an extant state and to avoid changes, that is preservation of the self, on the one hand; and the tendency to reach out for new goals to promote development, that is unfolding the self, on the other. By introducing this dialectical approach to understanding continuity and change in the development of the self, he also stressed the importance of the process character of development.

Aside from conceptualizing a person-centered exchange model in which endowment and environment converge to become a unified person, Stern proposed the idea of a special zone where the exchange between person and environment may take place and where the opportunity for personal experience also exists. This was an attempt to localize the process of introception, on the one hand, and to illustrate the permanent action–reaction cycles between person and context, on the other. Vygotsky (1986) very explicitly referred to Stern's concept of "personal space" when he developed his zone of proximal development, but Stern's concept appears not only more far reaching and more differentiated than Vygotsky's; it also emphasizes the dynamics during the exchange between person and environment in greater detail.

Stern constituted an area, which he called the "world a person is living in" (*gelebte Welt*), in contrast to both the subjective-inside world and the objective-physical world. The "world a person is living in" is conceptualized as being richer or larger than the subjective world, because the person's concrete exchange consists of more interactions, struggles with the environment's resistance, more active subjective selections than are perceived and memorized by the subject as the subjective experiences. At the same time, the "world a person is living in" is only a segment of the entire physical outside world, accessible to a possible neutral and objective observer. A person's proximal space, the "world a person is living in," then, is defined by Stern as the place of realization, where the person is affected by his/her environment and where the person shapes this environment according to his/her needs and age-related competences. Here, in the proximal space of the person, the interplay between person and environment could be studied properly. By concentrating on the proximal space of the person, Stern tried to take into account the relativity of the environmental influence on a person's subjective experience, but assumed, nonetheless, an additional *de facto* influence on a person's development which is not represented in the subject.

Following Stern's (1938) theory of personality development, the separate thoughts of relation which we have just considered in isolation, are never independent of one another; they are embedded in one complete pattern of thought which he designated as "meaning." Thus, the formal aspect of meaning can be circumscribed by the term Gestalt where the numerous single aspects of object and relation are moments within a particular structure in thought, in which the weight and intent of the individual components are determined by the whole. But the true meaning of "meaning" is approached only by referring to the dimension of depth. Those experiences which arise from immediate contact between person and world have a surface aspect, but they bespeak another aspect which lies behind it, and the endeavor to pry into the second is called seeking the "meaning" of person and world. This signification of thought-of-the-meaning thus holds for the depths of the person as well as the world. Finally, the activity in which this "thought-of-the-meaning" is fulfilled is called understanding.

Along these personalistic lines of Stern's developmental theorizing on a person's identity, each individual selects from his/her world those components which he/she incorporates so intimately that they become components of the self and hence factors in his/her self-organization. For each individual, however, there can exist only a small selection of objective aims that he/she is able to introcept (Stern 1938); within this range the self is actually unified, but at the same time this core is surrounded by other regions of external parts for which complete introception does not succeed.

In this connection the *unitas multiplex,* and personal contact with the world are fused. Since the self is *unitas multiplex* its structure depends above all on whether the factor of unity or multiplicity comes to the fore. The unity of the personality, which can never be relinquished, may become effective in such a way that the various subordinate areas and dynamics of individual striving form a whole at the very outset, supporting and modifying one another, or in such a way that its heterogeneity, perhaps constituting active revolt, leads to conflict, internal strain and retreat. Both self-meaning and world-meaning are accepted simultaneously.

The person achieves self-realization by internalizing the objective world-substance and thus turning it into his/her own self-substance. This permanent back-and-forth process from the inside to the outside, performing a centrifugal and centripetal movement from the person into the world and from the world into the person, neither the one nor the other, is termed introception. It is the elementary process whereby person and culture transact. According to Stern's (1938) personalistic approach, experiences that objectify and subjectify are thus like endless travels of discovery into the objective world and the subjective self; the self is thus not a fact but rather an act.

Ernst E. Boesch's Identity formation as structuring I–world-relationships

Boesch's (1991) cultural action theory—in line with Piagetian cognitive constructivism—is constructivist in nature but is neither a social constructivism nor a co-constructivism in the sense of the Vygotskian and post-Vygotskian traditions. Rather, it would be better described as a "phenomenological constructivism" (Overton 1998: 324). Moreover, he built his theory upon a model of a human being who is a meaning-making subject, that is, who is able to create and understand symbols, and who is capable of developing a theory of his/her own mind. Thus Cassirer's (1944) view of *homo sapiens* as *animal symbolicus* may fit Boesch's intentions most adequately (see Valsiner, 1998 for a short description of Cassirer's philosophical system of symbolic forms).

Along these lines of reasoning, Boesch (1991) argues that cultural psychology aims at an integration of individual and cultural change, an integration of individual and collective meanings, a bridge of the gap between subject and object. His transactional focus on development itself is described by a framework that entails two polar dimensions of developmental processes. One of these processes, called "primary structuration," involves the development of internal action schemes and the objectification of actions as culture (see Eckensberger 1995). In this process, individual meaning systems differentiate and become projected onto the cultural contexts. The other pole or "secondary structuration" entails collective cultural meaning systems providing historical changing contexts for the formation of individual meaning systems.

In Boesch's theorizing, culture forms action fields that determine opportunities, effects and meanings of personal activities. Action fields are thus not only "environments;" they rather reflect the subject's representation of those aspects of the material and social environment that are relevant to personal goals. The valences and boundaries that constitute fields of action are intrinsically related to the goals, purposes, and beliefs of individual actors. Changes in social rule systems, however, alter the range of possible actions, and eventually create new types of acts.

Cultures shape, constrain, and amplify not only opportunities of action but, likewise, opportunities of development. Much of what has been said above concerning the interfaces between action and culture has to be extrapolated to the developmental domain. That is, action fields also localize developmental tasks as well as paths leading to them; they constrain and, in a compensatory fashion, also augment the individual's potentialities for action and development. Here, Boesch's argument partly converges with the position of Vygotsky (1981), who considered a culture's externalized systems of representation as "psychological tools" that are incorporated into thought and activity and thus become formative elements of the individual's ontogeny. And cultural systems maintain and regenerate themselves through the regulation and control of development over the life-span. Across all functional areas and throughout all phases of life, developmental processes are shaped and canalized by culturally prestructured arrangements of stimulation and infomation, and by age-graded structures of demands and opportunities. As Boesch has put it, "human beings interact with the environment in a dynamic way, thereby structuring the . . . world as well as the self and its action potentialities" (Boesch 1991: 366).

I think Boesch's "I–world" relation here is, in fact, a double relation. From a phenomenological, internal point of view, "I" and "world" constitute a differentiation of consciousness into the subjective world and the objective world. This is the "I–world" that forms the center of inquiry for the investigator building a theory about the relationship of person and perceived culture, i.e. the intrapersonal structure. From the external point of view, "I" and "world" entail two entities: person and culture. This is the "I–world" that is the center of inquiry for the researcher concerned with communication and culture, i.e. the interpersonal. In each case action or rather trans-action in the pragmatic sense, which is in fact co-action, constitutes the fundamental *change mechanism* that explains the development of both person and culture.

I have now sufficiently introduced the main concepts of Boesch's symbolic action theory, so I will now turn to the central but most difficult issue of this chapter: the constitution of a subject's "I" or self-identity. To tackle this problem, I will first discuss the problem of self-identity along the more general terms of Boesch's theoretical frame. Second, I will discuss the role of external supports for identity. These, on the one hand, consist of subject–object relationships, while, on the other hand, there are "identity-props" of a cultural ideational kind. That is, identity formation seen from an action-theoretical perspective also refers to factual parameters: concrete action experiences, the individual's body, personal objects, and cultural rules, constraints as well as freedom. How individual identity then emerges from the transaction of these variables is, of course, a problem of complex structure formation.

In a similar vein to Dewey and Stern discussing the emerging self as act, the qualities of the Boeschian "I" are not sensorial, but actional. In fact, an action and an action potential can only be experienced by an "I." This statement seems to suggest two conclusions: first, although lacking objective qualities, the I-experience constitutes a basic content of our existential awareness; it may, however, lead to quite diverse structures and conceptualizations in terms of both individual action experiences and a kind of cultural framework. Second, if the I-experience implies the awareness of being an actor or agent, it will obviously be trained by the qualities of action. We would then have to assume that how people experience their "I" follows the shades and colors of their actions. However, there seems to be, in people's experiences, a surprising continuity with which they experience their "I" which, in turn, defines their identity. That is, through all kinds of situational inconsistencies, there remains a feeling of sameness. We somehow perceive our inconsistencies as nothing else than variations on a constant theme, similar in spite of the variability of its surface and the changing reflections of light. So we would have to understand and to explain how humans are capable of generating continuity within change. Thereby, we have to take into account that identity formation corresponds very closely to the person's effort to distinguish him/herself from his/her environment. That is, identity is formed in the context of an "I–world-relationship," implying that the "I" necessarily emerges in relation to the external environment where identification vs. distinction and integration vs. autonomy appear to work closely together.

Nevertheless, we can assume that identity constitutes a continuity through variations in manifestations; this must obviously imply recognizability in spite of variations. For a child, to recognize its mother who, for example, does not wear the same clothes all the time, may not require a similarity in appearances, but a minimum of indices permitting him/her to distinguish the mother from someone else. However, recognition is not enough, it allows orientation, and thereby action: there would be no constancy of objects or persons without a constancy in the related actions. Identity would thus be based upon the possibility of behaving in a permanent fashion towards an object or a person which, in turn, would require a consistency of inner action experiences. This, of course, would be related to action goals, which mostly relate to external realities. Therefore, "I" and "non-I" would be consituted jointly but with some time delay. But what is meant by consistency in Boesch's (1991) theorizing about identity formation?

First, consistency might be attributional, i.e. the internal signals an action conveys remain familiar, allowing me to recognize thoughts and feelings as mine. Thus, in the first sense, consistency would be concerned with ensuring a continuity of inner experiences. One can assume that different I-experiences induce, on the one hand, similar qualities of awareness, and on the other hand, similar I–world-orientations, be it real or imagined. Second, consistency implies the harmonization of specific goals with overall orientations, which, obviously, may range from relatively simple to complex coordinations. Consequently, inconsistencies will continously threaten the individual's action potential. It seems, then, that to integrate specific actions consistently into situational networks and overarching goal orientations will often be difficult, even jeopardizing the formation of one's own identity. However, we might also conclude the opposite. Could not the formation of identity consitute a kind of unifying instance capable of coping with the discrepancies in one's concrete action experiences? In any case, identity-forming actions entail the internal experience of an "I" capable of observing, evaluating, selecting, transforming and the like. Internal effects will be perceived by the individual as causes as well as results of external action, and thus external concomitants of action will become symbols of inner processes (Boesch 1991). Integrating those "I-action-awarenesses" over time will lead to the structure of the self, i.e. to both attributional consistency and systemic consistency.

But what would be the "mechanisms" of such identity forming constructions? Boesch (1991) points to what he called "self-fantasms." Among other anticipations which regulate individual actions, the future encompasses those self-values we feel not yet realized. They represent the "self to be"—often considered to be our "true self." In this sense it locates the ideal I–world-relationship which Boesch termed "self-fantasm." Boesch describes extensively how these self-fantasms emerge and function in intimate interaction with both the myths of one's group or community and the factuality of experience. All these are long processes; we know that the formation of anticipatory self-fantasms, although starting in childhood, will be more intensively pursued in adolescence and, of course, will then go on throughout the life span. From here, Boesch concludes that the self-consistency concerns essentially the maintenance or even the reinforcement of our self-fantasm, whose intactedness appears to be an important condition for our fundamental action potential. Self-consistency, in turn, follows the outlines sketched by self-fantasms which, as I described above, result from complex integrations of personal experiences with cultural models or myths. Overall, structuring one's identity involves continuous processes of selection and transformation. At the same time, identity structures so evolved have their impact on perception and action. Since identity consists of continuity over time, the assumption, then, is close at hand that objects of our actions contribute to identity construction.

Following Boesch's (1991) approach, we could detect such contributions in three ways: First, objects are both stabilizers and reinforcers of action; second, objects facilitate variations of actions; and, third, objects mediate between situations. Along these lines of object functions, there is a result of the permanence of objects which should be emphasized in more detail. That is, in the course of a person's relation to his/her object they are imbued with meaning. According to Boesch's symbolic action theory, meaning results from the denotations and connotations an object acquires through being integrated into "action systems," i.e. areas of activities which group different actions serving a common purpose such as family, occupation, or profession. However, I do not want to stress here the self-relevance of objects through their being the external pole of the "I-doing"-experience. In addition, manipulating one's jewelry or clothes symbolizes to a woman the power to control her identity by, on the one hand, promising fulfillment of aspirations, and, on the other hand, compensating real or assumed flaws. Along this line of resoning, Boesch recalls the magical qualities of objects. In fact, considering these meanings of body decorations, it is easy to see that adorning one's person may surreptitiously acquire an apotropaic symbolism. In this sense, objects establish an environment of meanings, often delicate and intimate, expressing itself even in unreflected banalities.

There is, however, another dimension of meanings whose impact on identity formation is important. Objects, of course, are not simply integrated into individual action systems, but into cultural ones as well. We know Lévi-Strauss' (1967) impressive account of the strategy of the Salesien missionaries who, by changing the alignment of villages and the shape of huts, weakened the cultural integration of Bororo Indians. In its material outlay, the village of the Bororos represented a cosmology as well as social structure. That is, the world of objects acts as a system of signs designating rules of behavior and of explanation common to everyone.

In sum, the stability or permanence of objects and, of course, the spaces they form or fill, provide the individual with a cadre permitting the building of complex action systems. Thereby they provide the conditions for those constancies in I–world-relationships without which the formation of identity would be difficult to conceive. Objects with "heavy" cultural "loading" symbolize, through their "polyvalent" functions and meaning (Boesch 1991), cultural structures; their possession gives prestige and possibly even power—perhaps materially, perhaps through connecting the proprietor with collective representations such as myths of his/her group.

However, mere constancy may not suffice for our action potential. One of the most important discoveries the child makes early in his/her life is that an object removed from his/her field of vision has not disappeared from his/her world (see Piaget 1970). This discovery initiates both searching as well as discarding actions, and both will be fundamental for the child's action potential. Discarding means being able to get rid of a thing which displeases one in some way or another. That is, it signifies a potential to transform a situation, to initiate variations in experience. Searching, on the other hand, confirms the potential to reestablish familiarity, to maintain constancy, to return to security. Then the world of our objects maintains constancies, and therefore, although facilitating variations, it still conserves appropriate actions. Thus, the variability of objects allows freedom within stability, whereby, according to individual, culture, and necessity, the first or the second may receive stronger emphasis. Sometimes, objects will be changed in exact correspondance with inner transformations. The beginning PC user will be given a used PC, but with increasing aspirations he will get a brand new, and even more powerful machine. The inner developments induce a search for congenial objects, while objects create the conditions for inner growth.

Both permanence and variability of objects may become of particular use in cases of existential transitions or critical life-events. Here, the object may take on a mediating function (Boesch 1991). It was Winnicott (1953) who coined the term "transitional object" to refer to those objects which allow a child to transfer its emotional investment from the mother to the larger external reality. Teddy bears and puppets are examples of such transitional objects. Because of the broader connotations intended, Boesch (1991) prefers the term "mediation object" for objects of relevance in phases of changing I–world-orientations. For example, the emigrant uses objects in order to maintain closeness to his/her culture of origin. He/she will take with him/her certain objects of subjective importance, such as presents or photographs recalling beloved persons, religious symbols reinforcing his/her faith, talismans or good luck charms protecting against adversities. Note also that, in collecting these items, he/she has effected selections, somehow distributing valences within his/her culture of origin according to his/her idiosyncratic preferences. Thus, he/she conquers a new degree of freedom in that he/she is able to personalize his/her environment to a degree which, had he/she remained home, he/she might not have dared to. The objects chosen mirror his/her perceived identity, and thus guarantee and preserve it across cultural boundaries.

Moreover, objects mediate in an innovative way. The immigrant, for example, will also choose those among the objects offered by the new culture, selecting from these both the immediately useful ones as well those objects which appeal to his/her interest, his/her readiness to identify with the new environment. All this applies not only to African Camras going to Paris or Romanian Germans going back to Germany (Wölfing 1996). We can observe similar choices in the transition phase from childhood to adolescence or from adolescence to adulthood (see Habermas 1996). Books, in my student days, were important mediating objects, symbolizing continuity, whereas bikes were important mediation objects, symbolizing freedom from control. Nowadays, computers emerge as objects mediating between adolescence and adulthood, presenting manifold symbolic valences (see Turkle 1995). Thus, the chosen objects appear to mediate between an "is-reality" and a "should-reality" of him/herself. Taken together, identity is formed in the context of an "I–world-relationship," implying that the identity necessarily emerges in relation to the external environment where continuity, variability, and mediation appear to work closely together.

Person–artifact transactions

In the late 1970s and 1980s, Simmel's cultivation principle was reinterpreted under transactional issues as an application of philosophical pragmatism to a theory of culture. Rochberg-Halton—together with Csikszentmihalyi—concluded that the potential significance of artifacts is realized in a transactional process of actively "cultivating" a world of meanings, which both reflect and help create the ultimate goals of one's existence (see Csikszentmihalyi & Rochberg-Halton 1981). For these authors, the most inclusive term to describe the modes of meaning that mediate people with objects is cultivation. Cultivation involves both senses of the verb "to tend:" to take care of or watch over, in other words, "to attend to;" and also to proceed or be directed on some course of inclination, that is, "to intend" some aim. Indeed, cultivation—the improvement, development, refinement, or resultant expression of some object or habit of life due to care, training, and inquiry—comes closest to the original meaning of the term culture. However, most contemporary theories of culture exclude this aspect in favor of a rather static "symbol system" approach, for example, in the structuralism of Claude Lévi-Strauss or the semiotic approach of Umberto Eco.

Following Rochberg-Halton (1986), when a craftsman cultivates his skill of improving a hand-made Swiss alphorn, for example, both the nature of that object and the nature of that person can be enhanced by the transaction. The meaning of the object, the Swiss Alphorn, then, becomes realized in the activity of interaction and in the direction or purpose that this activity indicates: physical and psychological growth. A much less obvious example might be the activity of reminiscence when looking at old family photos. First of all, this is an activity in which signs of loved ones or past experiences are communicated, certain moods associated with those people are induced, and a stream of thought about "how it was" is brought about from a person's current perspective on how things are now. The reminiscence evoked by the photo has its own peculiar flavor or pervasive quality. But this activity has another dimension. It also indicates intention—a direction, or a purpose, that is an essential feature of the meaning of the activity. That is, when a person intends something to come about, or attends to something, that activity tends in some direction—toward its outcome or purpose. The attention that a person invests in the activity is the means by which that outcome can be realized. Thus, the meaning of cherished possessions is realized in the transaction between person and object; transactions, according to Rochberg-Halton (1986) are psychic activities (or communicative sign processes) and not simply physical behaviors *per se*, although they involve physical behaviors; and there are different modes of transactions.

Influenced by Peirce's (1931–1935) "modes of being," Csikszentmihalyi and Rochberg-Halton (1981) distinguish three modes of transaction that seem essential to understanding how artifacts can come to acquire significance. Between the person and the thing, the first two elements of transaction, are the mediating modes. The tripart division of the mind—in terms of three modes of transaction, which in Peirce's sign theory are roughly the iconic, indexical, and symbolic modes of signs—has a long tradition in psychology, as Hilgard (1980) has argued in an article called *The Trilogy of Mind: Cognition, Affection, and Conation*. Most psychological theories including theories of meaning construction or identity formation have been dominated by the cognitive element to the relative neglect of the other two dimensions in the last forty-five years. However, for Csikszentmihalyi and Rochberg-Halton all three modes are essential to experience and the cultivation of the self and serve to mediate the person with the artifact. The same experience, however, will have different features come into prominence depending on what perspective one chooses to emphasize.

The first mode along which one might assess the nature of a person–artifact transaction implies the perception of the unique intrinsic qualities of artifacts. Csikszentmihalyi and Rochberg-Halton (1981) approach the *cognitive mode* from Dewey's (1934) distinction between what he calls perception and recognition. He describes recognition as a falling back on some previously formed cognitive or interpretive schema when confronted with an artifact, whereas perception involves an active receptivity to the artifact so that its qualities may modify previously formed schemes.

Along this line of argument, aesthetic experience as a cognitive mode of transaction is not limited to art alone but is considered a potential element of all experience. In fact, perception is essential to aesthetic experience and leads to psychological growth and learning. If culture, as, for example, artifacts, were simply a symbol system of convention, as some cognitive anthropologists argue, then aesthetic experience would only consist of recognition in Dewey's terms—or assimilation in the Piagetian sense—because the artifact of that experience "contains" meaning only as an arbitrary sign endowed with meaning by cultural convention and not because of unique qualities of its own.

Indeed, objective qualities of artifacts only serve the purpose of recognition, embodying neighborhood values, group norms, or religious beliefs about, for example, how homes and near-home territories are personalized (see Werner & Altman 1998). Deweyan perception, on the other hand, involves active receptivity to the artifact so that its qualities may modify previously formed schemas, habits, or even identities. An experience of perception in Dewey's sense means that the scheme, habit, or identity through which we interpret an artifact—to define ourselves through meaning transactions—is changed or enlarged, which is how learning and development occurs, by enlarging or changing the cognitive framework of meaning making or interpretation. It is this orientation to experience which is similar to the one Csikszentmihalyi (1996) describes as creativity.

Along these lines of reasoning, culture, seen as a process of cultivation, makes it possible to view meaning as transaction rather than as a subjective projection by a cultural or individual schema to an artifact with no meaningful properties of its own. Indeed, Dewey's view seems to account for something left out in most contemporary accounts of meaning, namely, the way something genuinely new can arise in experience; something not reducible to convention. His statement echoes somehow Simmel's view on the intrinsic "value" of objects for cultivation. What is really important here is that the artifact with which a person interacts has some influence on their meaning process or interpretation because of its own intrinsic qualities—for this is the essential way that learning and developmental change occur in Dewey's perspective. In fact, any activity can, and should, involve novel elements that make the experience unique and thus supports the cultivation of the self.

The *affective mode* of the transaction between persons and artifacts concerns how psychic energy is channeled. We have just seen how the intrinsic qualities of artifacts can have a decisive role in the transaction when a person allows those qualities to be realized as part of meaning transactions. Whereas Deweyan perception is what enables the individual to learn new things, to accommodate his interpretive schemes to the qualitative properties of the environment, attention is needed to realize a psychic transaction, that is for any meaning transaction to occur it is necessary that a certain amount of psychic energy be allocated to the object (Csikszentmihalyi & Rochberg-Halton 1981).

Attention then plays the key role in serving to limit and direct psychic energy. When a person interacts with an artifact, he/she selects it from the surrounding environment—including the cognitive or mental mind—through concentrating attention on it. Of course, there are many reverse instances when the artifact "selects" the individual and compels the person to pay attention as, for example, when the alarm clock harshly reminds us of the agreement we made with it last night to awaken at this ungodly hour. But mostly, it is the person who chooses to invest attention in a particular artifact, and most of our interactions with artifacts consist of habitual patterns of attention. In this way, the physical arrangement of our home can be seen as a pattern of attention and intention made concrete in the artifacts and the ambience they create; a pattern or design that in turn channels the psychic energy of the inhabitants. Homes objectively represent what the self is in terms of what artifacts psychic energy has been invested in; what, for example, we consider significant to possess.

If examined closely it can reveal the patterns of attention that help to structure our everyday life. For example, the organization of furniture and appliances shows where family members habitually spend time, what they tend to pay attention to, and what they wish visitors to see or not to see. Moreover, the total context of artifacts in a home acts as a constant sign of familiarity, both giving a feeling of security and telling us who we and our kindred are; what we have done or plan to do. In this way, significant artifacts reduce the amount of information we have to pay attention to in order to act with ease (Rochberg-Halton 1986). However, any experience with artifacts lies on a continuum ranging from boring sameness at one end to enjoyable diversity at the center and, finally, to anxiety-producing diffusion at the further end. The somehow optimal state of involvement in experiencing transactions with artifacts, or "flow," is in contrast with extremes of boredom and anxiety, which can be seen as states of alienated attention (Csikszentmihalyi 1996). Whereas flow experiences—or integrated attention that serves to direct a person's psychic energy toward realizing his/her goals—contribute to the cultivation process by stimulating growth through the intrinsically rewarding nature of transaction with the artifact, alienated attention represents a waste of psychic energy because it is expected without contributing to the process of cultivation.

The *conative mode* refers to the outcomes of person–artifact transactions. Here, one must consider the role of goals and intentions in the meaning of artifacts. To do this one has to address the purpose of cultivation itself, to examine what ends or goals meanings reflect. The importance of culture from this perspective is that it facilitates development, that is indicates developmental goals (or tasks) and acts, and has a purposive influence. The cultural environment of artifacts in the home, like culture in general, is not only a reflection of what people *are* but also molds what they may *become*. The pragmatic meaning of cherished possessions, for example, is that they serve to influence conduct toward certain goals. The term "pragmatic," as originally developed by Aristotle, and as reformulated by the pragmatists such as Peirce, James, Dewey, and others, meant the cultivation of a way of life through activities aimed towards the attainment of a feeling of well-being. It implied that developmental pathways to live well, as opposed to merely living, are dependent on a process of cultivating a web of meanings that make up one's life (Rochberg-Halton 1986).

The process of cultivation is motivated by belief in goals held to be ultimate by individuals. This does not mean that these beliefs are necessarily ultimate but only that they provide a provisional sense of purpose around which to shape one's life course. Ultimate goals provide a standard toward which actions are, or should be, aimed. Thus, when one values an intimate place, or a cherished photo, these transactions are intentional activities that reflect what one considers significant and which involve real outcomes. The sense of being emotionally attached to an intimate place one has visited or in touch with a loved one, expresses what we consider significant and reveals the purpose that motivates us to invest psychic energy in certain artifacts and meanings rather than in others. As the cluster of artifacts one values solidifies, so do the meanings one derives from transactions with them. Different selves emerge around goals embedded in cherished belongings or intimate places through cultivation. The artifacts one selects to endow with special meaning out of the total cultural environment of artifacts are both models of the self as well as opportunities for further development. In this way, artifacts serve to give a tangible expression, and thus a continued existence, through signs to one's relationships, experience, and values. Valued artifacts involve outcomes in the sense that these transactions reveal intentions or goal-directed purposes; that is, they tell us what "it all add up to," and how these goals are being realized.

Part II

Identity through culture

Chapter 3

The rediscovery of Georg Simmel's work on culture

The origins of the term "culture" can be traced back to the Roman philosopher Marcus Tullius Cicero, who claimed in his *Tusculum Disputations*, 2000 years ago: "Cultura animi philosophia est" (p. 13). This formulation makes sense only if "cultura" denotes a process, as it also does in "agri cultura." The cultivation of land, plants, and animals was the congenial basis on which Cicero postulated a cultivation of the mind, which we called philosophy. Cicero's approach had long receded into the collective memory of the European nations when the Baltic vicar Johann Gottfried Herder took it up 1800 years later in his *Ideas towards a Philosophy of History of Mankind,* which appeared in 1778. For Herder, culture also denotes a process, but one which he relates to the central goal of his age, i.e. enlightenment. The evolutionary concept of culture defined by Herder was to spread out to all European languages and, divested of its evaluative features, it also became a basic notion in a host of academic disciplines that took up the study of cultural matters throughout the last two centuries (see Koch 1989). Along the Herderian line of reasoning, Hegel came up with his idea of culture as "objective spirit," and, later, Moritz Lazarus and Heyman Steinthal in their *Völkerpsychologie* (1860) worked out a first conception of the embodiment of mind in culture. At the turn of the twentieth century, Georg Simmel (a student of Lazarus) focused on the centrality of the dynamic interaction between person and culture that can only be grasped through relational concepts. From his anti-individualistic standpoint, he replaced the categories of cause and effect by the logical form of a mutual relationship in which the person has an effect on culture at the same time as culture has an effect on the person. In fact, Simmel was reputedly one of the most brilliant thinkers of his generation and his intellectual impact is indisputable (cf. Frisby 1985, Kearn *et al.* 1990).

The era of the "cultured individual:" the 1840s to the 1920s

Many currents of thought—native and international—joined together in various ways after 1850 to form the intellectual context of cultural sciences in Germany (see Smith 1991). Thereby many of the main recognized philosophical movements such as the Enlightenment trends, post-Kantian idealism, Hegelianism, Comtean positivism, Darwinianism, British political economy and utilitarianism lent elements to cultural sciences. Along these lines of new paradigm developments, and in great contrast to the new established experimental psychology, in most branches of the social sciences the overriding trend has been away from the individual purpose to collective forces as the motor of human mentalities. The ideational background of this trend, as we know, is profoundly rooted in the Copernican and Darwinian deconstruction of the traditional anthropocentric view of the universe, and the emergence of the "cultured individual" between 1840 and 1920 constitutes a crucial addition to this cosmic deconstructionism in psychology (cf. Valsiner 2000).

Only a few German psychologists in the nineteenth and early twentieth centuries have been concerned with culture. However, this interest has not been reciprocated by the mainstream of their discipline (cf. Jahoda 1982). Psychology has, in many respects, remained individualistic and narrowly culture-bound, largely ignoring the wider perspectives provided by a new group of academic disciplines that took culture as their primary object of scientific study. The development of cultural sciences between the 1840s and the 1920s became an international phenomenon to which people of all major European nations and the United States contributed (see Smith 1991 for the development of the cultural sciences in Germany). In respect of psychology, *Völkerpsychologie* and its precursors like Giambattista Vico, Willhelm von Humboldt or Gottfried Herder are especially worth examining as case studies of the changing of the long-standing anthropocentric perspective in the humanities.

Some of the most remarkable developments were attempts to create a broad, unified cultural science that would overcome the differences between competing theoretical patterns and disciplines and provide a basis for effective social policy. The efforts to unify the cultural sciences were partly organized around a reaffirmation of the nomothetic orientation of the traditional liberal theoretical pattern, an orientation that had been maintained in many of the cultural sciences in part because of its utility in politics. The reaffirmation was felt to be necessary because of increasingly strong challenges to traditional nomothetic human science from the practitioners of *Geisteswissenschaft*, from the hermeneutic approaches of both Wilhelm Dilthey and the leaders of the German historical profession and, ultimately, from sociologists such as Max Weber and Georg Simmel.

To understand the reason why German cultural sciences in the twentieth century deviated in their theoretical approaches from their cognates in much of the rest of the world, one has to focus on the connections between particular theoretical patterns and the rise of radical nationalist ideologies. Thus, the identification of theoretical patterns with ideologies discredited these same ideas among social scientists outside Germany, especially after the victory of Nazism. That is one of the reasons why the early German cultural psychology—termed *Völkerpsychologie*—is dead. It did not, in any real sense, survive the 1920s, and it never achieved full recognition as an independent discipline outside of the German-speaking countries. Even in its heyday, during the last third of the nineteenth century, it was rather difficult to separate its central concerns from those of cultural anthropology as that discipline was defining itself. Nevertheless, German *Völkerpsychologie* was widely respected, if not imitated, among cultural scientists throughout the world (cf. Boring 1950).

What is true of psychology as a whole is equally true of cultural developmental psychology. The eighteenth and nineteenth centuries and the first third of the twentieth were in fact quite rich in alternative definitions of objects of study; objects that were cultural psychological in the broad sense of involving psychological aspects of the relation between the individual and cultural collectivity.

Among these alternatives *Völkerpsychologie* forms a variant that is interesting precisely because it is so very different from what was to become the dominant model. That difference is already apparent in the impossibility of supplying an accurate English version of the very title that this discipline used to identify itself. "Folk psychology" is an absurd mistranslation. "Cultural psychology" and "Ethno-psychology" come closer but are open to various objections. Thus, in order to avoid sterile terminological discussions I will use the term *Völkerpsychologie* throughout this book.

Völkerpsychologie has nothing to do with any form of racial or biological theories, nor has *Völkerpsychologie* anything to do with a romantic enthusiasm for a so called *Volksseele* characteristic of the Germans. On the contrary, *Völkerpsychologie* is an incomplete scientific project that addressed itself primarily to the psychology of groups in cultural and everyday life rather than individuals. *Völkerpsychologie* is indeed a psychology of social life, but at the same time it is a theory of socio-cultural evolution (see Koehnke 1990). Hegel's "objective spirit" as well as Herder's concept of *Volksgeist*, served *Völkerpsychologie* of the nineteenth century by inspiring metaphors for a new orientation towards culture. The guiding metaphor of the theories of objective spirit, represented by the Dilthey school and related positions of Spranger, Litt or Freyer, was that culture was the "coagulated spirit" that, through the hermeneutic-understanding view of the subject, becomes re-subjectifiable. There is adequate knowledge of the fact that there was a certain continuity in thinking from Hegel to Dilthey on cultural philosophy in the first third of the twentieth century. But it is often forgotten that as early as the mid 1900s, a comprehensive theory of objective spirit had entered into the scientific program of *Völkerpsychologie* as founded by Lazarus and Steinthal. Also, the literature on the emergence of *Völkerpsychologie* long ignored the differences between the classic contributors to the discipline or attributed the scientific progress solely to Willhelm Wundt (1912; for an overview see Galliker 1993). If the achievements of the two Jewish—like Simmel—scientists Lazarus and Steinthal were mentioned at all, they were seen only, and erroneously, in global form as providing the groundwork for Wundt's monumental *Völkerpsychologie* volume (see Danziger 1983). Almost a hundred years later, Richard Shweder, in his important collection of nine articles on *Thinking Through Cultures*, echoes the message of the early *Völkerpsychologists* when he described cultural psychology as the science that studies "how the mind and the world make each other up" (Shweder 1991: 11); unfortunately, he did not refer to the spiritual predecessors in the nineteenth century German *Völkerpsychologie*.

The embodiment of mind in culture: Lazarus and Steinthal's *Völkerpsychologie*

During the first half of the nineteenth century the terms *Volk* and *Volksgeist* became part of the vocabulary of a rising tide of German nationalism in which cultural and political issues became thoroughly entangled. However, in 1860 an attempt was made to reclaim these terms for scientific discourse by two socially marginal academics of Jewish descent, Moritz Lazarus and Heymann Steinthal. The literature contains a number of extensive accounts of the development and importance of Lazarus and Steinthal's *Völkerpsychologie* (cf. Belke 1971, Krewer & Jahoda 1990, Galliker 1993).

First, in an article in 1851 in the *Deutsches Museum,* Lazarus sketched out a program for *Völkerpsychologie* that in 1860 he formulated with Steinthal. Lazarus and Steinthal start from the assumption that human activity is rooted in sociocultural consciousness. Here they recognized tool use—like the Vygotskyian sociocultural school sixty years later—as the motivating force in the development of man. In 1860, they wrote that with tools, a number of inventive ideas gain realization and become powerful. This triggers progress and the mastery of nature. The tool and its product then affect the mind, stimulating and enabling it to more inventiveness.

Thus, for Lazarus and Steinthal (1860), the task of *Völkerpsychologie* is a dual one. First, it is the study of mankind as a whole, and of the development of the human mind. Here, the goal is to arrive at general laws governing the development of the human mind. Second, it encompasses the study of the specific characters of the various groups that constitute mankind, how they came to be constituted, and the changes they have undergone. That is, to investigate the factors producing differentiation resulting in the particular manifestations of the general laws among historical people. It is explicitly stated that these "laws" will be essentially the same as those of the natural sciences, i.e. "reducing things and properties to relationships" (Lazarus & Steinthal 1860: 24). However, the general aims of *Völkerpsychologie* were the synchronic (anthropological) and the diachronic (historical) study of the laws governing the development of the objective mind, and the analyses of the basic processes of individuals as a function of the objective mind. Lazarus sees the relationship of the individual to the collectivity as a central task for *Völkerpsychologie* and stresses that the collective is more than the sum of its parts. Referring to Herbart and anticipating Durkheim, Lazarus asserts the priority of the collective consciousness over the individual.

Lazarus further seeks to analyze the factors leading to the development of the objective mind, among which common language and joint activity are prominent. The relationship between the psychological activity of the individual and culture which that activity creates was conceived by Lazarus and Steinthal in a dialectical fashion. Thus, the individuals whose common activity created the objective reality of cultural forms are themselves to be seen as the product of these forms. In his *Synthetische Gedanken zur Völkerpsychologie* [Synthetic Ideas on Völkerpsychologie] in 1865, Lazarus wrote that "men's shared lives, their subjective activities, crystallize into objective content that then becomes the content, norm and organ of their further subjective activity" (Lazarus 1865: 41). The subjective activities constitute an objective content that is manifested in forms of thought, convictions and so on. They are disseminated in a society insofar as they stand above individuals and have an effect on them.

On the other hand, the objective spirit also manifests itself in "embodiments of thought:" works of art, writing, and buildings of all types. These contain, in a true sense, the objectified spirit. Subjective activities do not, however, objectify themselves only through links to material objects. Rather, these things themselves determine subjective activity, as they achieve a normative power that individuals, the creators of this objective spirit, cannot evade.

Thus, a person who at a certain point in time joins a community is not faced simply with a natural world, but also with a world of culture in which inherited societal experience is manifested. The individual can base the direction of his development on the experience embodied in a cultural object. It follows that the fundamental psychological processes which are of importance for *Völkerpsychologie* are the same processes that individual psychology operates with, and for Lazarus and Steinthal these had been adequately conceptualized in the processes of inhibition, fusion, apperception, assimilation, and so on, of Herbartian psychology.

Man thus finds himself in the paradoxical position of being creator and creature of culture simultaneously (Lazarus 1865). As a consequence, concluded Lazarus, human development is determined by the already existent life of the whole of humanity and the objective spirit lying within it. The objective spirit, through objectification of the subjective, supplies the prerequisites for the process of individual appropriation, which has its own laws. Objectification and appropriation are, according to Lazarus, complementary aspects of developmental processes. With this brilliant synthesis of objectification and appropriation, Lazarus outlined the first cultural psychological conception of person–culture development in terms of a fundamental circularity: the person–culture cycle.

Unfortunately, Lazarus did not succeed in presenting an integrated concept that would pinpoint the bridge—and test its load-bearing ability—thus allowing us to connect structural insights into objective forms with individual psychology. In fact, Lazarus had a grand vision about uniformities in the development of the objective mind and its particular manifestations within the *Volk* or national community that largely shape its psychology. It was a powerful idea but one that was, and still remains, difficult to research effectively. When it came to applying these theoretical commitments to the empirical material on language, myths, customs, and so on, Lazarus and Steinthal had little to offer.

Moreover, it was Wundt's (1886) scathing critique of Lazarus and Steinthal's work that signalled the demise of the original version of *Völkerpsychologie*. In working out the relationship between individual psychology and *Völkerpsychologie* Wundt tried to distinguish his own position from that of Lazarus and Steinthal.

What he mainly objected to in their project was its Herbartian basis. Psychological laws were not abstract principles, conceived on the model of classical mechanics, that could be applied analogously on the individual and on the social level. Rather, they were developmental principles that expressed the kinds of changes which mental contents underwent in interaction with a medium (Wundt 1886). That medium was environmental and social as well as physiological. The relationship between psychological laws on the individual and on the social level is not one of analogy but one of identity. The important practical aspect of this distinction was that Wundt's interest was not primarily one of superimposing a psychological interpretation on anthropology and history, as Lazarus and Steinthal's had been, but of using linguistic and ethnographic data to illuminate psychological processes in the individual. Their program for a *Völkerpsychologie* outlined in 1860 contained a conception of psychology which went beyond that of existing individual psychology. That is, psychology teaches us that human beings are in essence thoroughly cultural beings.

Overall, with his brilliant idea of synthesizing objectification and appropriation, Lazarus, for the first time, outlined a cultural developmental theory which was then elaborated sixty years later by Lev Vygotsky and his socio-historical school. In fact, the possible influence of the Humboldtian scholar, Gustav Shpet (1879–1937), on Vygotsky's thinking also remains largely unanalyzed (see Zinchenko 2000). As a student, Vygotsky followed a course given by Shpet and we may assume that he kept following Shpet's theorizing with some interest (Van der Veer 1996). What is interesting with regard to Shept is his discusssion of Lazarus and Steinthal's *Völkerpsychologie* in his 1927 *Introduction to Ethnic Psychology*. In a similar vein, Simmel designated culture as that which the mind has deposited in language, institutions, art and, last but not least, technology. Frisby (1992) argues therefore, that Simmel is one of the first cultural psychologists to examine the inner (psychic) consequences for individual experiences of the domination of the cultural things in everyday experience as the culture of human beings.

Simmel's life course

Georg Simmel was born 1 March, 1858 in Berlin at the corner of Friedrichstrasse and Leipzigerstrasse in the very heart of the city. He was, and remained, the product of a metropolitan civilization, overwhelming through a variety of sensual, intellectual, technological, poetical, and artistic impressions, all of which had their impact on the future author of the *Sociology of the Senses* and of the analysis of the metropolitan structure and intellectual life. Berlin was a spot that had all the conditions for inspiring a potential sociologist. Individuality had a rare chance to articulate itself in the merry-go-round of societal contacts and relationships and in the meetings of diverse social worlds: Christian, Jewish, academic, artistic, literary, journalistic. It was a place to encounter many different perspectives and structures. Although later professing the evangelical faith, Simmel was of Jewish background.

Simmel began his studies at the University of Berlin in 1876 with an initial interest in history. However, he soon moved on to the study of psychology under Moritz Lazarus—with whom Dilthey and Wundt had also studied—and anthropology before finally turning to philosophy (see Figure 3.1 for the overall origins of Simmel's work on culture and his impact on the social sciences at the onset of the twentieth century). Simmel finished his PhD in 1881 with a dissertation on Kant's theory of matter.

Simmel had great teachers. He studied history under Droysen, Mommsen, von Sybel, von Treischke, Grimm, and Jordan, psychology under Lazarus and Bastian, and philosophy under Harms and Zeller. However, it cannot be said that Simmel became an immediate adherent of any of these great men. He had too much individuality, too much that was specifically his own, to be a mere follower. He was original in the sense that, in his own characteristic way, he combined elements that were borrowed from the most divergent sources (see Spykman 1964).

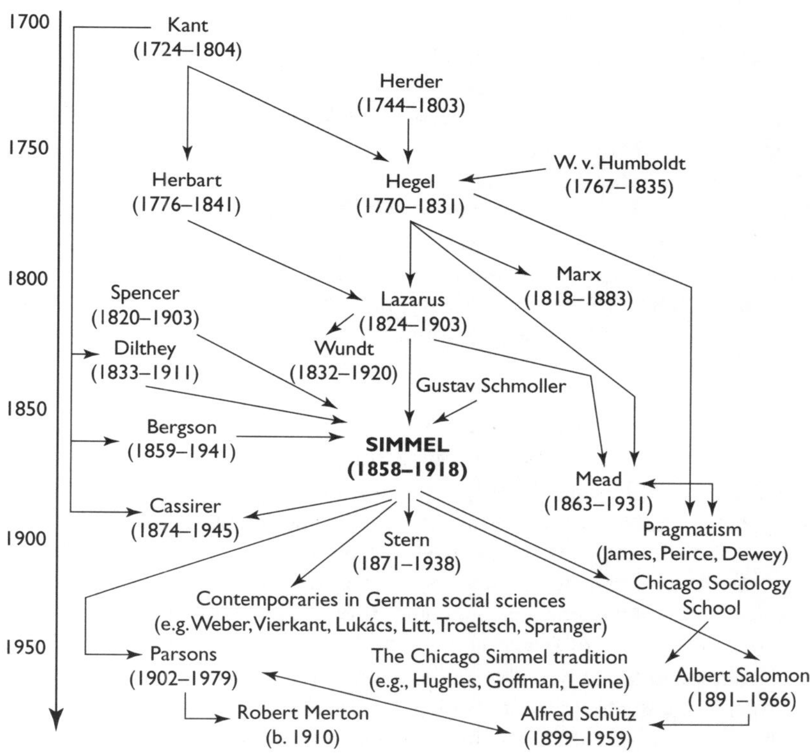

Figure 3.1 Origins of Simmel's work on culture and of his impact on social sciences at the onset of the twentieth century

Apart from his immediate teachers, the other formative influences were Kant, Cohen, Goethe, Schopenhauer, Nietzsche, Hegel, and Heraclitus. To Cohen's interpretation of Kant he owed a great deal, even if he did not fully accept it. Goethe, Schopenhauer, and Nietzsche, and the whole of the anti-intellectualistic movement of the nineteenth century, strongly affected his thinking. Heraclitus, for whom he had the most profound admiration, undoubtedly had a great influence on the formulation of his relativism, and there is too much similarity between Simmel's and Hegel's dialectic to attribute it to a mere coincidence.

In 1885 Simmel became a private lecturer (*Privatdozent*) at the University of Berlin. Simmel remained in this position until 1901 when he was nominated *Ausserordentlicher Professor*, a title which did not make him a full member of the faculty of philosophy at the Berlin Humboldt University. It was on the lecture platform that he showed his real greatness. As a lecturer he realized to the fullest his manifold talents. His lectures were not just learned, they were an inspiration. He combined a clear, logical analysis with an artistic, impressionistic approach. He gave his audience more than knowledge. He helped his hearers to live, to find adaptation to that vast cultural environment which is the European social heritage (Spykman 1964).

Albert Salomon (1891–1966), a scholar and PhD student of Max Weber, was invited to join the University in Exile, New York, later renamed the New School for Social Research, in order to represent the Weberian approach to sociology. Indeed, it is from his writings on Weber and on French social thought that he is best known. But Salomon's interest in Simmel was not just a consequence of the catholicity of his intellectual taste; he was once Simmel's student at Berlin and he gained a unique perspective on the classical sociologist, which he brought to his students and other audiences in his unpublished writings and seminars on Simmel.

Like many others from his native Berlin and around the world, Salomon sat in one of the big lecture halls where Simmel lectured and witnessed the master at work.

> In 1910, I attended for the first time classes at the University of Berlin. I remember vividly the lecture course Simmel gave. In the widest classroom, which streched from the Southside of the university with a view to Under den Linden to the Northside looking over the old chestnut trees to Dorotheenstreet, he lectured at the godless time from 2 to 3 p.m. in order to deter the hundreds of people who crowded the classes. He was disgusted with the fact that he was fashionable; but even at such an hour, there were hundreds of listeners in the largest classroom of Berlin University. Unforgettable was the impression of his personality. He was physically unattractive. When he began to speak, he was fascinating and repellent alike, as if surrounded by a halo of solitude and disgust. He really did not address the audience in the reciprocal give and take of a good teacher; he was talking in a monologue. His words came from somewhere, from an opaque experience like lightning, shocking and fascinating alike. He seemed to be a stranger, an adventurer in ideas and an actor whose

> gestures, of his hands in particular, feigned the spontaneity of his thinking in class, while he probably performed the same gestures every time he gave the course. Throughout my reading of Simmel's work and later in my teaching Simmel, I never got rid of the ambivalent reaction of fascination and repulsion.
>
> (Salomon 1943; see Jaworski 1997: 93)

For Salomon, the encounter was not an altogether positive experience. He was both attracted to and repelled by Simmel: attracted to the questions he asked and the manner of engaging those questions; repelled not only by Simmel's appearance but by his modernity. Salomon's rationalism, his faith that through reason one can grasp the whole truth, clashed with Simmel's psychologism, intuitionism, and other concessions to the modern revolt against reason.

However, Salomon brought his knowledge and conflicted appreciation of Simmel's writings to his New School courses, where Simmel was featured not only in history of sociology review courses, but in regularly offered seminars on Simmel, from the 1940s through 1966, the year of Salomon's death (Jaworski 1997). The Simmelian tradition at the New School continued in the work of Alfred Schutz, who "paid homage" (Wagner 1970: 49) to Simmel in some of his wartime papers on applied social theory, and then, later, in the courses of Peter Berger, Stanford M. Lyman, and Guy Oakes, among others.

Coming back to Simmel's work at the Humboldt University of Berlin, in the faculty of philosophy in the late nineteenth century there were three exponents of the three concepts of social science. Two of them were professors of the highest rank. All three were already of the highest merit, when the thirty-two-year-old Georg Simmel worked on his first book *On Social Differentiation* (1890). Seven years later, one of the three, Willhelm Dilthey, had published his chief work *Einleitung in die Geisteswissenschaften*—a book which includes a very critical account of the possibility and the meaning of sociology. Therefore, it is not surprising that Dilthey—who was also an implacable anti-Semite—found, some thirty years later, only a few favorable words for Simmel's sociology.

Quite unknown is the theory of another, but only adjunct, professor (*Extra-ordinarius*) of his faculty: Moritz Lazarus, who in the 1850s founded another new science which he called *Völkerpsychologie*. Simmel later characterized Lazarus as his most important teacher in his student days.

Next, I have to mention a third exponent of social science, also a professor at the University at Berlin, Gustav Schmoller. He was an economist and economics historian, the leader of the so-called "historian school of national economy." I don't want to elucidate Schmoller's methods in detail, but it is important to remember that the historical school worked with both positivistic-empirical and historical methods, but did not have the aspiration to build up its own universal theory. Only Schmoller, the economist, tried to be supportive of his young colleague.

The fourth concept, "sociology," emerged at the Berlin University with Georg Simmel (see Koehnke 1990 for a reconstruction of the relations between Simmel and the other three). Simmel's sociology, however, was not accepted in Germany at the time, in particular among Berlin's faculty of philosophy. In fact, Simmel's position is a compromise between Lazarus and Dilthey, between the idea of *Völkerpsychologie* and *Geisteswissenschaften*.

However, apart from his teaching program at the Berlin University, many indications of Simmel's interest in psychology during these years can be found in his twenty-five books and more than 300 articles (see Koehnke 1990, Frisby 1992, Frisby & Featherstone 1997). Among them, the year 1900 saw the publication of one of the most significant of Simmel's works, *The Philosophy of Money*, the intention of which was to construct a new story beneath historical materialism. For example, he set forth the dual claim that human consciousness derives from external material reality and that no simple unidirectional link can account for this process—in order to reveal the psychological preconditions of economic forms (see Simmel 1990).

Still within the context of his analysis of the cultural and psychological dimensions of modern life is his classic 1903 essay *The Metropolis and Mental Life* (see Simmel 1950). Here Simmel questioned the products of modern life as to their inner nature, as it were, the body of culture as to its soul by commencing with the psychological foundation of the metropolitan type, namely, the increase in nervous life, which emerged out of the rapid and unbroken change in external and internal stimuli.

Simmel remained a private lecturer in Berlin until the day of his departure for Strasbourg in 1914. However, the causes of this slow promotion at the University of Berlin can only be surmised. Certain difficulties with Dilthey are supposed to have had something to do with it, but what was probably largely responsible was the fact of his Jewish ancestry. The Berlin University was Prussian in its atmosphere and the Prussian view of things was not likely to lead to speedy promotion and official encouragement of Jewish teachers (Spykman 1964).

In 1915, in Simmel's unsuccessful bid for a chair in philosophy at Heidelberg University, the Heidelberg philosophy faculty pointed to his major achievements as the transformation and completely new foundation of the social sciences (see Frisby 1992; Frisby & Featherstone 1997). However, the call to Heidelberg was prevented by a report of Windelband to the minister of education in Karlsruhe in which the term "destructive" as describing Simmel's thinking played a basic role. How far Windelband's own anti-Jewish feeling was involved, is unclear (see Jaworski 1997).

Simmel finally received a full professorship at the University of Strasbourg in 1914. He disliked leaving Berlin, which, in spite of many disappointments, had become very dear to him. But financial reasons forced him to leave the place where he had worked and taught for nearly thirty years for a more-lucrative position in a less-congenial environment. The institutional manifestation of his marginality was both his Jewish background and his failure to be granted full-academic accreditation until the twilight of his life, and that in an unsatisfying appointment as a professor at the University of Strasbourg (cf. Levine 1971). He died on 28 September 1918 after having finished his last book: *Lebensanschauungen*. He was a European in the best sense of the term, incapable of narrow chauvinism, a lover of that European culture which was for him an indivisible unity.

Simmel's work in the Zeitgeist around 1900 and after

Simmel, of course, was aware of the antisemitism that blocked his advancement within the German university system. Indeed, the very fact that Simmel has been designated as a philosopher, sociologist, social and cultural psychologist, and cultural theorist and critic should sound a cautionary note for those who wish to subsume Simmel's work under any one of these titles. Jaworski (1997: 94) speaks of Simmel as a "philosopher sociologist, one and indivisible." It is true that, with regard to establishing the foundations for some of these disciplines such as sociology, philosophy, or even cultural psychology, Simmel sought to demarcate their distinctive features (cf. Frisby 1994).

Moreover, in the sphere of theorizing about culture, it should not be forgotten that the noun "culture" (*Kultur*) was applied in his lifetime to a whole range of disciplines and theoretical practices: to the philosophy of culture; to the historical study of culture; to the development of a sociology of culture; to a critique of contemporary culture and; by Simmel himself, to a distinctive philosophical culture, as well as more general references to the culture of individuals, social classes and strata, and so on (cf. Smith 1991). His student Georg Lukács (1991) claimed that the sociology of culture as it developed in the early decades of the twentieth century was only possible on the basis of the foundational work of Ferdinand Tönnies and Georg Simmel. The work of Weber, Troeltsch, Sombart, Scheler, and Mannheim may be viewed in this context. In some of Simmel's early work we can also see evidence of his confrontation with attempts to establish a moral cultural sphere. Germany itself, after unification, was also the site of a religious struggle over culture (*Kulturkampf*).

Virtually every one of these dimensions of culture within the academic sphere was the site of often-contested attempts to establish academic disciplines around the sciences of culture, be they historical, philosophical, sociological, anthropological, psychological, or whatever. By the late nineteenth century, the newest of these disciplines, among them cultural psychology (or *Völkerpychologie*), were struggling to demarcate themselves from the more general, all-encompassing foundations for human sciences (*Geisteswissenschaften*—the German translation of John Stuart Mill's "Moral Sciences" but epitomized by the philosophical works of Dilthey), or cultural sciences (*Kulturwissenschaften*—epitomized in the foundational demarcation of human studies from the natural sciences in the works of Windelband and, especially, Rickert, with both of whom Simmel was associated). Within the domain of the social sciences, Simmel's early career at Berlin University was supported by the historical economist Gustav Smoller and Simmel's attempt (1890) to establish sociology as an independent science (see Koehnke 1990).

In Simmel's case, the interest in cultural phenomena cannot only be traced to his study of anthropology, but also, more significantly, to the work of Moritz Lazarus who, together with Heymann Steinthal, was the founder of *Völkerpsychologie*. When Simmel published one of his crucial foundational essays on sociology—*The Problem of Sociology*—in 1894 (see Simmel 1950), he acknowledged to Lazarus the central role of his *Völkerpsychologie* which "forcibly directed me to the problem of the supra-individual" (Koehnke 1996). Lazarus's *Völkerpsychologie* aimed both to study the development and evolution of human culture and to analyze contemporary cultural phenomena in terms of language and meaning, sociocultural foundations and sociocultural formation.

Simmel draws, however, upon another feature of Lazarus's work, namely, a concern for the emergence of independent cultural phenomena arising out of everyday interaction in the sociocultural world. The constellations and configurations of individuals interacting with one another generate supra-individual phenomena that are condensed, distilled or crystallized into distinctive forms. It is a feature of Simmel's writings on culture that he continually has recourse to the exploration and analysis of cultural forms in their emergence in everyday mundane interactions between individuals, however fleeting they might be. Of course, Simmel also has an interest in the persistence of sociocultural forms over time and space, as well as their overwhelming presentation in objective forms that confront individuals as estranged entities. The systematic nature of such study should not be seen as a mere classification of cultural forms but rather as a critical confrontation with the dynamic, often antagonistic, contradictionary, and ambivalent development of cultural forms that are to be located within Simmel's major contribution to the study of modernity.

All of Simmel's conceptions of society are either directly grounded in, or presuppose, the concept of interaction or reciprocal effects (*Wechselwirkung*). The concept of interaction or reciprocal effects was already in frequent use in philosophy and elsewhere in the second half of the nineteenth century. Any indication of Simmel's sources must be qualified as possibilities, as provisional, unless a direct connection can be established. However, in recent discussions, Frisby (1992) has outlined the putative relevance of Gustav Fechner's work for the young Simmel. Certainly in Fechner's work we find a conception of the reciprocal effects of physical and psychological elements upon one another rather than the operation of forces in a single direction. It is certainly true that Simmel knew Fechner's work and that early on he established an ensemble of relational concepts for his social theory but it is just as plausible to argue that these can be found in the *Völkerpsychologie* of Lazarus and Steinthal.

We also know that in the late eighteen eighties Simmel was lecturing on Hermann Lotze's practical philosophy, in which the concept of interaction also figures (Koehnke 1990). Moreover, more readily verifiable sources for Simmel's sociology and concept of society are to be found in the work of Spencer, Dilthey, and Lazarus. Herbert Spencer, for example, was read intensively by Simmel in his early years, providing him not merely with an elaborate discussion of the concept of differentiation, but also with a number of the historical and ethnographic examples and instances which populate his earlier works (Koehnke 1990).

Undoubtedly, there is also a clear intellectual closeness between Simmel's ideas and Bergson's (1911) developmental thought on the concept of adaptation (see Valsiner 1998 for a summary of Bergson's view on adaptation and personality). In an autobiographical remark, Simmel stated that "he felt fortunate that he grew up in a historical situation of radical transformations in which Nietzsche and Marx, Naturalism and *l'art pour l'art* shook all dogmatic positions in philosophy, social sciences, and aesthetics" (see Jaworski 1997: 94). Under Simmel's direction Gertrud Kantorowicz translated Henri Bergson's (1911) *Creative Evolution* into German, and both she and his wife separately edited posthumous collections of his essays (see Kearn *et al.* 1990). Simmel felt an affinity with the new antimechanistic biology and vitalistic philosophy and psychology of Henri Bergson. Simmel engaged critically with his society and its cultural phenomena, producing an analysis that focused not upon abstract themes but, according to his contemporaries, upon all that which to us and to him appeared problematical for human beings at the turn of the century. In this line of reasoning, there is, for example, his deep commitment to fundamental problems, such as the development of individuality. There is also his attention to the long-term changes within history. Equally, he is concerned with the minutest and most momentary changes, such as the brief accentuation of one facial feature that in turn alters the entire configuration of the face. And we also have his interest in the interaction between the individual and society. In so concerning himself, he became the greatest philosopher of culture in our times (Hoeber 1918). And, of course, Simmel does not allow us to forget our unsolved problem, namely, the mutuality between individuality, culture, and development or fundamental change. Simmel opened up for us the question of how to conceptualize both the individual and sociocultural processes by his persistence in alerting us to the problem of developing individuality within modern society.

In spite of his fragmentalism, his marginality, and his inferior academic status, Simmel's impact on his academic contemporaries was immediate and far-reaching (cf. Levine 1971, Kearn *et al.* 1990, Jaworski 1997). In search of subject matter that would distinguish his theory from all other social science and humanistic disciplines, Simmel charted a new field for discovery and proceeded to explore a world of novel topics in works that have guided and anticipated the thinking of generations of sociologists (compare Figure 3.1). For example, the influence of Simmel on Marx, Weber, and other German sociologists (Dahme 1990), on some of the most famous representatives of the Chicago school of sociology such as Robert Park and Ernest Burgess (see Levine 1971, Frisby 1992).

Moreover, Simmel's impact on Ernst Cassirer and William Stern was direct and enduring (see Stern 1938). Both Cassirer and Stern—among other important academics such as Johann Jakob von Uexküll, Fritz Heider, Heinz Werner, or Martha Muchow—were members of Hamburg University. Around 1920, Hamburg was an important intellectual center for German academic life (see Valsiner 1998). Here, it is also an interesting and not well-known biographical note that Cassirer attended Simmel's lectures at the University of Berlin before he moved to Hermann Cohen at the University of Marburg (Paetzold 1997). Finally, his affinity to the cultural view of both American pragmatism and the symbolic interactionist school (see Rochberg-Halton 1986, Jaworski 1997) is obvious.

However, the valuation of Simmel is of recent date, especially in Germany, his native country. If we take a look at the history of Simmel studies in Germany and abroad and consider the impact of his works outside Germany, we find some remarkable differences. In the USA, Simmel's influence has always been very great and the reception of his works largely positive (see Levine 1971, Frisby 1994, Frisby & Featherstone 1997). The English translation of Simmel's work had already commenced by 1893. Of importance was the translation of his essay *The Problem of Sociology* in 1895. As the result of Albion W. Small's interest in Simmel's sociology, *The American Journal of Sociology* from 1896 to 1910 carried a series of translations of Simmel's essays and extracts from his works. In the USA, it was largely Small's initiative at Chicago that established Simmel as the most translated German sociologist in this period.

More recently, Jaworsky (1997) published the first book-length examination of the American reception of Georg Simmel. Jaworski draws on archival data, correspondence, interviews, and detailed textual analysis to explore the practical and strategic uses of Simmel's writings by a range of American social thinkers (see also Figure 3.1). These thinkers include the Chicago School figures Albion Small, Robert E. Park, and Everett C. Hughes; functional sociologists Talcott Parsons, Robert K. Merton, Lewis A. Coser, and Kaspar D. Naegele; and, more recently, Erving Goffmann and postmodernists Deena and Michael Weinstein. Goffman attended the University of Chicago from 1945 to 1953, when he took his PhD.

At the turn of the century, as urbanization, industrialization, and immigration in the United States changed the pace and shape of American life, ideological confusion, coupled with an inchoate and anachronistic system of graduate education, led unprecedented numbers of young intellectuals to travel abroad in order to attain some mental and moral purchase on problems at home. They traveled mostly to Germany, and from the 1870s to the 1880s to the universities of Berlin and Leipzig. While Albion Small was at Berlin studying with Gustav Schmoller, Georg Simmel was there studying philosophy. Small and Simmel would later meet, perhaps through Schmoller, a mutual friend (Jaworski 1997). Their intellectual relationship contributes a central chapter to the American Simmel reception. Later, Small played no minor role in the foundation of the Chicago School of Sociology. It was Small, not Thomas, who first invited Park to Chicago. After Park joined the faculty in 1914, with strong support from Small, he gathered about himself most of the graduate students in the department. Later, Small transferred the intellectual leadership of the Chicago department over to Park. Unlike Small, Robert Park studied with Simmel; his only formal instruction in sociology. He made Simmel central to his own practical interests and reform efforts. By focusing on Simmel's "interaction," Park shifted social analysis from an emphasis on inherent and immutable individual characteristics to social conditions and mutable personalities.

After the deaths of his Chicago teachers, Albion Small and Robert Park, Everett Hughes became the hub around which much Simmel scholarship turned (see Jaworski 1997). Among the Simmel scholars of the period after World War II—Salomon at the New School, Merton at Columbia, for example—Hughes was *primus inter pares*. His position as senior American Simmel scholar was part historical accident and part design. As a student of both Small and Park in the mid-1920s, both of whom knew Simmel personally, Hughes became the living link to the past. Certainly Robert K. Merton could not claim such an aura (for a complete analysis of Merton's Simmel reception in the mid-1950s, see Jaworski 1989).

But a more important reason for Hughes's significance is that he defined himself as a "Simmel man" and cultivated the study of Simmel at Chicago (Jaworski 1997). Hughes's lectures and seminars on Simmel continued the Chicago Simmel tradition and inspired the next generation, including Erving Goffman and Donald N. Levine. In contrast, there was no Simmel tradition at Columbia before Merton, whose involvement with Simmel was fertile but unsustained. However, Merton went to some pains to acknowledge the influence of Simmel among his recognized "masters-at-a-distance," and payed tribute to him in connection with several detailed analyses (see Sztompka 1986 for a more detailed discussion of the Simmel–Merton relationship).

Finally, for Talcott Parsons, Simmel was his exemplar for the solution of the scope of problematic sociology. While Parsons did not accept Simmel's specific formula for solving this problem, he did accept his general strategy (Jaworski 1997). Parsons' problem was to discover a way to move from the consideration of the action of a single individual to a consideration of all individuals in the community in relation to each other. Simmel's sociology was central to Parsons' solution to this problem, and this solution is a central part of his section on Simmel. Jaworski called it "Simmel's action theory contribution" (Jaworski 1997: 48). Rather than being peripheral to fuctional sociology, Simmel was a key architect of its intellectual and moral vision.

Post Simmel: on the current revival of interest in his philosophy of culture

The period after the First World War saw the continuation of translations of Simmel's works into Russian. In the United States, between the two world wars, the impetus for translations of Simmel's work lay solely within the Chicago School, either with Robert Park or Ernest Burgess, the founders of the famous Chicago School of Sociology introductory textbook, or as translations for circulation within the Chicago sociology department.

Interestingly, the largest number of translations appeared in Russian by the time of Simmel's death in 1918. Unfortunately, so far no one has seriously shed light on how Russian social sciences were influenced by Simmel's work (see Lohmann 1993 for the Simmel–Marx connection). But more remains to be done, and other Russian thinkers, perhaps Mikhail Bakhtin or Lev Vygotsky, merit similar comparison with Simmel. To make these relationships clearer, research on the Russian reception of Simmel is needed.

In Germany, by contrast, the situation with regard to reading and interpreting Simmel was rather different, if not quite the reverse, especially when we leave aside recent developments and consider instead the whole history of the reception of Simmel's theories (Dahme 1990). The 1950s saw the first new wave of interest in Simmel's sociology, stimulated most significantly by Wolff's (1950) edited collection, *The Sociology of Georg Simmel*. Almost a decade later, Etzkorn edited a valuable translated collection of Simmel's essays on culture and aesthetics (Simmel 1968). A useful collection of extracts from Simmel's works which once more made his work more accessible to students was that edited by Donald N. Levine (1971). One cannot say, however, that there was no interest at all in Simmel during the 1960s and 1970s in Germany; but the study of Simmel's works was not widespread. In fact, it was through this American sociological theorizing of the late 1950s and 1960s that Simmel's sociology was brought back to Germany. In the early 1970s, with the decline of the functionalistic paradigm, some few scholars set out to approve his approach to the study of society and to appreciate his importance as a classical figure of modern sociology (see Dahme 1990). This, in fact, prepared the way for the more nuanced reception of his work in Germany in the late 1970s and 1980s in which his more strictly sociological writings were placed in the context of his other writings on philosophy, psychology, aesthetics, and culture (see Frisby 1992, Frisby & Featherstone 1997).

The last decade has seen a marked renewal of interest in Simmel's work (see Kearn *et al.* 1990, Frisby 1994). Since 1989, the first volumes, out of a projected series of twenty-four, of a critical German edition of Simmel's works have begun to appear. The increasing attention given to Simmel's work during the last decade contrasts, however, with the more recent sociological theory textbooks in Britain and the United States, which often give only a passing reference to Simmel's writings. And it is in sharp contrast to some psychologists at the turn of the century like Stern or Lewin. In the psychology of the late twentieth century, even in the most recent cultural psychology textbooks, Simmel is completely absent.

Taken together, we are facing the apparent paradox that the reception of Simmel—who produced dozens of brilliant ideas—is generally ambivalent. He is enthusiastically assimilated by some authors whereas he is either rejected or neglected by others. On the one hand, he is praised for being a gold mine of good ideas, for having brilliant insights, for having anticipated role-theory, small-group theory, postmodernism, and many of the twentieth-century risks of society, for having said profound things about the dyad and the triad, and for having had deep insights into the modern metropolis. At the same time, the writers who praise Simmel also point out that he is unsystematic, that his methodology is confused, and that his writing and thinking are incoherent. Indeed, Simmel's work has a rather peculiar history of reception. Both during his life-time and even to this day he has been a stranger in the academic community. There are several reasons for the paradoxical situation with Simmel's work (see Dahme 1990 for an extensive discusssion of the disregard and low estimation of Simmel, especially in German intellectual culture). Here, I can just make a few comments:

First, the young Simmel favored an empirical and comparative method, and thus came into conflict with the mainstream of German philosophy and *Geisteswissenschaften* in the neo-Kantian and Dilthey tradition. His protracted difficulties in obtaining a professorial chair within the German university system testify to this. But the references to reality contained in his philosophy as well as his interpretations of modernity made him the philosophical "favorite" of the public. He offered unorthodox answers and explanations where orthodox philosophy either refused answers or abstained from giving them. Thus, many philosophers like Bloch, Lukács, and Cassirer who are still high in repute today were among his students (see Figure 3.1).

Second, at the same time, he increasingly gained importance for all those sociologists who joined in the program of establishing sociology as an independent academic discipline. Over a long period, Simmel—with Weber and Durkheim—was cited as the most important forerunner and founder of sociology as a special science. But in time, and especially after Simmel's death, German sociological scholars like Vierkandt and von Wiese came to be more interested in promoting their own image of sociologists. Thus citation of Simmel as the founder of German sociology ceased and Simmel's name was no longer mentioned in conjunction with the so-called new sociology. Even outside Germany, commentators on Simmel have frequently failed to do justice to his entire work, although it is precisely to the non-German Simmel researchers that the credit goes for preserving Simmel from falling completely into oblivion. At least in the USA, Simmel is primarily known as a sociologist. However, he would not have refered to himself as a sociologist; he certainly thought that he was a philosopher (see Kearn *et al.* 1990). In the 1990s, however, even in Germany, research on Simmel got under way (cf. Dahme 1990, Koehnke 1996, Lohmann 1993).

Chapter 4

Simmelian cultivation

The mutuality of person and culture

There exist a number of significant dimensions to Simmel's various attempts to define culture. From around 1900 onwards, his focus of attention shifts from studying man's sociation (see Simmel 1895) towards the process of the creation or cultivation of culture. Most significantly, culture as cultivation is, as it were, formed intentional subjectivity that emerges out of human life and its reciprocal interactions between person and culture and is created by human beings as objectified contents in language, artifacts, and so on. The concept of cultivation was introduced by Simmel in 1903 in his famous *The Metropolis and Mental Life* (see Simmel 1950) and was later elaborated in his essays *The Concept of Culture* (see Simmel 1990), *On the Essence of Culture* (1908a), and *The Concept and the Tragedy of Culture* published in 1911/12. The latter is perhaps the most well-known piece of Simmel's sociology of culture. Despite Simmel's pessimistic view at the end of his lifetime, his lifelong scientific question was how individuation emerges as a process of cultivation. This is a challenge that human beings alone meet, as only they have the ability to strive towards their own individuation. Today, the originality, comprehensiveness and deep attraction of Simmel's theoretical purpose still recommend him as one of the truly significant primary thinkers on questions of culture (cf. Frisby & Featherstone 1997). As a developmental psychologist, then, my main thesis, occasionally hinted at but never spelled out by Simmel scholars, is that one of Simmel's major contributions was the analysis of a bio-psycho-cultural developmental model of the emergence of human individuality.

Relationalism, as-if heuristic, and reciprocal interaction

One of the epistemological cornerstones of Simmel's philosophy is his constructionist foundations that make him realize that humans do not only *analyze* the world, they also *create* it with the same heuristic tools that they use for its analysis. This viewpoint firmly places Simmel in phenomenological and constructionist sociology. Accordingly, Kearn (1985) shows that in his thinking Simmel was grounded in the epistemological point of view known as the "Philosophy of As-If." Simmel, however, has not written any account of his use of the As-If.

Closest to this account is Chapter 1.3 of his book *The Philosophy of Money*. In fact, there is really only one book on the Philosophy of As-If: Hans Vaihinger's *Die Philosophie des Als-Ob*, published—also in the era of the "cultured individual"—in 1911. At the core of the philosophy of As-If are the following claims: The mind works independently of external reality. This independence manifests itself in the mind's capacity to treat the objects to be known-and-discovered—things as well as people—*as-if* they were what they are. The world as we know it is the result of people behaving "as-if." Interestingly, Vaihinger and Simmel arrived at very similar epistemological conclusions because they shared the same interpretation of the work of Immanuel Kant. Thus, the aim of this chapter is to present Georg Simmel's epistemology and some of the ways it shapes his philosophy of culture. With respect to more contemporary concerns of theorizing, it should be pointed out that more recent literature on both the "cognitive paradigm" (an excellent overview is provided by Howard Gardner 1985) and Michael Cole's (1996) cultural-mediational paradigm appear to be directly related to Simmelian theorizing. Here, the most recent literature in cognitive anthropology, such as Bradd Shore's (1996) *Culture in Mind*, should also be included.

Within Simmel's epistemology, the master function that is used for the creation as well as the analysis of the world—the object-to-be-known—is his relationalism (Kearn 1985). Simmel (1990) writes at length about it in his *The Philosophy of Money*. He points out that the relativizing function is, as far as he is concerned, "the foundation of our mind." Simmel shares with the Philosophy of As-If the view that the human mind functions independent of nature that is outside of it. These functions of the mind are what Kant called the *a priori*. While Kant saw these functions as immutable, Simmel saw them as changing, and he included them in a general process of evolution. The consequences of this independence of the mind are twofold: First, the picture that the mind creates for us when we analyze the world by using the functions of the mind is not necessarily a true reflection of reality; and, second, these functions of the mind *create* reality-as-we-know-it. Unlike Kant, Simmel insisted that it is the *whole* human being that is involved in the acquisition of knowledge, and he placed great importance on humans' inner life and the role it plays in the acquisition of knowledge. All these functions of the mind such as cognitions, emotions, and motivations include of course the familiar *a priori* cause and effect, time, and others.

Among those functions, however, is one that is peculiar, a master-function: It is the ability of the human mind to treat things—artifacts as well as people—as-if they were what they are not. By treating things "as-if," we create "fictions" (see Vaihinger 1911 or more recently Josephs 1998 for more details of the Philosophy of As-If). That is, the mind works independent of external reality. Thus, the As-If heuristic as well as other functions of the mind serve the dual purpose of, on the one hand, analyzing the object-to-be-known, and, on the other hand, creating the object-to-be-known. This as-if heuristic is used at the same time to *interpret* the world and to *create* the world. Simmel states his general relationalism by saying that:

> Whatever an object is to us, it is what it is because of and in relation to, another object. Objects exist to us only by virtue of another existing. This form of "one-object-emanating-from another", this "one-thing-determines-the-other" is the mode of operation of our mind with which it [the mind] creates the world.
> (Simmel 1990: 69)

And he continues: "The claim that things are related in such and such a way, has to be replaced by the claim: our knowledge-and-discovery has to proceed *as-if* things were related in such and such a way" (Simmel 1990: 73).

This is Simmel's most explicit statement of his relationalism. It shows that his relationalism is a "fiction" in Vaihinger's language. It also shows clearly that the as-if is a general principle in Simmel's epistemology. His relationalism applies to all things, human and nonhuman, and, most importantly, is clearly identified as an As-If procedure. Since it is a function of the mind to proceed as-if, and because the functions of the mind necessarily have to be used, they must be used, therefore, not only by the scientist when he analyzes the world but by everybody when we analyze our everyday world. These processes of the mind are not only used for analyses and the formation of knowledge but also for the *creation* of the object-to-be-known. As it will be outlined in this book, the implications of Simmel's epistemology for a culture-inclusive theory of identity formation are substantial.

One relativizing method that people use to create order out of the chaotic reality—such as the metropolis or the money market—with which they are confronted is to divide the object-to-be-known-and-discovered into a dynamic part which changes into a static part which remains unchanged. In other words, one of the ways in which people understand their world—and construct the world—is to view people as well as artifacts under the As-If assumption that they are composed of an inner, constant nucleus and an ever-changing phenomenon. We see things—and it echoes the dynamic between an identity's sameness and change—as the product of the relation of the constant and the changing. The one cannot exist without the other, only in relation to the other. Things move in relation to those which do not move, and things remain constant with respect to our relation to those which change or move.

This process of relating things is at the heart of Simmel's relationalism, and it is socially relevant as well because what is true of "things"—or artifacts—is also true of people; we see ourselves in relation to others. We look at ourselves as-if we were somebody else, and we understand ourselves by viewing ourselves in relation to "others" whom we can see as changing or as continuous, depending on whether we want to look at ourselves as stable or changing. The implications for culture-inclusive theorizing on identity formation are obvious: the dissection of things into changing and stable components has its epistemological base in the fact that humans view themselves as having an unchanging inner core which creates the developing or changing part of ourselves in combination with the sociocultural "flux of life."

In general, it is the function of our thinking to actively seek out the stable core, "the reliable," and then to place things-to-be-analyzed in this relation. In this way people create frames of references with which we orient ourselves in the wealth of fleeting phenomena. Simmel (1990) points out that modern science has moved away from the old viewpoint were the phenomena were stable, to a conception were everything moves and changes. He states that modern science has moved to a process-oriented, dynamic conception of the world. Simmel says that this shift from a stationary to a dynamic view is nicely exemplified by the shift from viewing the globe as a stationary object to viewing it as an object in a motion that is determined by its relation to other bodies.

According to Simmel, therefore, the course taken in the gaining of knowledge and in the making of discoveries is determined by two antithetical motivations. On the one hand, there is the motivation to be systematic and to preserve the system of knowledge—that is, for example, the continuity of one's personal identity—that has been achieved by not admitting knowledge that would disturb the systematicity. On the other hand, there is the motivation to be progressive, to push the limits of knowledge—that corresponds, for example, to the change dimension of personal identity. In logical terms then, continuity amounts to completeness whereas the open-endedness of change corresponds to incompleteness. Taken together, Simmel sees knowledge-and-discovery as never reaching a final conclusion. One of his reasons for believing this puts him in direct opposition to Kant—although he is usually classified as a Kantian or a neo-Kantian. Simmel took the evolutionary doctrine seriously, and he sees a changing and evolving mind.

The cyclic nature of thinking, and how it contributes to the creation of the world, was one of the concerns of Simmel that occupied his epistemology and his thinking in general. The idea of circularity or reciprocity shows itself in many forms. Simmel's type of relationalism is a form of what he calls circularity. His much-puzzled-over concept *Wechselwirkung* is another instance of it. Kearn (1985) translated *Wechselwirkung* not, as it most often is done, as "interaction" but rather as "reciprocal orientation." I agree with Kearn that reciprocal orientation expresses much more adequately the necessary character of what Simmel means by *Wechselwirkung*. However, I prefer the term reciprocal interaction, since *Wechselwirkung* is a bidirectional function, which focuses on the mutuality between the individual (subjective) mind and the cultural (objective) mind. It is also one of the main principles that create and regulate the sociocultural world-as-we-know-it, because human beings use the relativizing function of their minds, and by doing so they create relations between alter and ego—and alter and alter. Its result is *Vergesellschaftung*, or sociation; it creates society.

Along this line of reasoning, Simmel, at first, starts out from a regulative principle that everything interacts in some way with everything else. This principle of reciprocal interaction holds for society too. Second, the dynamic element of reciprocal interaction is often emphasized, as in the statement that "between every point in the world and every force permanently moving relationships exist" (Simmel 1890: 13). Later, he identified both principles as symptomatic of real tendencies in intellectual life, as a general tendency of modern thought, with its dissolving of substances into functions, the fixed and permanent in the flux of restless development. Third, in order to come to terms with this dynamic interaction of totality, he argued that the only appropriate concepts were relational ones. Fourth, any substantive unity that exists or is discerned is itself the result of reciprocal interaction. Taken together, these presuppositions from which he elaborates his various conceptions of society and individuation already indicate the centrality of a dynamic interaction that can only be grasped through relational concepts: reciprocal interaction, sociation, or the process by which we become socialized.

Simmel gained his concept of "interaction" through the analysis of Dilthey and Lazarus in which he found the well-known compromise that sociology can neither start out from the isolated individual, nor from society, nor from the opposition "individual and society." Simmel's position is a compromise between Lazarus and Dilthey, between the idea of *Völkerpsychologie* and *Geisteswissenschaften*. It is true and well known that not only does Simmel describe society by using the concept of interaction, but Dilthey does too (Koehnke 1990). Simmel, however, rejected Dilthey's "play of interactions" when it means that society is only the interplay of very many boundless interactions.

Here again it is Lazarus' theory of condensation which leads to a solution: interactions produce relatively fixed forms, both groups and forms of objective culture in a more unpersonal manner (Simmel 1890). In contrast, Dilthey only conceded interaction between individuals. Nations and groups, Dilthey said, cannot have a soul of their own and therefore no unified effect (see Koehnke 1990). Simmel replied that they indeed do not have a soul or spirit. For Simmel, the question about the unity of the soul was not the main problem. Individuals do not have any such single soul or spirit; but they do undoubtedly produce uniform effects (see Frisby 1985). In fact, for Simmel, the main question is whether they have uniform effects. And here he answered almost directly quoting Lazarus, who in 1865 dealt with this question in his *On the Relation between Individuality and Totality*, as part of a continuing discussion with Dilthey (see Koehnke 1990). The theory of interaction is found here in its first formulation and the main term of Simmel's sociology—*Wechselwirkung*—as well as other ideas that emerge out of a direct reception of Lazarus' writings. Thus, according to Simmel, the socialized individual always remains in a dual relation with society; he or she is incorporated within it and yet stands against it. The individual is, at the same time, within and outside society—for it and for him- or herself. In fact, the individual is determined, yet determining; acted upon, yet self-actuating (see Coser 1965).

Subjective culture and objective culture

In defining culture, Simmel's (1911) logical point of departure is "dualistic" or rather "dialectical," in a twofold sense: not only subject versus object, but conscious personhood in opposition to a natural world. The decisive passage bears quoting in full:

> Humans, unlike the animals, do not allow themselves simply to be absorbed by the naturally given order of the world. Instead, they bear themselves loose from it, place themselves in opposition to it, making demands of it, overpowering it, then overpowered by it. From this first great dualism springs the never-ending contest between subject and object, which finds its second tribunal within the realm of the mind itself.
>
> (Simmel 1911: 183)

The antagonistic directions then reveal themselves as a process of objectification:

> The spirit engenders innumerable structures which keep on existing with a peculiar autonomy independently of the soul that has created them, as well as of any other that accepts or rejects them. Thus, the subject sees itself confronting art as well as law, religion as well as technology, science as well as custom. Now it is attracted, now repelled by their contents, now fused with them as if they were part of itself, now estranged and untouched by them. In the form of stability, coagulation, persistent existence, the spirit becomes object, places itself over against the streaming life, the intrinsic responsibility and the variable tensions of the soul.
>
> (Simmel 1911: 27)

The process results in a radical and permanent tension—a *Formgegensatz* in Simmel's terminology—between vital, finite life and the relatively fixed, timeless forms it is destined to create as a precondition for its own expression and survival. This dense passage, with its exotic language of "spirit" and "soul," amounts to Simmel's version of the Hegelian objectification of mind: the human appearing as subject, with a subjective being, is opposed to the objective "natural world," and in this opposition creates a content and form for "life" and its "objects." And the "idea of culture," declares Simmel (1918), "dwells in the middle of this dualism." Here, two senses of the concept of culture seem to follow from these remarks. The one elaborates the metaphor of culture "as the path of the soul to iself," as a repression of the authentic subject. The other idea of culture suggests expression, development, and fulfillment of that which is essentially human. Culture becomes, quite directly:

> . . . the completion of the soul in which it takes the detour through the formations of the intellectual-historical work of the species: the cultural path of the subjective spirit traverses science and the forms of life, art and state, vocation and knowledge of the world—the path on which it now returns to itself as higher and perfected spirit.
>
> (Simmel 1918: 232)

Yet from this perspective "life" must also be something formed, and the activity of culture can offer it a "unity of the soul," that is the enticing prospect of a "solution to a subject-object-dualism" through the premise of setting the preconditions for qualities that could be designed self-development and personality.

However, Simmel's sense of culture is rich with paradox for, on the one hand, culture requires an unresolved dualism, while, on the other hand, it proposes to mediate or synthesize the dialectically separated poles of existence through cultivation. Subjective culture, driven towards perfection of its identity, "cannot by itself reach the perfection of culture," yet culture "is always a synthesis" of subjective life and the contents of life that "presupposes the divisibility of elements as an antecedent" (Simmel 1911: 186). Modernity accounts for such otherwise incomprehensible tension and potential confusion: as Simmel contends, "only in an analytically inclined age like the modern could one find in synthesis the deepest, the one and only relationship of form between spirit and world" (Simmel 1911: 192–193).

It would be most accurate to speak of a longing for synthesis and wholeness as characteristic of this most modern resolve. The clearest depiction of a second sense of the concept of culture comes at the end of Simmel's thinking on the subject in *The Conflict of Modern Culture*, where he decides to speak of culture not so much whenever it functions through mediation as cultivation, but rather:

> whenever life produces certain forms in which it expresses and realizes itself: work of art, religions, sciences, technologies, laws, and innumerable others. These forms encompass the flow of life and provide it with content and form, latitude [*Spielraum*] and order. But although these forms arise out of the life process, because of their unique constellation they do not share the restless rhythm of life, its ascent and descent, its constant renewal, its incessant divisions and reunifications. These forms are cages [*Gehäuse*] for the creative life which, however, soon transcends them. They should also house the imitative life, for which, in the final analysis, there is no space left. They acquire fixed identities, a logic of lawfulness of their own [*eigene Logik and Gesetzlichkeit*]; this new rigidity inevitably places them at a distance from the spiritual dynamic which created them and which makes them independent.
>
> (Simmel 1918: 11)

Along these lines of reasoning—and as early as social constructivism, symbolic interactionism, and pragmatism—Simmel (1990) in his *The Philosophy of Money* (originally published in 1900) dealt intensively with the paradoxical issue of man as being simultaneously creator and creature of culture. In grappling with the definition of culture, Simmel (1990) sees as central the question of the intersection of subject and object or of reciprocal interaction between "subjective culture," or *cultura animi*, and "objective culture," or *natura altera*.

Just as, from an epistemological standpoint, we draw our life-contents from a realm of "objectively valid entities" (Simmel 1990: 452), so, viewed historically, we draw the major part of them from the stock of accumulated mental labour of human beings. Here too we find preformed contents that are ready to be realized by individual minds but yet preserve their possibilities, which do not coincide with that of a material object. For even when the mind is tied to matter, as in tools, works of arts, books, and clothes, it is never identical with that part of them that is percetible to our senses. According to Simmel's (1990) *The Philosophy of Money*, the mind lives in them in a hardly definable potential form, which the individual mind is able to actualize. And Simmel continues: "Objective culture is the historical presentation or more or less perfect condensation of an objectively valid truth which is reproduced by our cognition" (Simmel 1990: 452).

That is, on the one hand, the name of objective culture can be given to things, extended, enhanced and "perfected" (*sensu* Simmel) so as to lead the soul to its own "perfection," or to constitute a part of the road to higher life of the individual or the sociocultural context. By establishing this category of "objective mind" (Simmel 1990) as the historical manifestation of the intellectual content of things in general, it becomes clear how the cultural process that Simmel recognizes as a subjective development—the culture of things as a human culture—can be separated from its content. This content, as I outlined above, acquires another physical condition and thus provides the basis for the phenomenon of the separate development of objective and subjective culture. If the objective mind of historical society is its cultural content in the widest sense, then the practical cultural significance of its individual elements is defined by the extent to which they become factors in individual development (Simmel, 1990). If we, for example, presuppose that Einstein's theory of relativity was only preserved in a book which no one knew, it would still be part of the objectified mind and a potential possession of society, but no longer a cultural value.

Since this extreme example can occur in countless cases, it follows that in society at large only a certain proportion of objective cultural values become subjective values. That is, the whole cultural development is richer in content than each of its elements (Simmel 1990). For example, the entire life-style of a community depends upon the relationship between the objectified culture and the culture of the subjects. In the small community of a less-rich culture, this relationship will be almost one of perfect equality; the objective cultural opportunities will not extend much beyond the subjective cultural reality. An increase in the objective cultural opportunities—particularly if it coincides with an enlargement of the group or the implementation of a new technology—will favor a discrepancy between both. However, the size of the social group does not yet in itself fully explain the divergence of the subjective and objective factors.

By "subjective culture," on the other hand, Simmel (1990) understands the degree of personal development thus attained. Objective and subjective culture, therefore, are coordinated concepts only if the former is understood in a figurative sense, namely if one ascribes to things an independent impulse towards perfection, a consciousness that they ought to develop beyond their natural limits. The human motivation which brings this about is then imagined to be only the means used by things, as it were, to this end. It is to create a symbolic parallel to this process by treating the development of things as if it were *per se* a teleological process, and then dividing it into a natural and a cultivated stage; the latter, as a self-sufficient state proceeding in its ascent, or a part thereof, by means of the intervention of human activity.

But when understood more precisely, the two senses in which the concept of culture is used are not at all anologous (see Simmel 1968). On the contrary, subjective culture is the overriding final goal, and its measure is the measure of how far the mental process has any part in those objective entities and their development. Clearly, there can be no subjective culture without objective culture, because individual development constitutes culture only by virtue of its inclusion of such objects. Objective culture, on the other hand, can, relatively speaking, become substantially—though not completely—independent of subjective culture, by the creation of "cultivated" objects, i.e. cultivating objects, as they should properly be understood, whose "value" as such is subjectively utilized only to an incomplete degree. However, the relationship between objectified mind and its evolution to the subjective mind is of extreme importance to every cultural community (see Simmel 1990).

The "individual law" as the epigenetic chart

For Simmel, in the case of individuality the entire historical heritage is at stake, and both man's biological existence and culture as a whole are implicated. In his essays on culture, Simmel reminds us of an issue that we have yet to solve, an issue which may be fundamental to our discipline. To me, the hidden relevance of Simmel's work on individuality and culture to a culture-inclusive psychology of identity formation lies in his examination of the question of how individuality develops according to its own "individual law." That is, the importance of subjective culture derives from the fact that human beings carry within themselves the intrinsic motivation to be cultivated. Culture in the subjective sense of the term, exists only in the presence of self-development, provided that this self-development relies on external means. The person acts his/her becoming out in the direction of his/her "individual law"—that is, so to speak, the epigenetic chart. Individuation through purposive cultural mediation is thus based upon a biological principle:

> The natural development . . . only leads to a certain point, at which it is replaced by cultural development. The wild pear tree produces hard, sour fruit. That is so far as it can develop under the conditions of wild growth . . . namely that phase in which only inherent energies are developed. This phase ends as soon as an intelligent will, with means at its disposal, takes up these energies and, with them, creates states which could not be attained by those energies unaided. If this seems to mean that the concept of culture is identical with that of purposive human activity in general, the concept needs to be qualified in order to pin down its special meaning.
>
> (Simmel 1908a: 40)

Thus, at this point, human will and intelligence have intervened and managed to make the tree produce the edible pear; that is to say, the tree has been "cultivated."

> In just the same way we think of the human race first developing, by virtue of psycho-physical constitution, heredity, and adaptation, to certain forms and modes of existence. Only then can teleological processes take over and develop these existing things, within the limits of their foregoing development. The point at which this change to a new evolutionary energy occurs marks the boundary between nature and culture.
>
> (Simmel 1908a: 40)

Thus, for Simmel, cultivation presupposes the prior existence of an entity in an uncultivated, i.e. natural, state:

> It also presupposes that the ensuing change of this entity is somehow latent in its natural structure of energies [the individual law], even if it cannot be achieved by the entity itself but only through the process of culture [i.e. cultivation]. That is to say, cultivation develops its object to that perfection which is predetermined as a potential of its essential underlying tendency. Hence we regard the pear tree as cultivated because the work of the gardener only develops the potential dormant in the organic constitution of its natural form, thus effecting the most complete evolution of its own nature. If, on the other hand, a tree trunk is made into a ship's mast, this, too, is undoubtedly the work of culture, but not a "cultivation" of the tree trunk, because the form given it by the shipbuilder is not inherent in its nature. It is, on the contrary, a purely external addition imposed by a system of purposes alien to its own character.
>
> (Simmel 1908a: 41)

This linguistic nuance obviously indicates that the fruit, despite the fact that it could not have come about without human effort, still ultimately springs from the tree's own "motive forces" and only fulfills the potentialities which are sketched out in its tendencies, whereas the mast form is added to the trunk from an instrumental system quite alien to it and without any preformation in the tendencies of its own nature.

Thus, for Simmel (1908a), all cultivation is not only the development of some entity beyond the form attainable by natural processes—i.e. the genotype—alone. It is development in accordance with an original inner essence, the perfection of an entity in terms of its own significance, its most profound impulse. Simmel, however, believes that this perfection is unattainable at the stage which he calls "natural," which consists in the purely causal development of initial inherent energies. According to Simmel:

> It comes into being, rather, by the combination of those energies and the new teleological intervention, an intervention in the potential direction of the entity

> itself, which may thus be called the culture of that entity . . . this means that only man himself is the real object of culture.
>
> (Simmel 1908a: 41–42)

And Simmel elaborates his epigenetic view further when he says that man's potential already has its own language. Whatever can be attained by the development of the soul is, according to Simmel, already present in its state at any time, "as an invisible inner pattern" (Simmel 1908a: 42). Along this line of reasoning, he argues that its "content" is actualized only in a vague, fragmentary way. However, it is a "positive feeling of direction" (Simmel 1908a: 42).

> Full development, as destiny and as capacity, is inseparably bound up with the existence of the human soul. It alone possesses the potential for development towards goals that are exclusively inherent in the teleology of its own being. However, it too cannot attain these goals purely through that growth from within which we call natural growth, but beyond a certain point it requires a "technique," a procedure directed by the will.
>
> (Simmel 1908a: 42)

Subjectivity rather than teleology

For Simmel, the individual with his/her potential of his/her psychic organization is still conceived of as radically open. Simmel speaks of "natural potentialities" and as such they exist "only as possibilities" (Simmel 1911/12: 57). Thus, he completely rejects a scientific tradition that saw human beings as determined by mechanical causality and pure epigenesis:

> . . . it is never inherent in the same way in the intrinsic meaning of their existence, it is never predetermined in their natural state as a kind of activity, in the way that the perfection attainable by the human soul is inherent therein.
>
> (Simmel 1908a: 42)

For Simmel (1908a), culture as cultivation also means the maximum development of a person's potential from its natural stage, following the "authentic intrinsic direction" of the particular personality while necessitating the "teleological intervention" or mediation to guide his "energies," i.e. the purposive element of cultivation processes. Indeed, the epigenetic chart is countered by Simmel's view of man as an individual who exists in that he acts purposively upon culture, i.e. the individual is *causa finalis*. Cultivation could, therefore, be described as a cyclical process of subjectification of objective culture, re-objectification of subjective culture, re-subjectification, and so on. In the same manner, the unity or lack of unity of the object that individuals create affects, in a psychological sense, the corresponding formation of their personality. Simmel (1990) postulates that whenever an individual's energies do not produce something whole as a reflection of the total personality, then the proper relationship between subject and object is missing. That is the internal nature of an individual's achievement is bound up with parts of achievements accomplished by others, which are a necessary part of the totality, but it does not refer back to the producer. As a result, the inadequacy that develops between the individual's self and that of his/her product because of greater specialization easily serves to completely divorce the product from the individual.

Following Simmel (1990), what is "meaning" is not derived from the mental mind of the individual producer but from its relationship with products of a different origin. Because of its fragmentary character, the product lacks the individual's mental "determinancy" that can easily be perceived in an artifact that is wholly the product of a *single* person—or for a *single* person. The significance of the artifact is then to be found only in the objective achievement that leads away from the subject. Thus, the more completely an artifact composed of subjective components absorbs the parts, and the more the character of each part serves only as a part of the whole, then the more objective is that whole and the more is its life independent of the subjects who created it. Generally speaking, a broadening of consumption corresponds to the specialization of production. The broadening of consumption, however, is dependent upon the growth of objective culture, since the more objective and impersonal an artifact is the better it is suited to more people. Such consumable artifacts, in order to be acceptable and enjoyable to a very large number of individuals, cannot be designed for subjective differentiation of taste, while on the other hand only the most extreme differentiation of production is able to produce artifacts cheaply and abundantly enough in order to satisfy the demand for them.

Coming back to subjective culture—which is termed in this book the internal or mental mind—results from cultivation of the developing uniqueness of the individual, which takes place through "interactions" with objective cultural contents—that is, so to speak, the cultural or external mind. "By cultivating objects, that is by increasing their value beyond the performance of their natural constitution, we cultivate ourselves; it is the same value-increasing process developing out of us and returning back to us that moves external nature or our own nature" (Simmel 1990: 447).

Thus, people cultivate not only their subjective culture, but also their objective culture. Again, cultivation is both *cultura animi* and *cultura altera*. Simmel reasoned that "cultivatedness is a spiritual state, but of such a kind as is attained by the use of purposively formed objects" (Simmel 1908a: 42).

And Simmel's "perfection" does not remain a purely immanent process, but takes the form of a unique adaptation, a teleological or rather subjective "interweaving of subject and object" (Simmel 1908a: 43). If then the development of the subjective culture:

> does not involve any objective artifact as a means and stage of its progress back to itself, then even values of the highest order are created, within the soul [subjective culture] or in the outside world [objective culture] . . . All these

> spheres of the inner and outer world are developed teleologically beyond their "natural" limitations; they thus, of course, become capable of functioning as cultural values.
>
> (Simmel 1908a: 43)

In fact, Simmel, replaces ideals of perfection, which human beings are supposed to achieve, with developmental trends. Following the interpretation of Simmel's notion of teleology by Georg Lohmann (1993), Simmel sees the determination of human ends not really teleologically but rather subjectively. Such a perspective leads to the conclusion that there is no absolute peak or endpoint in the development of human beings but rather that "the series of life-goals end at various different points" (Simmel 1893: 348).

Moreover, there is for Simmel no ultimate end which could not itself become a means. The loss of ultimate ends leads not only to a relational position but also to a fundamental relationalism, as it was outlined above. However, the somehow autonomous objective cultures are not such values *per se*, but are subject to criteria and norms derived only from their "objective content," not from the requirements of the unified centre of human personality. For this reason, Simmel notes, "it appears that there is a reciprocal determination of value by the objects" (Simmel 1990: 78).

For Simmel (1990) such a determination of relative value no longer requires any reference to the emotional ties of subjects to their objects involved. The relativity of value itself is simply a "mutual relationship" (p. 81); it is interaction (*Wechselwirkung*).

However, their contribution to the development of "human personality" is, according to Simmel, a different matter:

> However excellently they may serve our specific ends, their value for our lives as a whole, for the well-spring of our being in its struggle for development, may be very slight. Conversely, they may be imperfect and insignificant in the objective, technical perspective of their specific province, but may, for all that, offer precisely what our life needs for the harmony of its parts, for its mysterious unity. . . .
>
> (Simmel 1908a: 43)

Here we see the essence of the modernity, so to speak, of Simmel's definition of culture as cultivation. That is, individuals are not cultivated simply because they have formed this or that "individual item of knowledge or ability" (Simmel 1911/12: 56) within themselves, but only if all those things serve the development of that "psychological centrality which is connected to culture but does not coincide with it" (Simmel 1911/12: 56).

Moreover, an individual's efforts are aimed at particular "potentialities," and this is, according to Simmel, why the development of every person, viewed according to what can be named in them, is

> . . . a bundle of lines of growth that extend in quite different directions and with quite different lengths. However, it is not all these . . . which make a person cultivated, but only their significance for or their development of the individual's indefinable personal unity.
>
> (Simmel 1911/12: 56)

Looking more closely at the feedback process from the point of view of culture, one could say that what Simmel calls objective culture functions as the intermediary station between the not-yet-cultivated subject and the cultivated subject. Levine (1971: xix) summarizes this process as follows: "Cultivation is the process of developing a state of being in a creature which (1) would not come about naturally, but (2) for which he/she has a natural propensity, (3) by shaping, reconstructing, or creating objects external to it." As a consequence, Simmel gives a definition of culture in which these dynamic and goal-oriented mechanisms are included: "Culture is the way that leads from closed unity through the unfolding multiplicity to the unfolded unity" (Simmel 1968: 28).

The closeness of this general perspective to, for example, Heinz Werner's (1957) "orthogenetic principle" or William Stern's (1938) "unitas multiplex" is evident (see Chapter 2 for a description of both Werner's and Stern's concepts).

In fact, the value of objective culture consists precisely in the contribution it makes to human individuation. In Simmel's (1990) view we appear to embody a "bundle of developmental lines," all having varied potentialities; but that is only appearance, for man does not cultivate himself through their isolated perfections, but only insofar as they help to develop his indefinable personal unity. Thus, Simmelian "culture" is necessarily dualistic, necessarily objective and subjective, and it makes possible the process of forming the self—this "unfolding unity"—through reciprocal interaction between the objective and the subjective. In fact, Simmel points to the culture-inclusiveness of the self and self-development. Thus, for Simmel, the specific meaning of culture is fulfilled only ". . . when the person adds something external to that development, where the path of the soul leads through values and scales that are not themselves subjectively psychological" (Simmel 1911/12: 57).

In the same context in which Simmel (1911/12) discussed his model of cultural dualism or, more adequately, cultural reciprocity, he goes on to say:

> In the formation of the concepts "subject" and "object" as correlates, each of which finds meaning only in the other . . . Yet our relationship to those objects with which we become cultivated by incorporating them into ourselves is a different one, since they are themselves spirit. . . .
>
> (Simmel 1911/12: 58)

And Simmel's essay on *The Concept and Tragedy of Culture* continues:

> Those objectively intellectual constructs of which I spoke initially—art, morality, science and practical objects, religion and the law, technology and

> social norms—are stations through which the human subject passes in order to acquire the specific personal value known as its [subjective] culture. Individuals must include these constructs and constraints within themselves, but they must really include them within the individual self. . . .
>
> (Simmel 1911/12: 57/58)

For Simmel, then, the paradox of culture is that subjective culture, which is in a continual flow and pushes of its own volition towards its inner development, cannot, viewed from the idea of culture, achieve that development on its own, but only by the way of those "self-sufficient crystallized structures" (Simmel 1911/12: 58), which have now become quite alien to its form.

Subjectively driven cultural and mental mediation

In the following section, the domain of special interest is the idea of cultivation through subjective—rather than teleological—mediation. Simmel (1911/12) states:

> Thus, the subjective spirit must abandon its subjectivity but not its intellectuality in order to experience that relationship to the object through which it becomes cultivated. This is the only way in which the dualistic form of existence, immediately posited with the existence of the subject, organizes itself into an inwardly uniform referentiality. An objectification of the subject and a subjectification of the object occurs here, which constitutes the specific nature of the cultural process. . . .
>
> (Simmel 1911/12: 58)

Simmel goes on to say:

> That . . . it presupposes a parallelism or a mutual adaptation of both [subject and object] . . . The formula of culture . . . has been that subjective psychological energies gain an objective form which is subsequently independent of the creative life processes and that this form is once again drawn into subjective life processes in a way that will bring its exponent to a well-rounded perfection [i.e. the maximum development of a person's potential from its natural stage] of his or her central being.
>
> (Simmel 1911/12: 68)

With respect to the problematic relationship between subjective and objective culture, Simmel, in his essay *The Concept and Tragedy of Culture* points out that: "The object may move away from its mediating activity . . ." (Simmel 1911/12: 68).

Here, Simmel outlined, for the first time, the idea of the cultural mediation of subjective culture by objective culture such as artifacts, norms, and so on. And he continues: ". . . we can utilize cultural objects for our own ends, rather than pursuing them as ends in themselves" (Simmel 1990: 478).

Moreover, individuals are not only concerned with processes of mediating—purposively—the external into the internal, but also with problems of mediating subjective culture into objective culture. The dialectic interplay between subjective and objective culture represents not only former "subject–object activities," but also "instructions," i.e. feedforward mechanisms for new acts of cultivation (Fuhrer & Josephs 1998). In the case of objective culture, even when the creator of these structures is gone, the external "forms" he/she left can influence subject–object interactions in the same way as subjective culture can.

Moreover, Simmel analyzes individuals under a double perspective: under the perspective of their doing *(Tun)* and under the perspective of their suffering *(Leiden)*. The notion of suffering does not refer to experiencing physical and psychic pain only, but, more neutrally, to receiving effects from the outside and being affected by them mentally. Simmel uses, as we mentioned above, the concept *Wechselwirkung* (interaction) when analyzing individuals under the perspective of their social activities, the concept of *Erleben* (experience) when looking at individuals from the point of view of their being affected by the sociocultural structure. From here, Simmel (1911/12) talks about "mediating activities" in a double sense: first, he points to the individuals as creators of objective culture; second, he means the individuals as receivers of "effects" of the objective culture. As creators they invent sociocultural forms or use already established forms; as receivers they integrate the effects of the sociocultural products they have created themselves into their subjective culture.

The two concepts "interaction" and "experience" can be clarified further when looking at them from a dynamic perspective. Interaction refers to processes of externalization and objectification, whereas experience refers to processes of internalization and subjectification, that is processes in which individuals integrate the effects of the objective culture into their subjective culture or into the self. Simmel's systematic interest in both sides of individuality distinguishes him from other sociological scholars. His concern about the ways in which individuals experience the effects of the cultural structure within which they are situated permits him to answer the question concerning individuals' capability to maintain their autonomy and individuality in the face of the pressures of modern life (for a more detailed outline of how Simmel approached this research problem, see Lohmann 1993 and Nedelmann 1990). However, both subjective and objective culture are "generative" as well as "receiving" minds or—to use my term—*cultivating minds* with regard to both their feedback and their feedforward qualities in the process of cultivating the internal as well as the external. Thus, Simmel regards the process of cultivation as emerging out of the "use of purposively formed objects" in such a way that human beings create forms of culture that "take the process of perfection into real and ideal spheres beyond the individual" (Simmel 1908a: 40).

If this is the case, then, where does Simmel's theory of culture leave us? What can be regarded as its essential achievement? In my view, Simmel has opened up to observation the mutuality between person and culture. More specifically, the general insight underlying the concept of cultivation as a reciprocal feedback process refers to Simmel's conviction of the human being's unique capacity to complete his/her personality by internalizing influences external to his/her personal sphere. For example, material objects function as means or cultivating activities for his/her goal to successively elaborate his/her individuality. That is, Simmelian cultivation means the elaborative change of inherent opportunities that the developing individual cannot reach out to on his/her own without sociocultural "structures"—i.e. in my terms the external mind—external to him or her. What this also means is that establishing, expressing and transforming a person's subjective culture—i.e. in my terms the internal mind—through external, material things is a process that continues throughout the life-span. Here, Simmel presents his position in concise form:

> The never-ending change in the content of culture, and in the long-run of whole cultural styles, is the sign, or rather the result, both of the infinite fertility of life and of the profound opposition between the eternal evolution and transformation and the objective validity and self-assertion of those manifestations and forms in which, or by means of which, it exists. It moves between the poles of death and rebirth, rebirth and death.
>
> (Simmel 1918: 76)

Simmel's famous metaphor of the pear tree illustrates what he means by this developmental principle. In spite of the evolutionary bias of this perspective, it becomes clear that culture in the sense of cultivation has the effect of transforming subjects from being "closed unities" in the beginning of the process of cultivation and proceeding to the stage of increasing differentiation when assimilating objects from the sociocultural environment, i.e. the "unfolding multiplicity," until finally becoming "unfolded unities" after having succeeded in internalizing the external cultural influences into the structure of their personalities. That is, development as cultivation is seen as *causa finalis* (cf. Simmel 1968).

This process involves much more than the mere assimilation of a number of diverse cultural contents in the Piagetian sense. Above all, it requires that these contents be relevant to and integrated into the central core of the self. To use Levine's (1971: xix) words:

> Culture in the proper (i.e. subjective) sense of the term, exists only in the presence of the self-development of a psychic structure, provided that this self-development relies on external means. Cultivation could therefore also be described as a process of subjectification of objective culture and objectification of subjective culture. That is, objective culture also has to associate itself with its counterpart in order to survive in the long run. In turn, the value of objective culture consists of the contribution it makes to human self-development.

Overall, it was Simmel's personal option to consider the individual as a value (in relativistic terms) and to measure cultural reality against the extent to which a given culture enables the individual to develop his or her abilities or exposes him or her to suffering. This leads Simmel to his general concept of culture as a mediator of the soul in order to work out one's "individual law" (Simmel 1990). With the "individual law" Simmel begins his treatise on cultivation at the biogenetic level; processes of so-called normal development, involving the interaction of maturing structures within the limits indicated by the individual law, set biological conditions for the emergence of psychological capacities.

Simmel's probabilism and transactionalism

In bringing the metaphor of the *cultivating minds* even closer into the focus of modern developmental theorizing (see Fuhrer & Josephs 1998), I focus on Simmel's (1990) fundamental circularity of human development, according to which external structures can only be symbolically interpreted by analogy to internal structures, and these structures, conversely, only by analogy to sociocultural or external structures. The two analogy formations do not enjoy a relationship of mutual cause and effect, but occur simultaneously or produce one another mutually, and thus stand in a covariant relationship to each other.

Here, Simmel's reciprocal conceptualization of the relationship between cause and effect is substituted by the logical form of a mutual relationship. Simmel's transactional—he uses the term "reciprocal"—orientation, his preference for synchronism vis-à-vis diachronism distinguishes his approach fundamentally from the traditional concept of causality. His understanding of person–culture interactions implies a coexistence, which can be captured and described as a mode of magnificient simultaneity. Simmel's transactional conceptualization of the relationship between cause and effect is substituted by the logical form of mutual relationship. With this perspective, Simmel's view of causality along with his cultivation principle is neither direct nor linear. Rather, his causality conception is of reciprocal causality and it fits, for example, into Valsiner and Winegar's (1992) person–environment model of inclusive separation as well as into Rapaport's (1968) mutual causality conception (see for similar views Ford and Lerner's 1992 model of dynamic interactionism or the concept of transactionism; cf. Sameroff (1983). Simmel's probabilism depends on individual initiatives, subjective cultural experiences, and the constraints and opportunities within successive objective cultural contexts. The closeness of this perspective to Gottlieb's (1996) probabilistic epigenesis is quite evident (see Fuhrer & Josephs 1998).

Crudely speaking, future forms are (at least potentially) present at birth in the genetic code contained in the zygote. Neither cultural opportunities nor cultural constraints are contained in biological form, but rather are embodied in the material/ideal, patterned, symbolic, artifacts that mediate human developmental processes. In the case of both biological and cultural opportunities/constraints, of course, the final cause or telos (i.e. Simmel's individual law) is only an if-all-other-things-are-equal final cause. The actual developmental process is one of probabilistic, not predetermined, epigenesis (Gottlieb 1996).

In a similar vein, Simmel already claims that individual development cannot be validly understood outside the artifacts that are shaped by individual activity and that simultaneously shape the individual who is acting upon these products. Sooner or later cultural forms can be liberated from their connection with practical purposes and become objects of cultivation in their own right. They become artifacts, that is they are autonomous, in that individuals become devoted to them not for any practical goals but for their own sake. The structural potential within each set of forms can then be drawn out. Objects manufactured for adolescent consumers such as running shoes, retro trainers, or fashionable T-shirts initially manufactured to be used in sports become transformed into things used for individual purposes. For example, teenagers apparently wear Adidas retros not for the way the shoes look, but for what they communicate about the wearer as a person located in a sociocultural environment (Miles 1996).

Beyond any particular realization of objective culture, individuals are able to shape the sociocultural environment into a self-contained, irreducible world of experience with the support of either proximal cultural mediators (artifacts) and/or social partners (see the analogy to Vygotsky's idea of the zone of proximal development). The so-called internal mind consists of that complex of representations needed for people to act adaptively in accord with their psychobiological requirements. These "potentialities"—to use Simmel's term—come into being over time through interaction of specific experiences with various kinds of sociocultural structures. In one of his very last comments on the cultivation principle, for instance, Simmel reasoned: "Yet under all circumstances, this can only refer to a development towards a phenomenon which is laid out in the embryonic forces of the personality, sketched, as it were, as a . . . plan of the personality itself" (Simmel 1911/12: 56).

Although, in principle, any given sociocultural element can be constructed as an element in any individual's external mind, some contents lend themselves more readily than others to becoming part of a certain individual's internal mind. For example, for some adolescents artifacts become the sociocultural means by which a sense of self first develops, whereas for other adolescents the social interactions with others become the frame of reference for developing their "existing possibilities" (Simmel 1911/12: 57). Of course, this form of interpreting the becoming *cultivating minds* also connects with the motives of the cultivating person who is acting, but it subjects his or her cultivation to the *a priori* demands of thought, through which the transmitted structures are first formed into a sociocultural "form" (sensu Simmel 1911/12). Thus, with the cultivation principle, we broaden the understanding of predisposed tendencies in such a way that we assume a field of potentialities.

In the 1990s, Shweder and Sullivan coined an apt phrase—and it almost authentically echoes Simmel's writings—to describe the relationship between particular cultural meanings of artifacts and individuals: "the refashioning of inherited complexity" (Shweder & Sullivan 1990: 497). The phrase implies that human beings are born with a broader range of potentials than any other person can fulfill within the human life span. Choices always involve the exclusion of other possibilities. Thus, cultivating activities (*sensu* Simmel) through artifacts does not determine human potential but it can, and does, create strong biases for the development of some potentials over others. And it places limits on the likelihood that certain varieties of actions will be chosen or achieved.

Remember that Simmel's wild pear tree would never be able to produce more than very small, very sour, and woody pears. Cultivation develops and fosters the tree's natural tendencies to produce pears in a way that improves, according to certain sociocultural standards, the quality of the pears immensely. That is, the relative plasticity of the pear tree that exists because of the successive nature of change means that there is some possibility—albeit perhaps a small and potentially difficult one to attain—that a low-probability change may occur or may be promoted by social and cultural means to influence change in a given pear tree. In accord with the principle of relative plasticity, the production of a sailboat mast out of wood from the pear tree would, therefore, not be, according to Simmel, an example of cultivation, because there is no inborn tendency in the pear tree to become a mast. In fact, there must be a "fit" between the original epigenetic tendencies or the "embryonal forces" (Simmel 1911/12: 56) of the developing organism and the cultivation efforts from sociocultural environment. That is, the *cultivating minds* metaphor means that the nature of developmental changes is at best relatively plastic, and not absolutely plastic. In turn, relative plasticity means that change is a probabilistic phenomenon. One can say that, within certain biological limits, a particular set of individual changes is likely to occur given the nature of earlier states, current states, and the current environment.

Simmel, however, especially in his later work, uses the notion of cultivation in a more pessimistic stance. The products that come into being through processes of transactions can, and do, lose their connections and finally follow their own rules. In that sense, the sociocultural environment structures the individual's development but culture is not controlled by itself. Facing all the sailing boats following different tracks around him, Simmel (1918), at the end of his life, has somehow lost his optimism concerning the cultivation of the pear tree.

However, Simmel's thoughts on culture as cultivation lead us to conclude that the internal-external relation is psychophysically "isomorphic" (see also Oerter 1991). The "inner self" and the "outer self" are both physical and mental. In this way, Simmel avoids the problems inherent in Cartesian as well as strictly psychophysical parallelism when explaining these transactions. Rather, the individual, as "individual law," forms a bridge between body and soul. Thus, the relation between objective and subjective culture—in the sense of *causa finalis*—may be seen as subjectively meaningful. The total telos of the individual forms meaning; it is that "mediating activity"—sensu Simmel—between person (or life) and culture (or form) which creates meaning during the process of cultivation. According to Simmel's fundamental circularity of human knowledge, "external events" can only be symbolically interpreted by analogy to "inner experience," and inner events conversely only by analogy to tempo-spatial, i.e. "external" determinations. The two analogy formations produce one another mutually. How it is that cultivation may be understood in single cases is, however, a question that Simmel leaves unanswered.

Part III

The cultivating minds paradigm

Chapter 5

Identity, culture, and development under transactional issues

Identity is not a recent invention, like the Internet, that everyone suddenly began to want. People have always had identities. The modern difficulty with identity must be understood as resulting from a change in identity, or rather in the way identity is constructed, developed and created, or deconstructed again. Of course, names and addresses are labels that provide some help to define a person's identity. But they provide only a partial definition. An identity crisis is not resolved by checking one's wallet for one's name and address. People who have problems with identity are generally struggling with some more difficult aspects of defining their own identity, such as the establishing of both some integrity across various situational contexts and a kind of long-term continuity in their I–world relationships. Within culturally structured constraints, developing individuals select and construct their own developmental ecology and thus create and shape their personal culture. In times where globalization, rationalization, rapid societal change, migration, and multiculturalism are growing, the increasing hunger for identity is remarkable, although the desire for identity is different from some of the other modern appetites because identity implies being attached both inwardly and outwardly. Without these attachments, uprootedness results. Already in the late 1960s, Erik Erikson (1968) assumed that uprootedness might be an explanation for the popularity of the concept of identity in the late twentieth century. However, contemporary efforts to define and study identity vary considerably in their scope and in how they address these issues (cf. Kroger 2000). Today, theoretical and philosophical discussions of the self also abound outside the sociocultural tradition such as in cognitive science approaches (cf. Gallagher 2000). Rather than focusing on identity development in terms of the emergence of the self as a meaning maker (Kegan 1982) or on the social construction of meaning, with its emphasis on the self in cultural context (Shweder *et al.* 1998). The present book adopts a more pragmatic view on the formation of identity or the self.

Dynamic interplay between sameness and change

However, identity is a controversial concept and social scientists use the term "identity" in a variety of ways to explain an assortment of phenomena (cf. Kroger

2000). Nearly everyone is familiar with the popular vocabulary of the search for identity such as "finding yourself," "self-actualization," "identity crisis," and so on. Generations of psychologists have long been interested in the role played by "identity" in both social and psychological processes. The differing usages of the term identity by social scientists reflect an imprecise understanding of identity even among researchers. Identity is used as a descriptive term—"East German adults are in an identity crisis"—but also as an explanation—"since the fall of the "wall" an increasing number of East German adults have—a more or less—difficult time because they miss clear orientations to reconstruct their personal identity."

Moreover, within psychology various definitions of identity are used and each of these is linked to its own operationalization. This situation has led to different schools with their own theoretical and empirical tradition. Among these schools are the psychosocial approaches of the Erikson/Marcia tradition, Meadian and post-Meadian models of symbolic interactionism, or constructive-developmental attempts of the Piaget/Kohlberg tradition (cf. Baumeister 1986, Bosma 1995, Kroger 2000).

Contemporary efforts to define and study identity vary considerably in their scope and in how they address these issues. For example, there is wide disagreement about how to define identity, measure it, and study its development. Numerous difficulties also arise when one attempts to integrate the differing theoretical perspectives. A major reason for this "state of the art" is that, too often, identity researchers are overly restricted in their approach to studying identity. Thus, we still seem to feel that we have problems with identity even though we lack a clear idea of what identity actually is. There has not always been agreement on how best to conceptualize identity. With this book I hope to arrive at a more culture-inclusive understanding of the study of identity.

How is identity defined in general dictionaries? According to the seventh edition of *The Concise Oxford Dictionary* (Sykes 1982), identity is the absolute sameness, individuality, personality, and the condition of being a specified person. This definition, together with the definition of sameness, character, and being an identifiable person, form the main elements of the meaning of the concept of identity in connection to human individuals. Both meanings are related and can go together. Compare the example of an adolescent girl: despite the tremendous bio-social changes during the puberty years, she remains the same, unique person. However, it is not at all clear what exactly the girl's identity is. And, in the second thought, there is a paradox in the sense that something cannot change if it does not, in a certain respect, remain the same. Identity in this sense is often described as a dynamic interplay between sameness and change.

Another issue is also relevant here (see Bosma 1995). On the one hand, identity can be objectively identified by all kinds of data such as physical characteristics, name, date of birth, and even DNA fingerprints. On the other hand, "subjective identity" is the experiential side of "objective identity," for example, the awareness of these characteristics, of continually being one and the same person, distinct from others. However, IQ or DNA profile hardly matter on an interpersonal level. My wife focuses on other identifiers and from a subjective perspective I prefer to be identified by her by other, more psychological, characteristics. And in the work situation of my psychology department other subjective and objective identifiers are relevant.

So, what exactly is relevant—in different contexts—is hard to say. Both context and person play a role, "negotiate" as it were, which identifiers are relevant. That is, identity does not refer to a fixed set of context relationships but rather person and context mutually define each other. Consequently, identity and development are intrinsically related. It is, of course, impossible to talk about remaining constant without addressing change. They are really two sides of the same identity coin. It is precisely the fact of development that provokes the question of identity. Rather than considering identity as some sort of static endpoint, I propose to use a concept where one studies the dynamic tension between core and context in the midst of developmental change.

In this book, I present perspectives on this dynamic tension that capture the dynamic interaction between the intrapsychic and the extrapsychic. Identity involves the tension between something that is core or figure and something that serves as the context or ground to that core (cf. Valsiner 1997). Attunement between these two guarantees the continuity over time that I think of as identity. Moreover, the developmental dimension underlying identity can range from the moment-to-moment regulation or microgenesis that is made intrapsychically, or within interactions with social partners and/or artifacts, to qualitative changes within the "mesogenetic" (Cole 1996) or even ontogenetic scale.

Since, research on identity has to account for identity occuring in different scales of time, there is a need to deal with the core–context tension for each time scale. For example, in adolescence as a developmental period, young persons must adapt to a whole range of biologically, cognitively, and socially motivated "developmental tasks" (Havighurst 1948). Yet although they change, they still feel they remain generally the same. Often this can work itself out only gradually, over several years or decades. On a historical scale, the period of adolescence has only recently been viewed as a significant phase of identity development (cf. Erikson 1968). Reciprocally, historical or social changes influence the issues around which core–context attunement revolves.

Perhaps there are versions of these approaches that can be made compatible with cultural developmental psychology, however, the self or identity is not reducible to processes of the internal mind. A cultural developmental psychology approach to personal identity examines that part of our sense of identity that develops through meaning-making activities and through a history of symbolically mediated experiences with the practices of cultural communities. From the perspective of cultural developmental psychology, personal identity can be defined as the meaning-making activities or practices associated with being an "I" (a subject, a person) in a particular cultural community. Simultaneously, a cultural developmental psychology perspective recognizes that, for example, children are active constituents of their own cultures and that changes in their personal identities initiate changes in their relations with others and thus in their immediate cultural settings as media.

Returning to the insights of some of the field's early theorists (e.g., Simmel 1908a, Dewey 1938, Erikson 1968), it is evident that culture does not surround or cover the universal child. Rather, culture is necessary for development—it completes the child. Culture provides the media for "how to be" and for how to participate as a member in good standing of particular social contexts. The problem, however, is: in what way does culture transform into a person's identity? And in what way does personal identity transform into culture? The way in which the mind makes up the world has been undeniably neglected (see for notable exceptions Boesch 1991, Shweder & Sullivan 1990, Valsiner 1998, Wertsch 1998). To capture this problem we do not—as cultural developmental psychologists—have to search for the "order as found in cultural facts." Rather, by arguing along with Bruner, we have to study "order imposed by human beings" under developmental issues "that the central concept of human psychology is meaning and the processes and transactions involved in the construction of meanings" (Bruner 1990: 33).

The transactional word view

The transactional world view is an approach to the social sciences that was articulated most fully by Dewey and Bentley (1949), and, more recently, has been advocated by a variety of psychologists (cf. Altman & Rogoff 1987, Oerter 1998, Sameroff 1983, Wapner 1998, Werner & Altman 1998). There is considerable overlap between transactionalism and contextualism (Overton 1998), including coactional developmental models, such as the one which is depicted in this chapter. The overarching feature of transactionalism is its assumption that individuals change their environment through their actions in such a way that personal ideas, goals, and motives are transported into the environment and "materialized" there. Moreover, the essence of transactionalism is that psychological phenomena should be studied as holistic units. Thus, there are no separate actors in an event. Instead, there are acting relationships, such that the actions of one person can be described and understood only in relation to the actions of another person, and in relation to the situational and temporal circumstances in which the actors are involved.

Furthermore, the aspects of an event are mutually defining and lend meaning to one another, since the same actor in a different setting—or the same setting with different actors—would yield a different confluence of people and contexts. The aspects of one event are so intermeshed that the definition or understanding of one aspect requires simultaneous inclusion of other aspects in the analysis. A transactional approach assumes that the aspects of a system, that is a person and context, coexist and jointly define one another and contribute to the meaning and the nature of the holistic event. Thus, transactional approaches reject the use of separate components or parts. Instead, the preceding features are necessary and intrinsic definitional qualities of all psychological phenomena and collectively constitute an event, whole, or unity. For example, children are not separate from their actions or feelings, neither are they separate from other children nor the artifacts, nor the temporal circumstances that comprise unfolding events. In addition to its focus on intertwined aspects of an event, transactionalism incorporates temporal processes in the very definition of events. The transactional view shifts from analysis of the causes of change to the idea that change is inherent in the system. Change is viewed more as an intrinsic aspect of an event than as the outcome of the influence of separate elements on each other. Thus, temporal qualities contribute to the meaning of, and themselves acquire meaning from, events. Thus, in transactionalism, elements are not seen as pushing or causing one another, but rather as fitting together as total units.

The following example illustrates how meaning is a time-bounded phenomenon. Midnight may seem like an odd time to play basketball because adults are accustomed to daytime and evening basketball. However, in North American as well as in German cities, such as Hamburg and Berlin, basketball has become a device for reaching delinquent adolescents, giving them a structured activity as an alternative to drugs and violence. Holding the games at midnight contributes to their meaning by signifying that the community is reaching out to alienated youths. Simultaneously, the timing—midnight—acquires legitimacy as the success of the games grows over time. Moreover, by participating in these midnight games, adolescents develop some stability in their social relationships. They need to develop trust and familiarity, but they also need novelty and stimulation, excitement, and the unexpected. In this way, midnight games provide both stability and change in social activities and adolescents' identities. However, adolescents adapt to, seek, explore, and create changing circumstances in their identities and relationships while at the same time benefiting from the stability in these midnight basketball games as behavior settings.

Thus, in the transactional view as it is stated in *cultivating minds*, elements are seen as working together or fitting together as total units. Transactionalism in the pragmatic tradition assumes that psychological events unfold in a purposeful and goal-directed fashion but that goals can be short- or long-term and can change with time and circumstances. Finally, change in a transactional model may result in psychological outcomes that are variable, emergent, and novel.

A transactional-developmental model

This section addresses three issues. First, developmental biologists, anthropologists, sociologists, and developmental psychologists often argue with each other and among themselves about the nature and causes of development because they have quite different metatheoretical positions (cf. Cairns *et al.* 1996). However, in the case of one metatheoretical perspective, "developmental contextualism" (Lerner 1989), there is ample intellectual opportunity for multidisciplinary complementarity. Moreover, developmental contextualism stresses the reciprocal, or dynamic, influence of biological and psychological processes and cultural environmental conditions. In these conceptions, the reciprocal relation between the interrelated features of the person and his/her cultural environment are held not merely to interact in the linear sense used in analysis of variance. Instead, person and culture "transact" (Sameroff & Suomi 1996), "dynamically interact" (Lerner 1989) or "coact" (Gottlieb 1996).

Accordingly, genes and culture always maintain, constrain, and facilitate each other through their mutual influence, but these influences are flexible, not absolute. That is their transaction constrains development to a set of possible pathways, not a single one, and the size of the set of possible pathways varies with the specific nature of the genes and the cultural environment. By virtue of their reciprocal relation, each of the features is transformed by the other. The system of person–culture relations comprising human development means that at any point in the life span there is some probability that cultural means exist for significantly altering an individual's characteristics. This enables people to act to promote their own development, i.e. individuals produce their own development through (trans-) actions. It is of historical interest to note that Kurt Lewin and William Stern in Germany, and Russian developmental theorists such as Vygostky or Leontiev evolved a similar view in the first third of the twentieth century.

Second, I adopt a culture-inclusive view of developmental research (cf. Valsiner & Winegar 1992) which is, of course, familiar with developmental contextualism and transactionalism. Here it is suggested that individuals define themselves in relation to cultural processes and with regard to their I–world relationship. Whereas in exclusive separation, the

> person is separated from environment, with the connections between the two eliminated from analysis, in the case of inclusive separation of person and culture, the two parts of the whole are conceptually separated whereas the specific connections between them remain the focus of attention.
>
> (Valsiner & Winegar 1992: 5–6)

Exclusive separation follows the principle of Cartesian duality. Given this position, although the individual can perceive the body of another person, he/she cannot perceive that individual as subject. He/she knows his/her mind better than his/her body. He/she, however, can only know the body of the other, since he/she has no access to that person's consciousness. In contrast, the view of person–culture relations emphasizes inclusive separation as the starting point for triangulating identity and culture with developmental analysis. Consequently, any discussion of one set of issues necessitates a consideration of the other two. For example, how one conceptualizes identity will dictate the assumptions of how identity develops from cultural processes. Differences in how researchers define identity and deal with cultural processes will also increase in importance when the research is couched in terms of both cultural and developmental issues.

Third, individuals within a population are co-producers of their development and their cultural environment (Lerner 1989). That is, a given individual develops through the degree of realization—through purposive choice, selection, rejection, constraint, or other means—of the population-specific potentials for developmental change that inhere: (a) within the time-graded sequences and segments of cultural structures to which the individual is exposed; (b) within the genetic (micro-, meso- or ontogenetic) and other time-graded biological functions of human nature; and (c) within time-graded interactions of the prior two sources, with all three of the above varying as a function of a given person's activities in culturally structured environments over time.

Taken together, one can speculate, with some supporting evolutionary evidence, that both psychological development and biological change are rooted in the biocultural history of the human species (cf. Bronfenbrenner & Ceci 1993, Cole 1996). That is, the adaptational mode of *Homo sapiens* to its niche through cooperative social relationships, communal habitat, collective representations, and real or symbolic artifacts lays a basis for both ontogenesis and sociogenesis. This evolutionary, ecological interpretation provides the rationale for the following conceptual model of individual development as a bio-psycho-cultural process (see Figure 5.1). When I speak here of transaction as being at the heart of developmental analysis or causality what I mean is that we need to specify some relationships between at least two levels or domains of the hierachical developmental system.

The transactional-developmental model (below) represents the coactional processes that give rise to development in the evolving species biogenetic "text," changing cultural—social, material, and mental—structures of a given society, and both individual and collective activities. Accordingly, I postulate that processes of psychological development at the individual level can best be interpreted against commonalities and variations in such developments within culturally structured environments.

Following the transactional-developmental model in Figure 5.1, individual psychic functioning is depicted as a third level of activity, above the biological and below the cultural. Cognition arises as the social activity that takes place between these levels. Developmental understanding of the genotype has emphasized an epigenetic perspective denying any determining influence of genes on the psychology of the individual (see Gottlieb 1996). In fact, epigenesis means that:

> individual development is characterized by an increase of complexity of organization—that is the emergence of new structural and functional properties and compentencies—at all levels of analysis . . . as a consequence of horizontal and vertical coactions among its parts, including organism-environment coactions.
>
> (Gottlieb 1996: 68)

Looking at Figure 5.1, horizontal transactions are those that occur at the same level (e.g. gene–gene, neurons–neurons, cognitions–cognitions), whereas vertical transactions occur at different levels (e.g., gene–cytoplasm, cognitive activity–neurons, social activity–cultural tools) and are reciprocal, meaning that they can influence each other in either direction, from biogenetic to psychic and cultural,

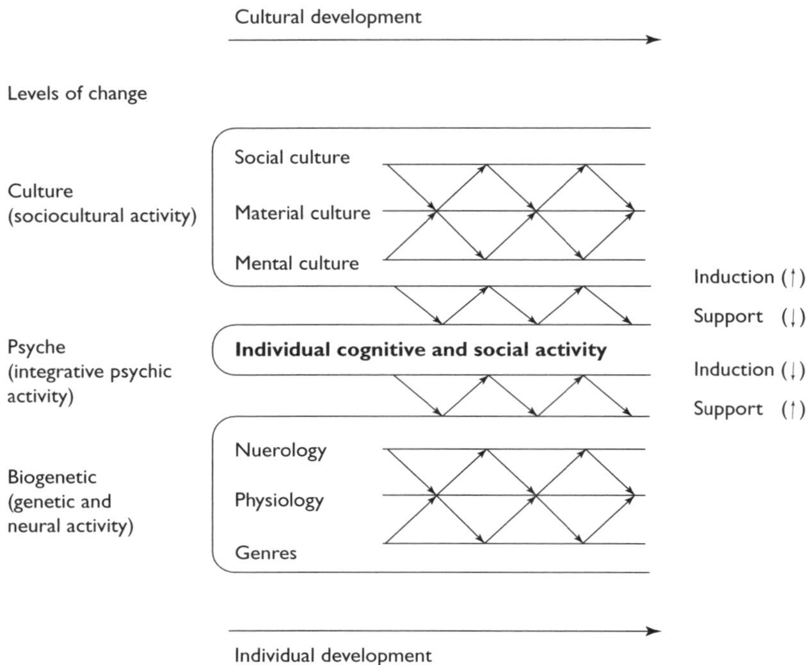

Figure 5.1 The transactional-developmental model integrating cultural, psychic, and biogenetic regulating systems

from cultural to psychic and, finally, to the biogenetic levels of the developing system (see Gottlieb 1996 for experimental evidence demonstrating crossover interactions between all levels of developmental analysis).

The essence of the probabilistic conception of epigenesis is the bi-directionality of structure–process relationships, as depicted in Figure 5.1. If, in this model, individual development remains probabilistic, it is only with regard to the fact that the interactive context created by the joint states of activity at the neurological and cultural levels is itself a probabilistic event. The coaction perspective requires that every event on the three change levels be interpreted as the outcome of a relation between individual (genotypic, phenotypic) and culture (see for a similar view Sameroff & Suomi 1996).

However, it is necessary to recognize a boundary between the organism and its culture, an interface where the integrative functions of the psyche can be specified. This is presented in Figure 5.1, where, instead of a single domain, two hierarchical domains or levels of development are depicted: the individual level and the level of culture. The biogenetic domain is defined as a hierarchy of structures and processes that, from the genes to the nervous system, may be represented by any number of relevant and specifiable levels of organization. The cultural domain, on the other hand, consists of those social, material, and mental aspects within a given culture that have relevance, for example, from the standpoint of individuals' developmental tasks. Here, social culture consists of institutions, including the rituals performed by them. Material culture consists of artifacts and the skills of producing and using them. And, finally, mental culture consists of systems of ideas and values believed in and the conventions governing their use and expression (see Posner 1989).

The arrows in the center of the figure depict the reciprocal relationship between cognitive and social activity and the biogenetic and cultural domains. This is a special case of coactionality, however, in that the relationship specified here takes the form of a recursive induction–support loop. On the premise that this relationship is actively established by the individual him/herself, processes of induction temporally precede those of support. In this sequence, integrative psychic activity recursively supports (or validates) itself through the alignment that it induces between biological and cultural activities. In this process, those aspects of biogenetic and cultural organization that are most vulnerable to change in the short term provide support for the new developmental and adaptive directions. If the conditions whereby this partial alignment was initiated are maintained, by virtue of coactionality, other systems within the hierachical domains of change eventually become correlated and further consolidate the new adaptive directions.

Again, what is emphasized here are the multiple avenues of developmental pathways that are generated through the coactions between increasingly more complex biogenetic, psychic, and cultural domains, their development, and the timing of stimulative cultural events that can act as triggers to the psychic activity, and *vice versa*. With respect to continuity and change in developmental patterns, organization inside or outside the psyche may play either a supportive role or impose constraints. Support is provided when conditions inside or outside the psychic apparatus are functionally aligned. In this case, psychic activity is correlated to these conditions and current developmental patterns are maintained.

In the second case, developmental challenges, such as coping with either developmental tasks and/or with critical life-events, occur that compromise this alignment, and those same conditions now impose limits on how the cultural environment may be redefined. To illustrate this, consider a situation in which a child is threatened by another group member. How this situation is eventually controlled by the child is necessarily constrained by a host of factors, ranging all the way from the social status of the protagonist and its physiological states to the specific physical–spatial milieu of its interaction. Within these constraints, however, cognitive activity may bring to the forefront configural aspects of the situation that create a "limited window of opportunity" for situation control. For example, this may consist in enlisting the support of the nearby mother to manipulate the social signals given to the aggressor or to take advantage of some physical–spatial options and some change in the interactive behavior as well. Depending on its outcome, a single interaction of this sort may have both short- and/or long-term effects for both the child and his/her aggressor, including a change in motivational states, personal identity, social perceptions, and the physiological substrates of these functions.

To the extent that these correlated effects would be validated and supported by parallel changes in the cultural environment (e.g. in the peer group, the parenting style), their psychic equivalent may also tend to resist modification. For example, the ingredients of the cultural code are the complex of characteristics that organize a society's child-rearing system and that incorporate elements of socialization and education (cf. Worthman 1993). These processes are embedded in sets of social controls and social supports. They are based on beliefs (mentifacts) that differ in the amount of community consensus ranging from mores and norms to fads and fashion. The content of such a cultural code is a core concern of sociology, anthropology, and cultural psychology (cf. Cole 1996). Human societies vary greatly in the experiences they provide for their children. Infancy is a time period when these differences are first apparent in birthing practices, feeding and sleeping arrangements, and the size of the family unit (cf. Munroe & Munroe 1971).

To what extent are cultural accounts of development compatible with, or opposed to, biological views? Given the backdrop of my previous arguments, the view that "it is culture, not biology, that shapes human life and the human mind that gives meaning to action by situating its underlying intentional states in an interpretive system" (Bruner, 1990, p. 34), has much appeal. However, whether or not developmental scientists give explanatory priority to the cultural context, they should remain aware of the fact that natural and cultural constraints interact, and permeate each other, in the formation of action, culture, and development (see Boesch 1991). Already the expression of biogenetic factors in ontogeny is mediated by cultural and psychic systems of action. The biogenetic regulation and canalization of developmental trajectories presupposes a complementary patterning of the range, intensity, and temporal ordering of critical exogenous factors.

This epigenetic pattern, however, is to a large extent formed by institutionalized agents as well as by the activity of the developing subjects themselves. Individuals often select environments according to personal preferences and competences which partly reflect genotypic dispositions. They thus expose themselves to particular influences or experiences to which they respond in ways that, in turn, correspond to their genotypic constitution (see Plomin & McClearn 1993). The developmental ecology thus becomes an extension of the individual's phenotype. By the same token, plasticity of developmental trajectories cannot be considered a fundamental feature of development, but nevertheless reflects potentialities of developmental control within a given cultural, social, and historical context. Indeed, this principle does not imply that the ranges of developmental variations are unlimited.

However, there are historical and cross-cultural differences where changes in child behavior are emphasized or ignored. Indeed, informal education can begin at many different ages, depending on the culture's attributions to the child. Some middle-class parents, for example, have been convinced that prenatal experiences will enhance the cognitive development of their children and consequently begin stimulation programs during pregnancy, whereas others believe it best to wait until the first grade before beginning formal learning experiences. Such an example demonstrates the variability of human developmental cultural environments and the openess of the regulatory system to modification. As pointed out in the Lewinian tradition of theorizing, Barker (1968), Bronfenbrenner and Ceci (1993) and Valsiner (1997), among others, pointed out that culture affords unique opportunities and constraints for both continuity and change in developmental processes.

Unlike psychic activities directed at the material aspects of the cultural environment, like tools or spatial arrangements, social actions involve other individuals that share the same psychological and behavioral capacities. Accordingly, the basis of the organization of action in this environment may be rapidly transformed as new constraints and opportunities emerge in the temporal flow of social interchanges or deconstructions in the physical environment. In light of the constant flux in social interaction, relationships, and social structures, maintaining and establishing new person–culture relationships requires that activity within the different systems of the individual organism—genetic, hormonal, or neurological—be in the service of establishing them. Thus, the unifying banner of "development" is seen as a process of transaction between, on the one hand, individual human beings as active, holistically functioning biopsychological agents of their own development and, on the other hand, the equally dynamic multilevel cultural systems in which they live their lives.

Coming back to Georg Simmel's wild pear tree, what existed as a potentiality in the tree is cultivated to an actuality through human, purposive intervention. Despite some limitations of Simmel's bio-psycho-cultural metaphor when it is confronted with more recent examples of developmental behavior genetics, it can help us to thoroughly understand developmental processes via cultural means. First, individuals and their development can never be described and explained in a context-free or culture-free sense but rather must be described in a culture-inclusive manner. Development always takes place in the dynamic interplay of transactions in which every aspect of the individual–culture-system is defined in terms of one another, not as separate elements. That is transactions de-emphasize the operation of universal regulatory principles that predetermine the course of development of a phenomenon, although they accept the idea that psychological events are intentional and goal-directed. However, these goals are flexible and are not assumed to be underlain by a limited number of predetermined organicist principles.

Second, development, as a process by which new forms of organization emerge from those forms which preceded them in time, needs the qualitative change of something external to the internal basis of development. That is, developmental transformation is not an inherent property of either the individual or its cultural environment but becomes possible because of the linkage between the two (cf.

Valsiner 1997). Inside and outside, though related, are qualitatively different despite similarities in their functional qualities for the developing individual (cf. Fuhrer 1993a). This characteristic provides a strong objection to the assumption of fusion between the person and the social world in developmental theories and theories in cultural psychology (cf. Lawrence & Valsiner 1993). Sometimes, and here we switch again to Simmel's botanical metaphor, the developmental partners which we have loosely called "inside" and "outside," cannot transact directly with one another. A third partner—such as Csikszentmihalyi and Rochberg-Halton's (1981) three modes of transaction—is needed to make at least the decisive but now indirect transaction between the two partners possible.

Third, development is characterized by constraints placed on the process by the person and the culture. Not all cultural processes are made for feeding into developmental processes. Moreover, not everything can be made out of a person. There must be a "fit" between the subjective potentials and cultural efforts to work on those potentials. In fact, cultivating one's own mind becomes the cultivation of these individual potentialities through culture. This view stands in sharp contrast to the idea that development represents a predetermined unfolding of genetic programs without recognizing the relevance of the individual's sociocultural potentialities for change and diversity. The cultivation principle, therefore, recognizes the possibility of multiple trajectories of development. Here, however, we run into a difficulty because Simmel has a maximization process in mind. The developing person, however, according to Herbert Simon (1957), satisfices, rather than maximizes; that is, he or she looks for a course of development that is good enough, that meets a minimal set of requirements. In that sense, the bio–individual–cultural cultivation procedure—like parenting, schooling and the like—is not in control of all conditions that have an influence on the product, whether it is a pear tree or a child.

Thus, the cultivation principle fits with a transactional view of development when it expresses the mutuality of subjective and objective culture through cultivation. In fact, many developmental psychological designs often overlook some of the third factors or cultural mediational influences. In other words, these factors mediate and influence the process of the reciprocally-related constitution of the development of the internal mind as well as the development of external mind (i.e. material, social and mental culture). In extending Simmel's pear tree analogy, I would suggest that if the pear tree is growing in poor soils, fertilizer spread by a third party (farmer) would improve the development of the tree. This points out that the tree, or the child, the cultural environment, or the child's parenting system, and the cultivating influences such as artifacts or social partners, all interact.

The meaning of the pear tree itself grows into something much more than it was in its uncultivated state. Meaning, in other words, is not simply fixed, but rather has an existence in and through a process of cultivation, a process involving the development of some artifact or habit of life due to care, inquiry, or suffering, and whose goal is the greater embodiment of living reasonabless. Meaning is action, even transaction, or "triadic semiosis" (Rochberg-Halton, 1986) that not only includes subject and object as constituents but also the three modes of transaction between them. For this reason, culture is the cultivation of meaning that includes, in accord with Rochberg-Halton, the inherent quality or *qualitative possibility* of that which is cultivated, the *existential otherness* involved in the transaction, and the real generalization toward which the *process* is *aimed*, that is the outcome of cultivation. How meaning is formed in living cultivation will now be outlined in the next chapter.

Chapter 6

Cultivating meanings as mediating possibilities for the self

The most important question of this book that now needs to be answered is still open. It is whether cultivation as a meaning-making practice can provide the uniqueness, continuity, and consistency that is so vital to the formation of one's identity. While the theoretical attempts mentioned above were mainly concerned with guided structure formation, they paid little attention to man's self-related creative activity, where meaning-making practice means that people themselves experience their identity as meaning processes.

Cultivating mediating possibilities for the self

In the *cultivating minds* paradigm, I view culture as a medium for generating possibilties, i.e. a generative medium for the agentic, self-referential, creative self. If meaning transactions can be carried out symbolically in it or through culture, each and every actor is an active and self-developing producer of their own developmental possibilities, and, in turn, their own identity. Thus, transactions with one's cherished possessions, for example, either actually or symbolically can be seen as meanings or sign expressions of the self. Unlike "concrete" aspects of identity, symbolic aspects are not necessarily observable to outsiders, because they are based upon active "analogies," interpretations or "substitutions" (see Boesch 1991). If a personal object such as a diary, a photograph or a musical instrument is important to a person, this means that he/she interprets the object in the light of the reference system of personal intentions. This interpretation turns the object into a sign of personal identity where signs (in the narrow sense defined by Peirce 1933) are at the same time symbols. As symbols, signs refer back to their objects on the basis of convention. This is why symbols are culture-dependent.

In all of these cases of symbolic molding of physical objects, it is ultimately impossible to find out whether a thing is a "model of" a pre-existent individual identity characteristic or whether the object is a "model for" a newly generated aspect of identity (Csikszentmihalyi & Rochberg-Halton 1981). If the physical environment of the child has the single purpose of promoting the development of cognitive schemata, interaction will be viewed as necessary in order to set off cognitive structure genesis; but the interaction is purely object-structural in nature. This means that the substitution of an object X with an object Y would not make any significant difference to the subject. In this way, Piaget's (1970) theory, for example, is not "trans-actional" in the pragmatic sense. Neither Piagetian—nor Vygotskian or post-Vygotskian—objects have any intrinsic characteristics—as held by Dewey (1934) and later by Boesch (1991)—that would structure identity as meaning-making practice.

By this line of reasoning, every action is the selection and production, the expansion, or even the re/creation of possibilities for development, and the whole point of intention is to govern which of all the available possibilities is realized, expanded, or re/created. However one acts, he/she could have acted otherwise (Boesch 1991). If, then, every action is also a choice to select, to expand, or even to create a possibility, it is also something that will be right or wrong, just as propositions are either true or false. Of course, it may be right or wrong either in the technical or the moral sense. The criteria in either case will not come from any external or alien source but rather from the same sociocultural context in which the action is constituted.

Multiple mediations: the quadrangular cultural mediational model of identity formation

In the quadrangular-mediational model of identity formation, meaning transaction may be viewed as semiotic process (compare Figure 6.1). Following the concept of triadic semiosis (see Peirce 1933), in this process meaning emerges from the effect that a sign or symbol triggers in the consciousness of its interpreter. In its totality, the quadrangular cultural-mediational model (see Fuhrer & Josephs 1998) represents a multiple mediated, co-developmental systems approach.

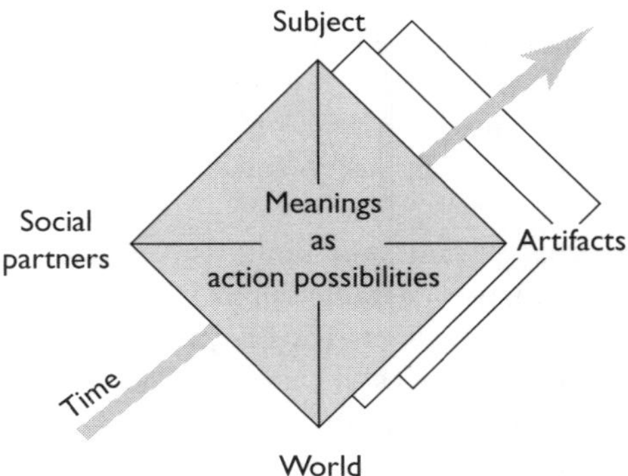

Figure 6.1 The tetradic mediational model of identity formation

First, one might speak of four (interrelated) "systems" of analysis for a cultural-mediational view of identity as tetradic—instead of triadic—meaning transactions. Each is a system because each is an organized and dynamic complexity. The first system is the subject, with a distinctive biological make-up and a unique history of experience. The second system is the social partners with which the subject collaborates. The third system is culture in its symbolic sense, culture as artifacts. The fourth system is the objective world.

Second, the link between the four "systems" is of the co-creation type. The subject and the objective world serve as mutual creation, with the world mediated through holistic proximal units such as social partners and artifacts. There is, at least in the quadrangular version, not only a "direct" link between subject and world but simultaneously an "indirect" co-creational link through both social partners and a medium constituted of artifacts. That is the four systems are fundamentally interpenetrating and mutually constitutive, which is to say that they co-create each other.

Third, the quadrangular model is characterized by its holistic and dynamic nature. Thus it favors a transactional view of development (see Fuhrer & Josephs 1998).

Fourth, the model mirrors, at least in part, Kurt Lewin's (1943) conditional-genetic analysis which entails investigation of the processes of development as new phenomena emerge. The analysis of conditions under which these phenomena are brought into existence constitutes the core of the conditional-genetic analysis.

Thus, the cultural-mediational quadrangle slightly extends Michael Cole's (1996) basic cultural-mediational triangle both to the social partner side and towards the co-developmental quality of its component parts. The tetradic-mediational model, which captures the truly multiple and parallel nature of both artifactual mediation and social mediation which are interpreted as mediational possibilities for the growth of the self, hypothesizes that actions proceed qualitatively differently depending on the subject's socioemotional relationships with others. At the same time, the quadrangle reduces certain aspects of the triadic structural model of mediation as it was conceptualized by Engeström (1996). In contrast to his model, a tetradic mediation seems more concise in representing the basic mediational means within a holistic self-developing system of meaning transactions. Finally, neither Cole nor Engeström's triangular systems pays due attention to the fact that development often accompanies the regulation of identity (see Bruner 1990).

In this book, in contrast to the triadic semiosis often adopted from Peirceian pragmatic philosophy, I propose a tetradic semiosis of identity formation through cultivation. If an individual interprets his objective world indirectly, then the objective world functions as a sign (first correlate) that is either co-interpreted or co-created by social partners as interpreters or creators (second correlate)—here is the extension of triadic semiosis *à la* Peirce—or itself stands for something (third correlate; artifacts as symbols). The second or third correlates (triadic) or the two together elicit in the interpreting individual a cognition or emotion as a fourth correlate (tetradic). This is the new, subjective meaning upon the background of a current, or changed, I–world transaction.

For example, a grandmother (subject) may cultivate her husband's wedding ring and that of her own grandmother as identification objects (artifacts). She gives the rings to her grandson and his fiancée. The rings are signs (first correlate) that in grandmother's eyes stand for five generations of family continuity (second correlate) or, in her grandson's eyes, become a social substitute for the person of grandmother (third correlate). Later in the process of meaning transaction, the fourth correlate is made up of the grandmother's reactivated memories of people and events and of the cognitions and emotions triggered through appropriation that allow her to cultivate her unique personal identity. Via meaning transactions, grandma finds ever anew her individuality and continuity and thus secures her identity. In this way, the development of grandma's identity corresponds with the transformation of the meanings that artifacts (grandma's rings) take on in tetradic transactions. For this reason, it is reasonable to assume that identity processes take place through tetradic mediation. Identity becomes the transactional process of meaning that—in semiotic terms—is a tetradic sign process.

In contrast to models of triadic mediation *à la* Cole (1996), the multiple tetradic mediational model focuses upon I–world transactions mediated by artifacts and social partners at the same time. These mediations may be very complex, as, for example, when a teenager "negotiates" his changing identity, as depicted in Figure 6.2, A to D, by the variously structured quadrangles, together with his/her peers. Teenage behavior is developmentally-related when young people select, use, re-create, or co-create the world of their consumer goods or their leisure-time settings in such a way that they reinterpret their denotations in mediations as meaningful "subjective-functional analogues" (Boesch 1991). If an object such as a pair of inline skates or a photograph of Elton John is meaningful to a teenager, this illustrates that the meanings of the object have been co-created in the frame of reference of his/her personal experience and also in meaning-bestowing mediations with peers. Figure 6.2 illustrates these meaning transactions within socio-culturally mediated I–world relations.

Here, a teenager sees himself face-to-face with a peer (see Figure 6.2A)—to whom the adolescent has a more or less close relationship—and with whom he/she can negotiate the meanings of his/her I–world relationships, and thus his/her identity. This takes place when his/her peer introduces him to typical, fashionable and trendy teenage artifacts.

With this, the peer as social partner has at least three tasks. He may present the artifact (see Figure 6.2B), and then he must form a social relationship with his age-mate. The subject–partner system allows the subject to use the artifact in its meaning in a way that it is subjectively and functionally re-created (see Figure 6.2C).

Finally, the teenager as subject is in a position to use the artifact to define symbolically his/her identity independently (see Figure 6.2D). The transactions, as they are illustrated in these four figures, however, proceed differently depending

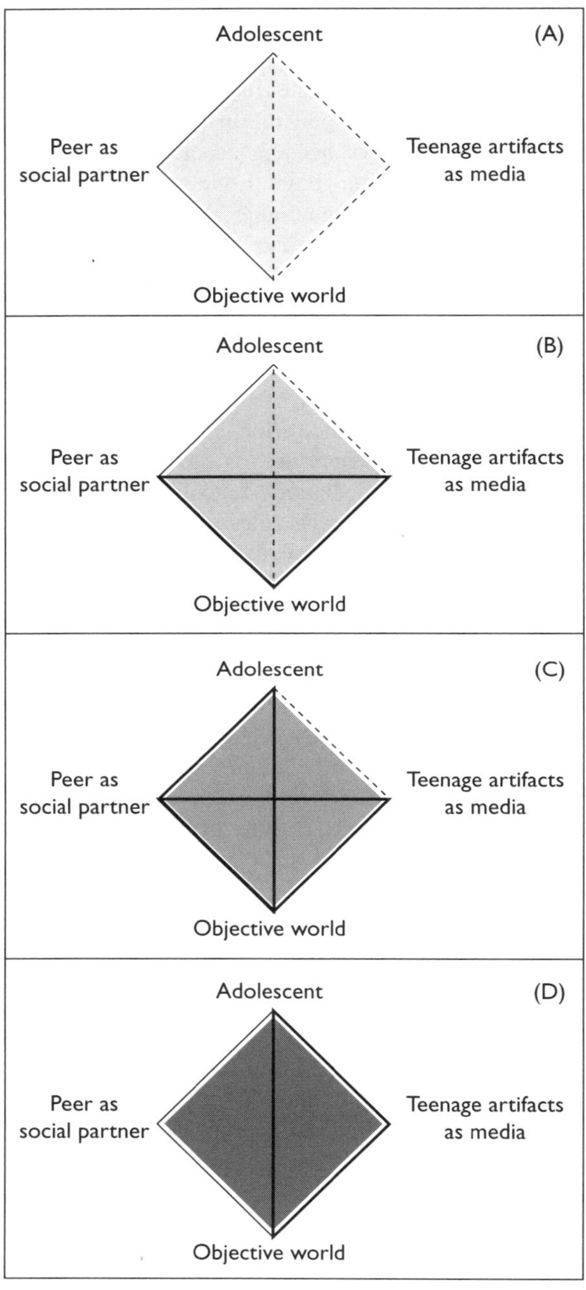
Adolescent
(A)
Peer as
social partner
Teenage artifacts
as media
Objective world
Adolescent
(B)
Peer as
social partner
Teenage artifacts
as media
Objective world
Adolescent
(C)
Peer as
social partner
Teenage artifacts
as media
Objective world
Adolescent
(D)
Peer as
social partner
Teenage artifacts
as media
Objective world

upon the adolescent's socioemotional relationships with his/her peer. That is social partners constitute an essential component of the tetradic transactional system to no less an extent than mediational artifacts or tools, but the effectiveness of other persons is heavily dependent upon the subject's emotional tie with them (see Rogoff 1993). The example makes clear that adolescents can create their own self via their—partly self-created or co-created—tetradic mediations.

The tetradic mediational model of meaning transactions, in which the variously structured quadrangles represent qualitatively different meaning constellations, describes the process of identity formation in the form of mechanisms and determining principles. As such it is quite a big step away from topographic, state-oriented models of identity where the need for a developmental perspective, i.e. structured change over time, is neglected. In the tetradic model such sequences are described as "trans-actional" in the sense of Deweyan pragmatism or according to dynamic systems theory in developmental psychology (Sameroff 1983).

This reciprocal mechanism is one aspect of the identity-formation process as a process of meaning transaction. Another aspect concerns the iterative nature of this process. Following these lines of theorizing, human beings are "tetradic constructors" of meanings. A child is born not only into a sociocultural environment, but also into one that is meaningfully organized. Artifacts, such as objects and places as media either have culturally specified meanings for people, or develop them in accordance with the folk model of meanings at the given time. Following the Vygotskian approach, this inevitability of the development of meaningfulness of the sociocultural environment stems from the human use of signs in controlling their environments and themselves. Adults and older children either have already developed their own personal understanding of the sociocultural environment around them, or are in the process of establishing such an understanding.

In contrast, the newborn is at the very beginning of that developmental course. His advance along these lines involves strong reliance on the denotational understanding of social partners around him: parents and other adult relatives, older siblings, or peers. The developing child is a co-constructor of the cultural meaning system, since he is a target of his social partners" purposeful and culturally organized actions. However, the child's input into the cultural environment is not direct, but rather indirect, i.e. mediated by the sense-making systems of

Figure 6.2A–D Multiple mediation in an I–world transaction developed for the purpose of cultivation: (A) intentional mediation of personal identity, in which the person defines his/her self symbolically via a particular artifact; (B) the existent ability of a social partner to support the person in defining self symbolically via a certain artifact; (C) social cooperation, in which the person co-constructively defines his/her I-world transaction mediated by an artifact; (D) the person—more or less—independently defines his or her self anew in its I–world relationship via the artifact

his/her social partner (see Figure 6.2, A to D). The cultural meanings are not transmitted from the environment to the child's social partner and from them to the child in an immutable form. Instead, each participant in this mediational process is a co-constructor of the cultural meanings, i.e. the mediational possibilities for the self.

Based on the cultural-mediational quadrangle one could assume that, for example, an adolescent as he/she collaborates with social partners and artifacts may account for many of the observed differences in developmental outcomes among adolescents of different ages. Ontogenetic or age-related diversity may then be accounted for by the different symbol systems and social contingency structures that order a child's experience within the different age-group cultures in which he/she participates (e.g., Fuhrer & Laser 1997, Kegan 1982, Miles 1996, Turkle 1984). According to Figure 6.3, this means, generally speaking, that the "output" of Step 1 or State 1 is the new "input" for Step 2 or State 2; the subject's (S) State 2 not only depends on the artifact (A) in State 1 but also on both the subject's State 1 and the social partner's (SP) State 1. In a similar way, the artifacts of State 2 depend upon both the subject's State 2 and the social partner's State 2. Each of these transactions can be considered as an iteration. Thus, the subject's identity constellation which is defined by all these ongoing transactions in State 1 is, in turn, changed by these transaction into a person's identity structure—as it is graphically represented—in the State 2 transactions.

Finally, State 2 transactions form the starting point for the next transactions, and so on. Identity formation is thus a sequence of multiple mediations among subject and social partners, with which they co-actively collaborate, and the artifacts which function as cultural opportunities. This means that identity as it is represented here does not solely refer to the left-hand side of Figure 6.3 (the subject's State 1), but to the process of meaning-making in which subject, social partner(s), and artifact(s) mutually constitute each other. Identity refers to a relation, not to an entity or essence. This conceptualization of meaning can be illustrated by the example of the teenage boy who spots a shiny new bike in a store window, is overcome with desire for the bike, and then begs his father to purchase it for him. Meaning is neither the stimulus object (bike) nor the individual self (boy) but rather lies in the coming together of the self and object at, developmentally speaking, a particular time and place. As such, meaning-making refers to the co-development of these qualities as a person evolves in a cultural context.

Therefore, first of all, identifiers—the target variables—according to this reasoning on identity formation, should have a personal and a contextual (social partner, artifact) meaning. The selection of concrete variables then depends on the type of person–social partner–artifact relation that is chosen as a subject of study. Another desideratum, especially relevant in developmental research, has to do with the time span under study. The relevance of identifiers, personal and contextual (social partner, artifact), could be different for different age-groups and/or study sites. Even facts such as name and birth date or ethnicity could change in meaning transactions over the life span. Most identifiers probably show clear age-related

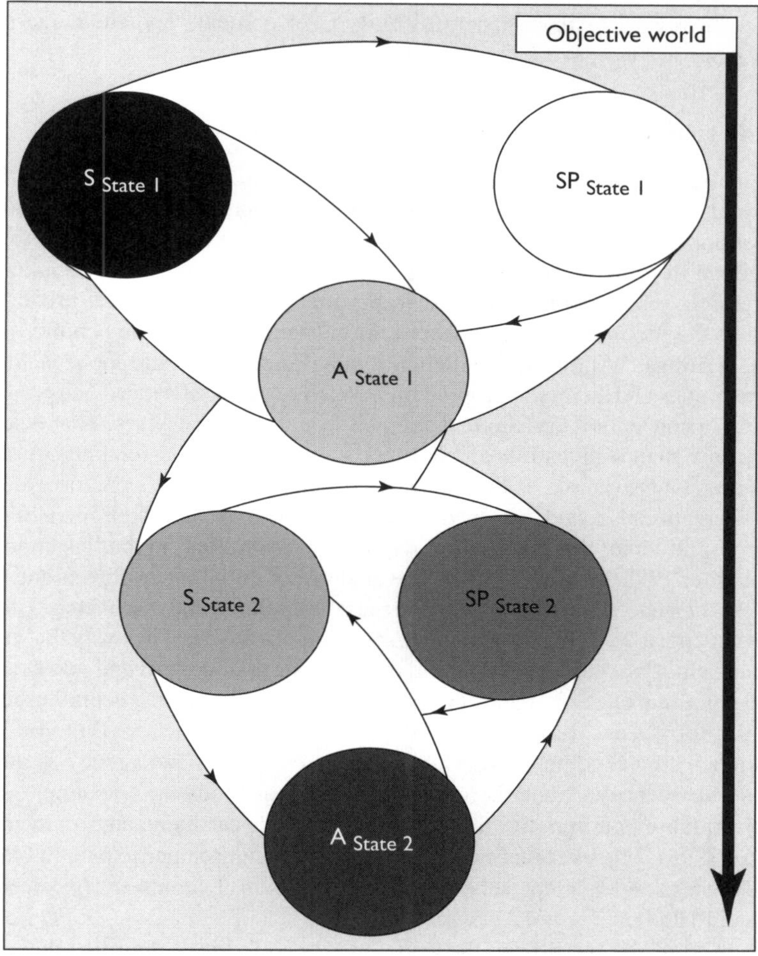

Figure 6.3 An example of a dynamic systems model of subject–partner–artifact transactions in a meaning-making activity

changes in personal and contextual meaning, or are especially relevant for specific age-groups. Historical or societal changes also influence the meaning of identifiers (see Baumeister 1986). So, target variables could have a limited relevance, only for a specific age-group in a specific situation or activity setting, for example, a particular brand of surf boards in a particular peer-group context in adolescence down at the Southern Californian beach sites. Other identifiers could be relevant over a longer age span and in more than one context. So, the targets should be selected not only on the basis of their personal and contextual meaning but also with regard to their generalizability over contexts and their age-related relevance.

Modes of cultivation

Originally, Simmel distinguished between two modes of cultivation, which I interpret as modes of cultivating meaning transactions: production and self-expression (see Oerter 1998 for a similar view). These modes can be described and explained in terms of two dialectical pairs: reification–appropriation, and self-expression–sense-making. At least in Simmel's (1990) work, the predominant mode is the production mode whereas the self-expression mode is more implicit in his writings. Within the production mode, Simmel refers to the *reification* of inner abilities and their re/appropriation through re/subjectification. The production mode is a conception that Simmel adopted from Hegel and Marx. That is, culture represents man's divesting of his inner workings and his re/appropriation of the same. One example of this transaction mode is children's creation of living and recreational spaces as mediational possibilities and their own ultimate re/appropriation of these spaces as "cognitive possibilities" in the Piagetian sense (see Fuhrer 1998, Wohlwill 1985). The qualities of the simplest objects and spaces that children encounter in everyday life must be explored and discovered. The child must act upon these objects, in a practical or cognitive sense, in a way that accords with the child's act objectified within them. Feelings of control and power arise as basic emotions of externalization. Externalization is thus also a central process of identity formation. It mediates the experience of self-efficacy (Bandura 1997), which is a crucial component of continuity, consistency, and agency as qualities of a secure identity. Along these lines of reasoning, children, for example, should be given more opportunities to help structure their near-home environments (see Fuhrer 1998). This is sometimes practiced when children participate in planning playgrounds, kindergartens, school yards, or classroom environments (see Weinstein & David 1987).

I now shift the focus from the artifact to the individual; *appropriation* within the production mode means the opposite process of reification. The subject appropriates artifacts by integrating them into his/her internal mental structure. In terms of cognitive constructivism *à la* Piaget, it is a matter of appropriation by reconstructing artifacts as mediational possibilities. The basic emotional processes produced by internalization is self-security. Appropriation makes the artifacts part of a person's identity. It is in this way that an environment that is known and emotionally related to a person becomes an intimate place for him/her. Thus, out of appropriation two other components of identity emerge: self-confidence and self-assurance. With regard to children's encounters, for example, their basic activity is exploration, which makes new things familiar. For instance, in the modern urban setting, children use opportunities for exploration in all kinds of "behavior settings" (sensu Barker, 1968) such as shopping malls, game centers, parks, and, of course, streets (see Fuhrer 1998).

The second transaction mode is much more implicit than explicit in Simmel's work. This mode is the ability to express oneself, i.e. the *self-expression mode.* Simmel (1990) understands this in the meaning given to the classical Aristotelian view by Herder or von Humboldt—that life expresses itself in forms. It is then from others' feedback on our expressed actions that we form an impression of ourselves. Here, we can interpret Simmel's thesis to say that self-expression does not have immanent meanings. Instead, meaning is co-created within processes of sense-making and social negotiations. Through the process of the social co-creation of meaning, the individual can experience himself in the reaction of his/her social partners as someone changed or as someone else. Following this line of reasoning, teenagers attempt to raise their self-esteem by means of self-expression to such an extent that their behavior may become exaggerated or even problematic. Graffiti, for example, is a symbolic and socially exaggerated form of expressing the self. Graffiti is the attempt to gain "recognition" in the public sphere, to gain an identity and to assert oneself. Places are used as a means of self-actualization. Sennett (1990) describes meaning-making transactions of people active in the graffiti scene as follows: graffiti artists express their "I," find self-confirmation in their own signs and experiment *via* the environment and with themselves. Through the artist's transaction with his/her graffiti he/she cultivates his/her self, and graffiti consists of representations of the self, just as the words one utters or the thoughts and emotions one has are representations of the self (see Chapter 8 for a more detailed description of graffiti as a medium for cultivation).

Our transactions with cherished possessions are communicative dialogues with ourselves (see Rochberg-Halton 1986). Cooley or Mead might say we engage in conversations through these signs, communicating with internalized representations of the generalized other, embodied in one's own personal things. In accord with Rochberg-Halton (1986), the home is a sign-practice, a craft to be cultivated. It forms an important part of both the individual and family self as well as representing the wider culture. Experiencing oneself by making sense of others' reactions to one's self-expressing act is the core process of forming identity. Only those domains to which one is committed and which can thus be integrated into one's own internal mind and harmonized with one's intentions, goals, and needs become a part of identity forming meaning transactions of the sense-making type. This assumption is expressed directly in the statement "I can [cannot] identify with." Sense-making discovers and/or constructs similarities between the environment and the person. It protects the actor from the feeling of alienation in a world with features different from those of the transacting person. Making sense of how mediating developmental possibilities, and in turn oneself, out of others' actions has the effect of strengthening and forming identity. Thus, the basic emotional processes of expressing oneself and making sense of others is familiarity and place attachment (see Fuhrer 1993a). Looking at children's activities, play is certainly the main self-expressing activity. In play, children together with their artifacts and social partners transact with a reality constructed by the child according to his own personal goals and motives (see Vygotsky 1978). Thus, providing opportunities for play of every type means stimulating sense-making processes. Moreover, a chance for children's externalization beyond play is found in the opportunity to define action possibilities as new possibilities of re/shaping environments by changing their topography or re/defining the rules of the play as they grew older.

These transaction modes continue to leave "signs" in the world through objectification, either in the production or the self-expressive mode. In their representations, the person can see the effect that they have. The term "representation"—in the symbolic sense used by Boesch (1991)—means that objectifications in the form of artifacts are part of a "connotation net," or a net of subjective-functional meanings. Instead of a connotation net, one might also speak of "semantic space" (Osgood 1964), which suggests a possible operationalization of connotation. Along these lines of reasoning, reflection is encountering the inner world in the outer world in order to confirm the self. Via meaning transactions, mental structures and feelings become solidified in artifacts as sociocultural mediating possibilities for his/her self. This means that personal objects such as musical instruments or sports equipment are never mere confirmations of the fact that one plays music or sports, but always also possibilities for the person to redemonstrate his/her ability and skill. These possibilities are incentives to generate development. Each object or place that is a subjective-functional value mediated possibility within I–world transactions thus implies both confirmation and confrontation. The challenge is issued towards differentiation and integration of the I–world relation (see Boesch 1991). The essence of externalization or reification is, according to Simmel, both the production of things and the self-expression of oneself in acts. This process constitutes the core of human activity the results of which are preserved in culture or serve, at least in many cases, the maintenance of culture. Externalization, however, thus includes all goal-directed, intended activities that shape and alter environments, and, therefore, create mediating possibilities to act upon these environments to form one's self.

While the two modes of cultivation are linked together, they complement each other to form an integrative whole. Each of the four components is involved in any meaning-making transaction contributing, with different weights, to the process of creating mediating possibilities. However, culture in general and activity settings in specific cases sometimes have constraints that restrict transactional opportunities and, therefore, the creation of mediating possibilities. For example, in Western cultures appropriation prevails over reification because the economy is based on consumption (see Rochberg-Halton 1986). That is, the dominance of consumption in everyday life suppresses processes of reification. From this view, a very general definition of mental health can be derived insofar as mental health is a state and a process in which the four basic components of identity forming meaning transactions are somehow in balance.

Meaning possibilities as media for the cultivating self

After this re-examination of identity formation as a process of cultivation, in particular, the mediational relationship between internal and external aspects, and the role of mediating possibilities for the growth of the self, I shall now go on to elaborate them by incorporating the cultivation principle as an essential mechanism of human development along with some well-known assumptions proposed by recent developmental contextualistic metamodels (cf. Ford & Lerner 1992). With regard to the cultivation principle, reference will be made to research based on the identity through possessions model, since the search for identity or the self is a pervasive theme of human nature.

The preceding considerations have led to a concern about the structuration of three levels of the developmental system, because all levels of the system may be considered potentially coequal in this respect in the developmental systems view depicted in the Figure 5.1. But what makes development happen? Looking at Figure 6.4, the biogenetic level represents the biological potentialities of human beings. They may serve to sustain already achieved socio-cognitively constructed possibilities (maintenance function), but they can temporally regulate when a feature appears during development (facilitative or supportive function), and it may be necessary to bring about a socio-cognitively constructed possibility that would not appear under the occured experience (inductive function). Moreover, culture offers opportunities for development at the psychic level. With these opportunities (and constraints), however, the socio-cognitive activities (as meaning transactions) at the psychic level may bring to the forefront configural aspects of cultural opportunities that create a limited range of meaning possibilities for psychic development.

For example, the child's socio-cognitive activities at any time is a product of the transactions between the psychic possibilities, or the child; the cultural opportunities; and the biogenetic potentialities. On the cultural side, culture contains a range of opportunities for the child, but the particular regulating experiences that are active at any given point in time are in response to the status of the child's psychic possibilities. In fact, psychic-conscious systems constitute the environment for cultural systems, while cultural systems constitute the environment for psychic-conscious systems. Analogically, psychic-conscious systems constitute the environment for biogenetic systems, while biogenetic systems constitute the environment for psychic-conscious systems. These self-referencing systems evolve in a transactional or co-actional fashion. Consequently, psychic-conscious systems and both biogenetic and cultural systems emerge together through mutual differentiation based on self-referencing operations, and each facilitates the growth of the other in a transactional or co-active fashion.

To understand the intrinsic connections between identity, culture, and transactional developmental processes, Simmelian notions seem particularly suited to capture the ways in which a person's identity is, at least partly, externalized in the

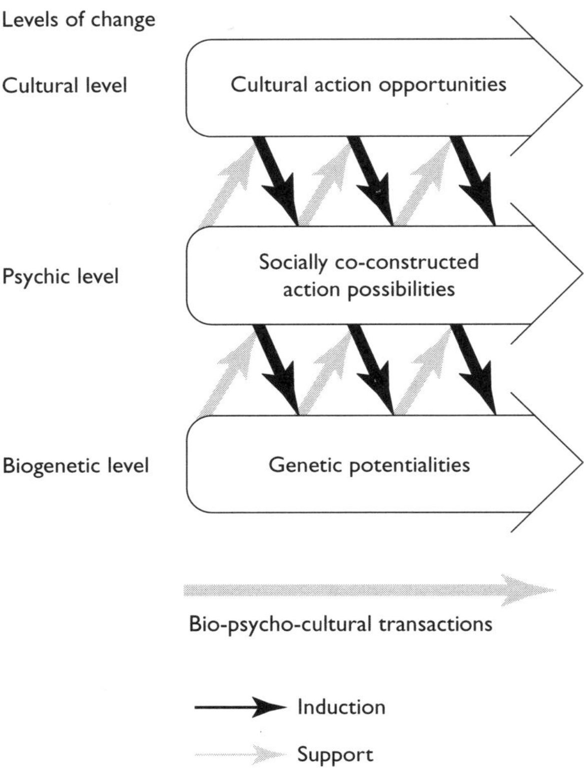

Figure 6.4 Transactions between biogenetic potentialities, socio-cognitive possibilities, and cultural opportunities

form of "objective culture" which, in turn, will be incorported into his/her personal sphere and thus become a formative element of the individual's self. Viewed substantively, the interaction between "subjective culture" and "objective culture," constitutes some of the foundations for a fuller understanding of his/her cultural analysis of individuality and his/her individual analysis of culture. Thus, Simmel regards the process of cultivation as emerging out of the use of purposively formed artifacts—as part of material culture—in such a way that human beings create forms of culture that take the process of individual developmental change into real and ideal spheres beyond the individual contents. Indeed, as the selections from Simmel's writings indicate, the mediation between these minds—that is the purposively functioning person–culture cycle is seen as a process of cultivation where identity is described as phenomenon where the "internal mind" and the "external mind" (culture) make each other up (Fuhrer 1993a).

Aside from the steady elaboration of his social philosophy, Simmel (1968) was concerned with how a personal identity or self is formed out of the multiplicity of cultural structures. Just as concrete sociocultural products are only finite and imperfect realizations of the ideality of some individual mind's expectations, so individuals are only limited realizations of their ideal selves. The attainment of personal identity is thus not a matter of arbitrary subjectivity, but rather a developmental process towards the successive elaboration of an epigenetically given form via objectification. Here we have to recognize that the development of personal identity, although it pertains to the subject, can be reached only through the mediation of cultural means such as artifacts (Fuhrer 1993a).

But how does one select between competing mediating possibilities for the self? Looking more closely at the process from Simmel's view of culture, one could say that what he calls objective culture (which parallels somehow the term "meme;" see Csikszentmihalyi 1996) functions as the intermediary station (or medium) between the not-yet-cultivated subject and the cultivated subject. That is, cultivation is the process of developing a state of being in a creature of mediating possibilities which would not come about naturally, but for which human beings have a natural propensity, by re/shaping, or re/creating objects external to it. As a consequence, Simmel gives a definition of culture in which these dynamic and goal-oriented mechanisms are included: The total telos of the individual—as *causa finalis*—forms meaning; it is that mechanism between person and culture which creates mediating possibilities through meaning-making transactions. Applying Simmel's idea of the cyclical process of cultivation to the question raised above, one can say that memes can only be symbolically interpreted by analogy to "inner experience," and conversely inner events only by analogy to external, cultural determinations. The two analogy formations produce one another mutually.

When applying this view to the question of how a personal identity is constituted through artifacts as mediating possibilities for the self, it becomes even more obvious what Simmel (1990) means when talking about the tragedy of culture. The very idea of culture consists in creating artifacts which are meant to be integrated into the subjective culture of their creators and to be submitted to subsequent generations of individuals. In his/her role as cultural receiver the subject becomes the addressee of the destructive effects of artifacts he has created him/herself in his/her role as cultural creator. In the long-run, the interruption of this reciprocal feedback process affects both sides negatively. The more individuals react towards the threat of objective culture with retreatism and cultural deviance, the greater the likelihood of subjective culture and objective culture becoming dissociated.

Maintaining a coherent biographical sense of identity over an individual's life span has become an increasingly arduous task, because it has to transcend the diverse and shifting kaleidoscope of artifacts between which individuals constantly move (cf. Kroger 2000). In part at least, the unique and stable personal attributes which are supposed to form the core of our identity have to be made concrete, reproduced and recreated in and through artifacts. It is in this sense that children and adolescents are thoroughly immersed in an environment of cultivating artifacts. Even before the infant is born, its parents have begun to project an environment of clothing, toys, and furnishings that will begin the cultivation process. The child's self arises in a setting that is constantly "addressing" it, telling it who it is through its surroundings, telling it how to become he or she. However, from its beginnings, child development involves transactions between internal and external structures and these transactions imply a two-way activity. The external becomes internal and becomes transformed in the process of internalization. But because, from its very beginnings the child actively cultivates his/her environment, the internal becomes external and the external becomes transformed in the process of externalization. On the one hand, the child can influence the social partners who influence them; that is, development involves reciprocal relations rather than only unidirectional ones. Moreover, not only do children influence those who influence them, but through "circular functions," children also get feedback as a consequence of their influences on others. On the other hand, rather than passively react to a prefabricated sociocultural environment, individuals re/shape, and re/create their environments in unique ways. Such reconstructive transactions with one's cherished possessions, for example, either actually or symbolically, can be seen as mediating possibilities or sign-expressions of the self (Fuhrer 1993a, Rochberg-Halton 1986). That is, when the self transacts with some material artifact, that artifact becomes a mediating possibility for the self. Therefore it is adequate to say that the self is a transaction between an interpreting individual and an object, and in this sense it is in two places.

Along these lines of reasoning, I assume, for example, that valued possessions are living signs, whose life consists in the transaction between person and thing. As living signs, objects must be cultivated to retain their significance; as cultivated objects, things can grow in significance over time and take new layers of meaning which, in turn, are part of developmental processes. That is, as mediating possibilities things, places or settings cultivate and can create new mediating possibilities for individual development (see also Fuhrer 2000). An old fence separating two neighborhoods, for example, can play a significant role in children's play as a vehicle for cultivation (see Wohlwill 1985 for an overview of the famous work of Martha Muchow on the life space of the urban child). For Muchow's children in a working-class neighborhood of the city of Hamburg, the fence plays a major role, and that is quite different from the one intended for it where it serves as a barrier for adults. The children, instead, perceive it as an object of major attraction, as well as a challenge, for practicing and exhibiting all manner of athletic skills, experimenting with novel ways of transcending it, and of descending down into the landing area. Or a piano, to take another example, might be merely a silent bulk of status-furniture for one family, but in the hands of a young Mozart it can act as a physical means for the growth and transformation of self, and culture as a whole. Even as we cultivate things, they cultivate us, i.e. they become a part of our self (see Belk 1992). Here, Erich Fromm's question fits nicely: "If I am what I have and what I have is lost, who then am I?" (Fromm 1976: 96).

In a similar vein, in the field of environmental psychology Proshansky *et al.* (1983) stressed their concept of "place identity" (i.e. a substructure of self-identity) the contribution of the built environment to a person's self-development. They pointed to the necessity of including material cultural means in the understanding of processes of acquisition of and change in one's self-identity. In no way is the importance of the social process devalued; rather, the social process is shown to be embedded, restricted, and enriched by the physical setting in which it takes place. Transforming one's own identity is mediated through cognitions and processes that relate to the regulation of person–environment relationships, which also influence the relationships to other persons and the experiences one has with regard to oneself. In the studies by Chawla (1992), Cooper Marcus (1992) or Fuhrer (1998) places such as hideouts, forts, and small leftover spaces in the home or outdoors were spaces frequently used by children and adolescents to cultivate themselves. Here, too, their outstanding quality appears to be that children can cultivate these spaces in undisturbed privacy and shape them, as mediating possibilities, according to their will. Thus, a child's play, for example, is most satisfactory when it allows him/her the greatest possibility to manipulate his/her environment according to his/her "need to be cultivated."

In a similar vein, Frisby (1985) points out that fashion is a sociocultural form which juxtaposes the feeling of individual identity alongside the security of commonality with others. In fact, from this perspective the whole history of society is seen to be a compromise between adherence and absorption in a social group and the need for individuation and distinction from the members of such groups. The individual needs to feel that he/she is different from everybody else, in order to play upon the social circle's sensitivity for difference. In this sense, the fashionable teenager is envied as an individual and yet approved of as a member of a cultural subgroup. Thus, clothing styles that may be considered by adolescents to be individually inappropriate are readily accepted as dictates of sociocultural fashion. Inevitably, however, fashions have a rapid turnover time, due to the impatient tempo of modern life. Fashion, then, provides a support mechanism in a society whose individuals often lack independence, and who are in constant need of sociocultural support while constantly cultivating and recultivating their minds. Thus, the concept of the "cultivated individuality" differs from the concept of individuality as it is only concerned with the individual's capacity to receive and integrate elements of his/her sociocultural environment into his/her personality structure.

With regard to cultural developmental psychology, the above mentioned phenomenon of paralyzation parallels Erik H. Erikson and James E. Marcia's well-known descriptions of the subjective experience of identity crisis (cf. Marcia *et al.* 1993). For example, active experimentation (i.e. a form of cultivation) is not the only form an adolescent identity deficit may take. Instead, the person may shrink from making choices, adopt an avoidant stance, and ruminate alone. Orlofsky *et al.*, for example, say that during identity crisis some adolescents are active, engaging, and creative while others are "paralyzed by inner turmoil of indecisiveness" (Orlofsky *et al.* 1973: 211). If a case of paralyzed indecisiveness becomes chronic, such as prolonging adolescence toward early adulthood, it becomes appropriately described as identity diffusion (Marcia 1989), which, in turn, is characterized by a fragmentation of the self. By self-fragmentation, Kohut (1977) refers to a developmental delay in the formation of an integrated or cultivated self as the result of an inadequate response of self-objects as artifacts. This does leave the individual with feelings typical of some forms of identity diffusion. That is "feelings that one is not real, that one is not cohesive, that one has no continuity in time, that one is not whole" (Kohut, 1977: 33). Developmental psychology so far, however, has shed little light on how, for example, artifacts mediate the process by which adolescents successfully cope with identity diffusion or even with self-fragmentation. We would assume that artifacts such as personal possessions may take on a "mediating function" (Fuhrer & Laser 1997) similar to Winnicott's (1971) "transitional objects" or Boesch's (1991) "bridging objects."

In contrast, in cultural studies, theorists routinely use notions of decentering and fragmentation as a way to think about the self (Gergen 1991). For example, Sherry Turkle (1995) sensitively describes how virtual communities on the Internet such as multiuser domains (MUDs) serve as places for the construction and reconstruction of identity. MUDs make possible the construction of an identity that is so fluid and multiple that it strains the very limits of the notion. On the MUD, Turkle says, some people create a living environment suitable for their ideal self. Others create a character or multiple characters that are closer to embodying aspects of themselves that they hate or fear or perhaps have not ever consciously confronted before. As with television, you are engaged with the screen, but MUDs are interactive, and you can take control of the action. As in acting, the explicit task is to construct a viable mask or persona. Yet on MUDs, that persona can be as close to your real self as you choose, so MUDs have much in common with cultivation or even with psychodrama. In its virtual reality, we self-fashion and self-create, we cultivate ourselves through the Internet culture. And since many people simply choose to play aspects of themselves, MUDs can also seem like real life.

Turkle's (1984) past research into the experiences of individuals working with computers have led her to assume that these evocative objects open a new way of remaking or cultivating the self. That is MUDs are a context for constructions and reconstructions of identity and they are also an environment for the de-construction of the meaning of identity as "one" (Turkle 1995). While MUDs are certainly not the only places on the Internet in which to play with identity, they provide an unparalleled opportunity for such play. A MUD can become an artifact for discovering who one is and wishes to be. In this way, the games are somehow laboratories for the construction of identity. Thus, the Internet has become a significant soiocultural laboratory for experimenting with the constructions and re-constructions of the self that characterize post-modern life.

Through theories that stress the decentered subject, post-modern self-developmental psychology confronts what is problematic and probably illusory in both traditional notions of a unitary self and the development towards a single-self. Thus, the fragmented self of post-modern self-theories stands in a sharp contrast to the cultivated individuality concept which stresses Stern's (1938) idea of unity in diversity (i.e. "unitas multiplex"). With regard to Simmel, in his earlier writings he clearly stressed the idea of the fragmented self (Simmel 1890). There, the young Simmel favored a sociological view of individuality which had a quite negative flavor. In his later writings, however, Simmel (1968) stressed a definition of individuality which developed from closed unity through the unfolding multiplicity to the unfolded unity. It is, in fact, an empirical question if in today's media-saturated world, where identities are no longer built solely within the close-knit communities of family, neighborhood, school, and work transform the human psyche, resulting less in psychic unity than in psychic divergences in mind, self, and emotion.

Taken together, choices in terms of mediating possibilities are generally dictated by subjective meanings which, in turn, refer to a person's intentionality or *causa finalis*. Generally, cultural opportunities that do the job with the strongest facilitating demand on a person's intentions will survive. Sometimes selection, and even more so shaping and creation, are based on internal consistency which, in turn, is an essential component of personal identity. Cultural opportunities (with which individuals transact as mediating possibilities) survive because people store them in memory, internally as well as externally, and then reproduce them through their transactions. Taking Simmel's idea of cultivation, cultural opportunities, whether consisting of artifacts or ideas, instruct us to act (i.e. cultivation's feed-forward mechanism), just as genes do. Much of our psychic energy is devoted to trying to select among them and reproduce them. Generally, we feel that this activity represents our own desires. Here is where Simmel's cultivation principle enters the scene. That is the importance of subjective culture derives from the fact that human beings carry within themselves the intrinsic motivation—rooted in Simmel's "individual law"—to be cultivated. Culture in the subjective sense of the term, exists only in the presence of self-development, provided that this self-development relies on external, objective means. The person acts his/her becoming in the direction of his/her individual law—that is, so to speak, the epigenetic chart. In a sense, then, it is true—adolescents may want to buy the latest chart, the newest brand of fashion—but what choices do they have actually? As long as their minds have been influenced by the cultural opportunities—as mediating possibilities—in question, they inevitably feel that to replicate them is in their personal interest. However, it is not easy to know when we are serving the runaway replication, or even creation, of cultural opportunities, and when we are doing something because it is best for us. It is impossible to rid ourselves completely of the artifacts and ideas populating the minds, the internal as well as the external. But with the other sources of illusion—the world created by genes, by the culture, by the self, by significant others—we can at least take cognizance of our limits, step back and evaluate where our psychic energy, i.e. the intrinsic motivation to cultivate the external towards the internal mind, and so forth, is being directed, and why. Even if we stop there and go no further, we will have claimed a certain amount of freedom in both the reproduction and creation of possibilities as media for our lives, and we will better be prepared to face new challenges. This principal is true already by virtue of its logical form. It does not imply, however, that the ranges of developmental variation are unlimited.

Discovery and creation

To say that we have made a discovery means that we have come to recognize something about the nature of the world or ourselves. That which is found is something that already exists. Now it is recognized, appropriated and understood. Discovery is the process of making the unknown known. Discovery is the way of scientists. The process of creation, on the other hand, is to bring into existence something that has never before existed. It entails selecting from among virtually unlimited opportunities and constructing from the elements chosen something deemed to be of value. Creation is the way of artists and engineers.

The construct of identity as discovery is closely linked with the philosophical concept of the daimon or "true self." The daimon refers to those potentialities of each person, the realization of which represents the greatest fulfillment in living of which each is capable. These include both the potentialities that are shared by all humans by virtue of our common specieshood and those unique potentials that distinguish each individual from all others. The daimon is an ideal in the sense of being an excellence, a perfection towards which one strives and, hence, it can give direction and meaning to one's life. In a similar vein, the identity as discovery is incorporated into Maslow's work on self-actualization. Self-actualization is defined as the:

> ongoing actualization of potentials, capacities and talents, as fulfillment of mission (or call, fate, destiny, or vocation), as a fuller knowledge of, and acceptance of, the person's own intrinsic nature, as an increasing trend toward unity, integration or synergy within the person.
>
> (Maslow 1968: 25)

Consistent with the discovery metaphor, the experience of self-actualization is said to be accompanied by a distinctive set of intrinsic rewards. It should also be noted that Maslow referred to peak experiences, often associated with self-actualization, as "acute identity experiences." Since the daimon is identified with the person's potentials, the task of identity formation is to discover or recognize the character of the daimon, that is his/her own character (compare the analogy to Simmel's individual law in Chapter 4). It follows that only a limited range of the possible resolutions to an identity crisis will be consistent with the "true self," and could, therefore, be considered as successful resolutions. It should also be understood that the discovery of the daimon does not ensure that it will be actualized. People may default on living in truth to the daimon for any of a variety of reasons. They may be limited by the constraints and barriers of their cultural environment to activities necessary for the satisfaction of needs that take precedence over the pursuit of self-fulfillment. They may also succumb to external social pressures directing them into other activities. To the extent that the daimon is unrecognized or defaulted to, the individual will be missing out on the most important source of purpose or meaning of life.

The construct of identity as creation is most clearly represented in the existential philosophy of Jean-Paul Sartre. For Sartre (1956), there is no "true self." The self is seen as emerging from "nothingness" by an act of personal choice. Identity formation, then, is an act of creation. It entails making choices from among an almost limitless array of alternatives and becoming what one has chosen to become. This sounds like people can become anything that they choose to become. But this feeling of omnipotentiality is not an unmixed blessing. With all of one's options open, there arises a fear of indefiniteness, a fear that one will never accomplish anything and become no more than a dilettante. The fear of indefiniteness in turn gives way to desire for commitment. But here too is ambivalence. To make a commitment, particularly where there is the concern that any choice is arbitrary, is to risk making a poor choice and thus find oneself moving in an unrewarding, unfulfilling direction. Thus, in the absence of an intrinsic nature, the numbers of opportunities are limitless and the choice of one option over all the others becomes arbitrary. To default on the necessity of choice is to experience existential dread. And the responsibility for the choices made must be one's own, the burden cannot be shifted to another. To abdicate that responsibility, to allow someone else to direct the nature of one's commitments is, to live in bad faith (Sartre 1956). Here, it is where a fear of stagnation arises. The fear of stagnation gives rise to a renewed desire to maintain a sense of omnipotentiality, with the result that a new cycle is begun involving a fear of indefiniteness, a desire of commitment, a fear of stagnation, and so on. Although the term identity appears to suggest a fixed personal quality, and thus seems inappropriate to a discussion of developmental processes, the process aspects of identity transactions are most evident in the dimension of exploration as individuals move from the lack of awareness of alternatives, possibly to an avoidance of awareness, to their active consideration, to a putting aside of identity questions, whether successfully resolved or not.

Taken together, if identity formation is a process of discovery, the primary focus of responsibilty for working through the identity crisis rests firmly on the developing individual. Possible resolutions must almost certainly emerge from within the person. Significant others should be supportive of the search, but any specific suggestions they make will likely be of only limited utility. In contrast, if identity formation is a process of creation there is a greater opportunity for shared responsibility. A larger role can be played by guiding figures since their suggestions may well be more realistic and more "creative" than the ideas a developing person can generate for him/herself. If, then, identity formation is a process of discovery, a greater reliance may be placed on intrinsic rewards in guiding the eventual resolution of the identity crisis. Feelings of eudaimonia constitute the criteria for success and significant others are not called upon to play a judgmental role.

However, if identity formation is a process of creation, there is a larger, more crucial role for extrinsic rewards in guiding the eventual resolution. This may require outside figures to exercise more of an evaluative function since they may be able to make realistic predictions of future success and, in addition, their expressions of approval may constitute part of the extrinsic rewards. Moreover, if identity formation is a process of discovery, it is important to respect the internal timetable of the developing individual. Progress likely will be made only when the person is psychologically prepared to take the next step. Indeed, it can be argued that the steps to be taken and their timing are themselves aspects of the daimon. In contrast, if identity formation is a process of creation, it may be possible to accelerate the resolution of an identity crisis by making the pieces of a potential solution available earlier. Of course, it is entirely plausible that each person may choose his/her metaphor for identity formation, some preferring the identity search, others looking to create or construct their own identity. It may be most appropriate for us to conform our efforts to be helpful to their preferences. In any case, we might infer from this that the parameters of our potentials for self-realization are relatively broad. Within the parameters set by the daimon, therefore, the processes of identity formation may well be an act of creation (see Waterman 1990 for a similar view).

Chapter 7

Behavior settings as media for children's cultivation

To understand why children participate in the contexts in which they actually participate to cultivate themselves, I synthesize in this chapter the cultural developmental thinking of Georg Simmel with the notion of "behavior setting" as it was introduced into developmental psychology by the Lewinian scholar Roger G. Barker. The two approaches, however, have developed separately; each has attracted attention, but no-one has tried to incorporate the contribution of the other to create an account of human developmental processes that recognizes the essential relation between individuals and their cultural settings with regard to identity formation. From the conceptual background of the previous chapters, behavior settings, individuals, and their development are interpreted as interrelated processes that constitute each other, and social scientists' delimitations between components parts of persons, their development, and the world are intentionally blurred. The attempt to rethink development as cultivation leads to the question of what makes behavior settings attractive vehicles for the study of children's cultivation.

Goal opportunities and social forces: behavior settings

In psychology, both Lewin's (1943) and Barker's (1968) theorizing exemplify many aspects of a transactional perspective. Lewin considered psychological processes to be embedded in physical and social settings, forming a "life space" or "psychological field." He departed from a strict transactional perspective by assuming quasi-stationary equilibrium states towards which life spaces develop. Although readily accepted in principle, these ideas have not always been translated into theoretical and empirical work. An exception, however, is the ecological research by Barker and his associates (see Schoggen 1989). Ecological psychology, or eco-behavioral science, as Barker later named the discipline, had its beginning in 1947, when Roger Barker and Herbert Wright opened the Midwest Psychological Field Station at the farming community of Midwest (code name), Kansas. The original modest purpose was to study the development of children in a town small enough to observe and measure. Barker and Wright's

(1955) studies moved from an attempt to characterize behavior settings in one community to comparisons of behavior settings across several communities. In the 1960s, Barker opened a counterpart to Midwest in Yoredale (code name), England, and over a decade compared the demise and rise of behavior settings in the sister towns (see Barker & Schoggen 1973). The Midwest–Yoredale comparative research was undertaken in the hope that the similarities and differences identified in the public life of the two towns might reflect differences in both goal opportunities and social obligations between the, larger, US and English cultures.

Along with the application of naturalistic methods, there evolved a new perspective on human behavior according to which behavior and environment were seen as occurring in inseparable units called behavior settings. In Barker's terms, these behavior settings are natural phenomena with both a specific, denotable space–time locus and people displaying regularly occurring behavior patterns. There is a similarity in structure (called "synomorphy") between these behavior patterns that occur within the arrangement of the physical objects; and these patterns exist independent of any particular person's perception of them, i.e. they are preperceptual ecological entities (Barker 1968).

Rather than to record all human actions in a particular town, Barker and Wright (1955) discovered that places like villages, towns, or cities can be studied in small-scale environments, that is, in the format of behavior settings. Whether one considers neighborhoods, small towns, or metropolitan centers, they are assemblies of behavior settings where people are essential components. Barker and his co-workers discovered that it is easier to predict children's behavior on the basis of the behavior settings they entered than the behavior profiles of the individual children.

While much of developmental psychology viewed children's environments as passive arenas and handled them (conceptually) as a kind of black box, Barker and Wright proposed that behavior settings lead dynamic lives, governed by their own sets of rules, opening goal opportunities, and capable, moreover, of coercing certain behavior from the people who enter them. Crowded streets, a playground, a shopping mall—each has its own imperatives. This linking of behavior with environment has led to the claim that the psychological field station gave birth to an ecologically oriented psychology. Barker and his co-workers discovered that human habitats consist of a series of nested ecological units, ranging from single synomorphs to more complex assemblies of synomorphs (see Figure 7.1). They began experimenting with ways to measure these attributes and came up with a series of scales, which became the principal units of measurement in eco-behavioral science (see Barker 1968).

Synomorphs

Synomorphs consist of single behavior–milieu parts, that is, they encompass physical and behavioral attributes that are similar in structure (e.g. a child sitting

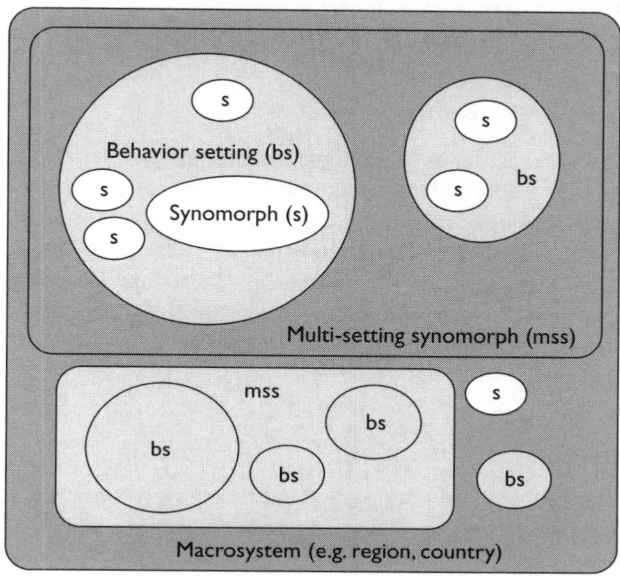

Figure 7.1 Behavior settings and their relations to smaller and larger ecological contexts

at the school desk, a teacher writing on the blackboard). Synomorphs are the smallest human–environment units, and they have a greater degree of interdependence between themselves than with parts of other behavior settings. Two or more synomorphs form a behavior setting.

K-21 behavior settings

While most behavior settings such as playgrounds, grocery stores, and school classes are easily identified, it is often difficult to know intuitively whether, for example, the lunch counter at a drug store is a separate behavior setting from the pharmacy counter. Thus, a scale was developed to determine whether two putative behavior settings were actually separate or whether they constituted a single setting. The K-21 scale consists of seven subscales (7-point Likert scales) that are added together. The K-test of interdependency is based upon ratings of the degree to which (a) the same people enter both settings, (b) the same leaders are active in both settings, (c) both settings use similar spaces, (d) both settings use similar behavior objects, (e) the same molar action units span the two settings, (f) both settings occur at the same time, and (g) the same kinds of behavior mechanisms occur in the settings. A rating of 1 represents the greatest similarity, a rating of 7, the least similarity between synomorphs on the measure in question. If the sum is 21 or more, the behaviors are considered separate behavior settings. If it is below 21, they are deemed too interdependent to be separate.

Multi-setting synomorphs

If a certain part of a community contains synomorphs with less than the specified degree of interdependence, that is if any of these synomorphs are too independent of other synomorphs of a certain community part, or too independent of the whole bunch of synomorphs, then this community part is, by definition, more than a single behavior setting. This criterion serves to exclude as behavior settings such synomorphs as churches, schools, and many other institutions. These behavior–milieu structures are not behavior settings, but clusters of behavior settings, that is multi-setting synomorphs.

Macrosystems

Last, synomorphs, behavior settings, and multi-setting synomorphs are embedded in sociogeographical contexts. These largest human–environment systems can be described in terms of Bronfenbrenner's (1979) macrosystem. Within Barker's work there is no term for these largest systems, which are defined by cultural boundaries. Although there is no concept that captures contexts larger than multi-setting synomorphs, Barker's work recognizes such cultural macrocontexts (see Barker & Schoggen 1973, Schoggen 1989).

Contrasting social interaction in the behavior settings of an American town (Midwest) and a town of similar size in Great Britain (Yoredale), Barker and Schoggen (1973) reported differences not only between the two towns but also between the two macrocontexts in which they are located. For example, behavior settings designed especially for the benefit of children increased substantially in Midwest but decreased slightly in Yoredale, whereas the reverse relation occurred in the behavior settings where children benefit members of other age groups (Barker & Schoggen 1973).

In contrast to Bronfenbrenner's (1979) work, however, Barker and most of his co-workers do not draw much attention to either multi-setting influences on development or to "ecological transitions" that take place whenever a person undergoes a change in role within a setting or in a different setting during the life course. However, Allan Wicker (1987) has focused on ways to account for changes in the level of functioning of behavior settings and for setting growth and decline.

Behavior settings are parts of communities that are generally recognized by citizens. Thus, many psychological and behavioral processes in public life domains unfold the "format" of behavior settings (Barker & Schoggen 1973). Unfortunately, much of the study of people acting in behavior settings has been focused on the structure and the coercive forces of those behavior settings upon individuals, and of the behavioral aspects of these individuals *en masse*. The study described in this chapter brings the single individual back into the focus of attention. Here, an attempt is made to capture both the behavior setting as a sociocultural community of practice and the individuals' actions in one single process. The behavior setting and the individuals' actions are not separate elements; rather the behavior setting as a whole is a confluence of inseparable individual and collective actions that depend on one another for their very definition and meaning. That is individual and behavior setting are in a transactional relationship with each other (see Stokols & Shumaker 1981).

Moreover, behavior settings (interpreted in the traditional Barkerian way as sociocultural systems, events, or entities) consist of opportunities for goals and actions (Barker 1968). In a particular behavior setting different people may achieve the same goal. For example, in a playground setting kids are collaborating with each other with play material to cope successfully with the games. Furthermore, different people may achieve a different cluster of goals in the same playground.

Thus, any behavior setting exists only when it provides its participants with the particular goal opportunities their unique nature requires. Otherwise, the behavior setting will cease (see Wicker & King 1988). However, social forces indicate one kind of link between people entering into the behavior setting and the "standing pattern" characteristic of behavior in the particular setting (Barker 1968).

These standards of the behavior settings' appropriate behaviors are important means in guiding children's actions. These forces imply obligations for setting participants and they can be strongly coercive. The power attaching to the members of behavior settings who occupy responsible positions within those behavior settings, such as the mother who takes care of the kids within the playground, is well known. For example, if a kid enters the playground his/her behavior is somehow channeled into this behavior setting's specific patterns of behavior.

Thus, within a behavior setting there are routes to (official) goals that are satisfying to the participants. In the playground there are (official) paths for finding physical play material or even for reading books, but there are no paths, at least no socially accepted paths, to goals like buying cookies, watching TV, or surfing on the Internet. Barker (1968) hypothesized that some setting participants, mostly staff persons, old-timers, or, in the playground case, adults who might be identified by the children as authorities, act as control persons. All these things may increase the children's level of self-consciousness, that is the sensitivity to their own actions. Here is where the identity issue comes into the children's focus of attention (see Fuhrer 1993b).

The fact that a behavior setting is typically both located in a man-made environment (i.e. the milieu) and regulated by social norms and rules (i.e. the setting program) tells us that behavior settings are cultural rather than "natural" settings. I thus suggested that behavior settings be regarded as cultural constructions whose structure can be understood in terms of "life-spaces" that were collectively shared among setting occupants within a particular cultural group or community (Fuhrer 1990).

In accord with Wicker's (1987) theoretical reformulation of Barker's "pre-psychological" view of behavior settings, the revised framework also recognizes an additional level of analysis beyond that of the person and the behavior setting, that is the larger cultural environment that constitutes the context of behavior settings (Fuhrer, 1990). Thus, both behavior settings and the larger cultural world in which these behavior settings are embedded are of a culturally structured environment (see also Valsiner, 1997, for a similar view).

Generally, cultural events have an intrinsic double aspect. They give meaning, that is objective conceptual form, to the social and physical environment both by shaping themselves to it and by shaping it to themselves. Actions, things, places, and temporal dynamics are interlocked in such a way that actions gain meaning by virtue of the actors and actions that exist within it. Thus, it is not surprising that there is remarkable consensus among cultural communities in describing person/group–environment–transactions in terms of behavior settings (Stokols & Shumaker 1981).

However, doubts have often been raised about these assertions, specifically about whether behavior settings can be validly described as kinds of "collectively shared life spaces" in the face of individual variation (Fuhrer 1990: 533). For example, a behavior setting like a market place or a volleyball game has more than a collectively shared meaning, that is the denotative setting qualities as captured by Barker's K-21 scale. It is important to recognize that behavior settings are full of personal and group-specific experiences; and these connotations are not expressed by the denotative level of the K-21-setting analysis. Although this symbolism of settings on the connotative level is extremly complex, it merits considerable attention (see Boesch 1991).

Children cultivate behavior settings to cultivate themselves

In the most general terms the present endeavor is an effort to integrate the theoretical perspectives of Roger G. Barker, and Georg Simmel. The cultivation paradigm of the present theory is explicitly structuralistic. In other words, it emphasizes the fact that both the developing child and his/her environment are structurally organized. That structured nature of the child and the child's environment is not static and immutable; it is dynamically transformed as the child develops in transaction with the behavior settings in the surrounding culturally structured environment. However, a number of basic notions upon which this theory is built must be made more explicit.

In applying Simmel's (1908a) view of cultivation to Barker's eco-behavioral science, one notes that children do not simply *use* behavior settings to take part in some more-or-less prescribed behavior patterns. Rather, they transact with behavior settings as vehicles to cultivate themselves. That is they externalize their ideas, goals, and plans when they act, more or less, in accord with the behavior setting.

However, by changing either the standing behavior patterns or the physical milieu, children, to varying degrees, transform a behavior setting; they cultivate the behavior setting. For example kids often engage in alterability play, involving modification either of the physical milieu, the play objects, or the playing rules. The contrast between *cultivating* the behavior setting by self-specific actions *à la* Simmel and just *using* it *à la* Barker illuminates the basic difference between the two approaches.

Bringing these two theoretical perspectives together, however, one sees that behavior settings as media of cultivation denote a model of development that entails two critical issues. First, development is seen as the outcome of an individual's own potential for self-specific development aimed at cultivating external environments to make them a part of the self. Second, such externally oriented self-specific actions produce not only change in the environmental context of development, but change in the individual as well; behavior settings as culturally structured environments become vehicles for cultivation. Thus, it is cultivation that links the changing individual and the changing environment.

This view of development corresponds closely with "development as action in context" as a paradigm for developmental research (see Silbereisen *et al.* 1986a). The cultivation model of development, however, differs from this paradigm with respect to the central role of the self as a manifestation of subjective culture and objective culture (in the sense used by Simmel 1908a). In fact, if one views development as cultivation, then the overarching goal of development is the continued growth and concretization of the self, a process that is reached only in transaction with purposively created objects, settings, and other components of the culturally structured environment like social groups. For example a musical child may need a piano lesson to enact his/her musical talent, just as others need a football game or an adventure playground to activate aspects of their selves.

Thus, development as cultivation within a given behavior setting can be part of a larger socialization process providing necessary elements for aspects of the self. For the child, being socialized into school (as a multi-setting synomorph) also means being socialized in school lessons (as behavior settings). Thus, it may not seem so far-fetched to say that behavior settings can be actual manifestations of the self. However, children differ significantly on how behavior settings become relevant media for the definition of their selves (see Proshansky *et al.* 1983).

In the absence of more extensive research by developmental psychologists on the qualities of behavior settings for children's cultivation, I refer instead to Muchow and Muchow's (1935) interesting precursor of this approach (see also Wohlwill 1985). Martha Muchow's work on the life space of children was among the earliest, and is still one of the most outstanding, approaches concerning children's experiences of urban environments. Consistent with frequent observations by others, the children Muchow observed made use of public spaces intended primarily for pedestrian and vehicular traffic—notably city streets—for their play, while avoiding areas specifically set aside for them such as developed parks. Similarly, they spontaneously selected undeveloped areas in a city block, adapting them for their play activities, while avoiding developed areas.

Particularly intriguing is Muchow's comparison between adults' and children's uses of an area serving as a relatively little-used loading and unloading facility for canal ship traffic. Of similar interest are the observations of children's exploration of a large department store, including the analysis of stratagems employed to slip past the guard at the gate in order to gain access to it.

This type of study, combining an ecological focus with a naturalistic approach, has been all too infrequent in this area. Notable exceptions are, for example, Roger Hart's (1979) studies of children in a small Vermont village, Herb Wright's city project on children's activity range in two Kansas towns (1967), and the work that a few German developmental psychologists have done with children in Berlin and, especially, Herten (see Görlitz *et al.* 1998). Muchow's work nicely illustrates the significant role of vacant lots and undeveloped areas in children's play. These milieus are used not only for ballplay and other games but also for activities such as climbing, and digging.

In a similar vein, certain research on child behavior in the outdoor environment points to the significance of settings that are not highly structured in terms of the physical layout and arrangement of significant elements and the behavior appropriate to and supported by these settings (see Wohlwill & Heft 1987). The work that Hayward *et al.* (1974) have done on children's behavior play settings of different types is illustrative in this regard. The study provides useful information, notably on the use of adventure playgrounds, which designers have favored for some time. Hayward *et al.* (1974) pointed out the value of the adventure-type playground, with its openness and lack of fixed structure for creative and imaginative, as opposed to purely physical play, and thus its suitability for children beyond the preschool level.

Generally, the common refrain in the research on children's outdoor play has been that children, particularly of school age, and boys more than girls, tend to prefer physical milieus such as streets, empty lots, quarries, and undeveloped natural areas for their play, as opposed to more structured, designed, and equipped playgrounds (see Wohlwill & Heft 1987). With regard to adolescents, the work by Silbereisen *et al.* (1986b) also illuminates the relevance of behavior settings that are characterized by a loose relation between the physical layout and the behavior patterns of the setting. They pointed out the significant role of niches that open possibilities for actions toward "unofficial" goals, i.e. acting "against" or "beyond" the social rules and/or the physical-structural qualities of the behavior setting. These kinds of informal functions are exemplified by such actions as hanging out in shopping centers or boisterous behavior at swimming pools.

In sum, I assume that a series of self-specific transactions is initiated by children either to transform existing behavior settings or to look for congenial ones. Here again, the distinction between *cultivating* and *using* is important. The latter seems dominant in the environmental psychology literature on child development (see Weinstein & David 1987, Wohlwill & Heft 1987). In other words, if one likes behavior setting X to act in (and selects it), then one prefers it to others, whereas the cultivation idea links preference with the opportunity for self-specific transactions with the environment. Thus, the development-as-cultivation paradigm has fundamental implications for both theory (e.g. children's transactions with behavior settings to self-cultivate along lines not foreseen by adults' understanding of "what children want") and application (i.e. frustration of many efforts by city planners to design "developed areas"; Hart 1987).

Of course, cultivation will vary with the availability of behavior settings, especially with the degree to which behavior settings are segregated by age. One might assume that small villages or rural towns have both different sorts of behavior settings and different rules of segregation among age groups from metropolitan areas (Barker & Wright 1955). For example, behavior-setting surveys done at Midwest in the early 1950s showed that the town was remarkably open to the coming and going of children.

Some 60 per cent of all behavior settings were open to children, whereas adolescents could enter 79 per cent of them. The analysis of the number and type of behavior settings frequented by individuals at all periods of the life span provides a good illustration of this type of study. The changes are documented with age in both type and number of settings occupied by the residents of Midwest.

Above all the major shift from family to community settings occurs after preschool, peaking in adolescence and reversing in adulthood and old age. These data mean that a child who lived to adulthood in Midwest would at some time during childhood and adolescence have an opportunity to become acquainted with most of the community behavior settings of the town. In most behavior settings, a Midwest child associated with people of a wide age range. He/she, therefore, continually experienced the ways and roles of younger and older persons.

Thus, living in Midwest brought continually expanding action opportunities. This was not as true for children of other Midwestern communities nor for children in other cultures (cf. Barker & Schoggen 1973). In terms of cultivation, behavior settings are thus useful in demonstrating that opportunities within a more or less stable environment are limited. Within larger contexts, however, such as neighborhoods and towns, children can select from among a broad range of settings that fit their developmental tasks (Havighurst 1948), such as learning both a variety of cultural technigues (e.g. reading, writing) and age-specific social skills (e.g. playing and working in groups). Thus, I assume that the selection of behavior settings depends on age and self-specific developmental orientations of the self.

Along these lines of theorizing, the qualities of both the physical milieu and the setting program are important aspects of behavior settings in terms of their attractiveness to children's self-specific needs and with regard to cultivating "possibilities" for the growth of their self. In terms of cultivation, at least two qualities of behavior settings are important: variability and openness. The former is viewed as the potential that the physical milieu and its props offer for physical manipulation and alteration. The latter refers to the number of different action opportunities that a behavior-setting program offers to potential users.

On the one side, a physical milieu of low variability is, for example, a play unit without any opportunities for alteration. On the other side, behavior-setting programs with high openness are typical, for example, of shopping centers, with their wide range of action opportunities. One can assume that children's cultivation is nourished by such qualities as variability and openness of behavior settings and that their social development is fostered. There is also ample evidence that low-structured or medium-structured behavior settings are preferred to well-structured ones; the latter provide almost no challenges (see Wohlwill & Heft 1987).

Microscope on children's daily life

Environments on the urban scale are not very readily dealt with by psychologists. This state of affairs is even more obvious when we turn to the work on children's experience in urban behavior settings. In much of the earlier work by Barker and Wright, small towns were chosen because they lent themselves to analysis in terms of behavior settings, which were relatively few in number. A notable advance in this regard, however, is represented by the work of Gump and Adelberg (1978), who presented an analysis of preadolescents in a neighborhood within a large city in terms directly comparable to that employed for Midwest.

In the present investigation, among other goals, I attempt to analyze children's outdoor activities in terms of behavior settings as cultural media (see Fuhrer & Quaiser-Pohl 1999 for a more extended version of the study). In contrast to the extended outline on behavior settings and cultivation, however, the focus in the study reported here is narrowed down from dynamics to residuals. The methodological approach adopted for the present study required an identifiable environmental behavior unit, that is a spatially compact unit so that the children would reside relatively close together. The members of my team and I chose to look for a medium-sized rural town that exhibited as many urban traits as possible. Such requirements would seem to contradict each other, but Midland (code name) was ideal. Midland is a fairly typical rural town located in the Bernese Mittelland (Switzerland) with a population size of 10 100. The railway divides the town into two parts. In the center of the town is the expected dense group of stores and schools. The train station, small industries, apartment houses, and a large public swimming pool extend southwards and detached family houses and apartment blocks extend northwards. Socioeconomically, two per cent of the inhabitants are farmers, twenty-five per cent blue-collar workers, and sixty-eight per cent white-collar workers. A total of 184 Midland school children aged ten, twelve, and fourteen years participated in the study. The sample included 93 girls and 91 boys.

We selected the children by controlling variables distilled from the literature review as being potentially significant factors in terms of leisure activities (see Wohlwill & Heft 1987): age, sex, and socioeconomic status (SES). The SES (medium-low vs. medium-high) was defined by the type of school in which the children were enrolled. Children who attended primary school were classified into the lower SES group, whereas those who were enrolled in secondary school were part of the higher SES group. This distinction, however, was possible only for the 12- and 14-year-old children because the 10-year olds all attended the same type of school—primary school. During August 1992, the children filled out a self-administered diary for seven consecutive days during their entire waking time. Each child was given a form as physically compact as possible on which to record the day's activities, the time when each was begun and ended, the location in which the activity was embedded, and the people who accompanied the child. The major dependent variable was the time children spent in particular types of public-behavior settings.

With regard to the cultivation model of development, the behavior settings were then categorized along the two dimensions described above: the variability of the physical milieu and the functional openness of the behavior-setting program. That is all behavior settings were assessed for both variability and openness on a three-point rating scale (low, medium, high) by two independent raters with interrater reliabilities of $\kappa = 0.68$ for variability and $\kappa = 0.65$ for openness. Behavior settings with low variability were the two large food stores, several restaurants, and the disco. Behavior settings characterized as medium variable were streets, youth meetings, and club festivities. A behavior setting of high variability was that of cooking on a open fire in the woods. Behavior settings with low program openness were theaters, cinemas, and restaurants. Examples of behavior settings with medium openness were public festivities and youth meetings. Last, behavior settings with high openness were the public swimming pool and several small neighborhood streets.

The most preferred settings in terms of variability and openness

I shall first give a short overview of the mean percentage of time that Midland children spent in behavior settings differing in both physical variability and program openness (see Figure 7.2). The corresponding standard deviations (minutes per week) for physical variability (PV) were: low PV (SD = 3.54), medium PV (SD = 5.13), and high PV (SD = 0.21). The variability indices for program openness (PO) were: low PO (SD = 1.18), medium PO (SD = 1.84), and high PO (SD = 4.81).

Figure 7.2 shows that children spent most of their time in behavior settings that were characterized by either medium variability of the physical milieu or a high openness of the behavior patterns that were prescribed by the behavior-setting program. Thus, the Midland children did not prefer completely changeable spaces as is often claimed in the developmental literature. Rather, they used spatial milieus that are not totally physically changeable. To these children, behavior settings are most attractive when their physical variability is neither very high nor very low and their programs are highly open.

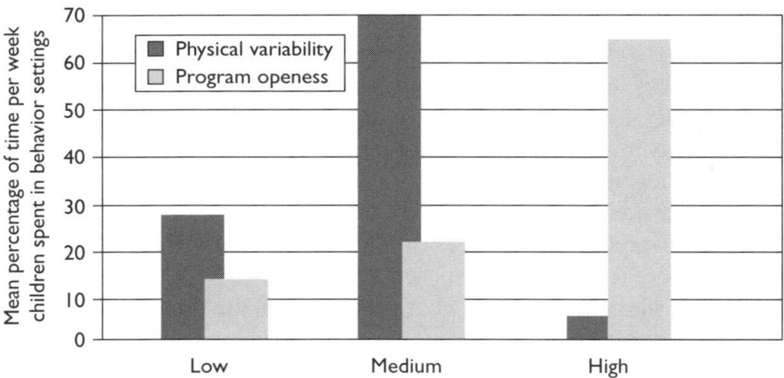

Figure 7.2 Mean percentage of time per week that children spent in behavior settings differing in physical variability (low, medium, or high) and program openness (low, medium, or high)

The impact of the predictor variables (age, sex, and SES)

Second, we tested the relations between the predictor variables and the time that children spent in behavior settings differing in both variability and openness. Because the requirements for multivariate analyses of variance were not given in the study, Wilcoxon matched-pairs signed-ranks tests were performed for either variability or openness, sex and SES being used as predictors. Then a Kruskal-Wallis one-way analysis of variance by ranks was performed for either variability or openness, age being used as predictor. Post-hoc tests were performed when significant age effects were revealed. The major dependent variable was the time (in minutes per week) that children spent in behavior settings differing in both physical variability and program openness.

Table 7.1 summarizes the main results of these nonparametric statistical tests. Binomial tests were then performed to check whether the significant effects were random among all other effects. The three binomial tests revealed that the significant univariate effects for each predictor variable were not random ($p < 0.05$ for each analysis).

Thus, age, sex, and SES are related to the time that children spent in behavior settings differing in both variability and openness. The sex effects indicate that: (a) girls spent more time in behavior settings of low variability (mean = 210 min) than did boys (mean = 180 min); (b) girls spent more time in settings of low openness (mean = 95 min) than did boys (mean = 20 min); and (c) boys spent more time in highly open behavior settings (mean = 510 min) than did girls (mean = 390 min). The age effects showed that: (a) 10-year-olds spent significantly more time

Table 7.1 Results of Wilcoxon and Kruskal-Wallis tests regarding the time that children spent in behavior settings differing in both physical variability and program openness as a function of sex, age, and socioeconomic status (SES)

Predictor variables	*Sex*			*Age*			*SES*		
Dependent variables *Time spent in settings of*	*df*	*z*	*p*	*df*	c^2	*p*	*df*	*z*	*p*
Low variability	1	–2.00	0.05	2	2.01	0.37	1	–0.78	0.44
Medium variability	1	–1.83	0.07	2	2.84	0.24	1	–2.51	0.01
High variability	1	–0.73	0.47	2	10.37	0.01	1	–0.37	0.71
Low openness	1	–2.14	0.03	2	0.15	0.93	1	–0.77	0.48
Medium openness	1	–0.21	0.83	2	9.77	0.01	1	–2.58	0.01
High openness	1	–2.06	0.04	2	11.42	0.01	1	–1.88	0.06

in behavior settings of high variability (mean = 30 min) than did both 12- and 14-year-olds (mean = less than 3 min for each of these age groups); (b) 14-year-olds spent significantly more time in behavior settings of medium openness (mean = 280 min) than did both 12- (mean = 140 min) and 10-year-olds (mean = 100 min); and (c) both 10- (mean = 490 min) and 12-year-olds (mean = 535 min) stayed significantly longer in highly open behavior settings than did 14-year-olds (mean = 300 min). Last, the SES effects indicate that: (a) children of lower SES spent more time (mean = 540 min) in behavior settings of medium variability than did children of higher SES (mean = 360 min); and (b) they also stayed in behavior settings of medium openness significantly longer (mean = 220 min) than did children of higher SES (mean = 100 min). This last finding seems to imply that high-SES parents are somehow "better" parents and that they are more concerned with protecting or monitoring their children.

In accord with studies of both child behavior in the outdoor environment (see Wohlwill & Heft 1987) and adolescents' preferred leisure-time behavior settings (Silbereisen *et al.* 1986b), the findings showed that children generally go to transact with behavior settings of high program openness, that is behavior settings that do not prescribe any behavior-setting-specific actions. I assume that highly open behavior settings are exactly the kind of settings in which many children, although they may differ in their self-specific needs, can cultivate themselves in transaction with the particular behavior setting. Highly open behavior settings, therefore, have exactly the qualities of social gathering places for children. The children in the present study, however, did not prefer the physically most flexible behavior settings but rather mostly participated in behavior settings of medium variability. It is assumed that the reason children have for preferring behavior settings of medium variability is the medium potential that such behavior settings have for complexity, challenge, and novelty. These "collative" variables (Berlyne 1960) do not refer to the visual complexity but rather to the behavioral complexity of the behavior settings. With regard to physical variability, this finding is quite in accord with the research on curiosity and the often observed finding of an inverted U-function between environmental complexity and the intensity of exploratory behavior (see Görlitz & Wohlwill 1987).

In contrast, children prefer behavior settings of high program openness with which they might compensate their search for functionally complex behavior settings by the desire for physically less complex behavior settings. More or less stable physical environmental prerequisites can be seen as a complexity-reducing orientation context (Kaminski 1986). In fact, physically more restricted behavior settings might be precisely the behavior settings that give a certain level of security that, in turn, children need to test program-specific rules, or to "break" the "official line" of the behavior-setting program as a means to cultivate themselves (e.g. Muchow & Muchow 1935). With regard to program openness, therefore, the present findings are not consistent with the inverted U-function as mentioned above.

Furthermore, the analyses revealed a sex effect on the time that children spent in behavior settings differing in both variability and openness. Obviously, girls prefer behavior settings that are of low variability and of low openness as well. One can only speculate about the reasons why girls spent more time in physically less challenging behavior settings than did boys. Research on sex differences in environmental exploration indicates that boys explore larger territories than girls do (see Wohlwill & Heft 1987). Parental restraints and environmental fears (relating to security problems in public places) have generally been suggested as responsible for sex differences. Whether these arguments are valid interpretations or not, girls, unlike boys, either preferred or were encouraged to use behavior settings in which their actions were highly supported by both the physical milieu and the behavior-setting program. I would speculate that girls, in general, show a lowered self-confidence when coping with environmental challenges than boys do. In a similar vein, Hart (1987) describes differences between the kinds of settings that boys and girls create for themselves. Boys tend to "build" the behavior settings (e.g. forts), whereas girls concentrate on the furnishings and arrangements to elaborate the interior spaces of these behavior settings. Hart also rejects a psychodynamic explanation for these differences as too simplistic and argues that they reflect sex-related social roles that boys and girls are encouraged to adopt. Among adolescents, however, the gender-typic needs for visiting particular leisure places is more complicated (see Cotterell 1998).

In contrast to the sex differences mentioned above, the age effects are less consistent. Moreover, the results are not completely in accord with previous findings that children prefer more challenging behavior settings as they grow older (see Wohlwill & Heft 1987). However, if one interprets behavior settings as "places for development" (Silbereisen *et al.* 1986b) then the age differences make sense. As children grow older they may favor settings that facilitate social interaction with peers. For adolescents, meeting their peers, especially affiliating with peers of the opposite sex, can be a "risky" thing. Thus, taking into account that learning to interact with peers of the opposite sex is a challenging process one finds it understandable that 14-year-olds spent more time in behavior settings that are neither very open nor highly variable than did 10- and 12-year-olds. Again, semi-open behavior settings can be seen as a complexity-reducing orientation context that encourage novel social encounters in older children.

In contrast to the differences of both age and sex, influence of SES on the time that children spent in behavior settings of both medium variability and medium openness are less clear. In the literature, effects of SES are usually explained by differences in parental restraints on children's use of outdoor places (e.g. Hart 1979). Behavior settings of both medium variability and medium openness are shopping centers, youth meetings, and all kinds of festivities. Thus, among other action opportunities, social interaction with all kinds of people represents a common goal of these behavior settings. One could speculate why children of lower SES spent more time in these types of behavior settings than children of higher SES. I would assume that parents of higher SES are more concerned about protecting their children from negative social conduct than parents of lower SES are. Moreover, higher SES parents are more restrictive with their children than lower SES parents are with theirs when it comes to the use of behavior settings in which their children run a greater risk of meeting unknown, perhaps "undesirable," people.

Directions for future research

With Simmel's concept of cultivation, I introduced a concept that seems likely to elaborate Barker's behavior setting concept with regard to its potential for human development. That is cultivation is seen as the outcome of a person's self-oriented transactions aiming at changing behavior settings to the needs of specific developmental orientations of the self and these transactions not only alter the specific behavior setting but change the individual as well. In contrast to other contextualized developmental approaches (see Silbereisen *et al.* 1986a), cultivation as a paradigm for development points to the significance of children's self-specific transactions with their behavior settings; above all, it requires that these behavior settings be relevant for the central core of the self. Along this line of theorizing, it is my impression that several areas are potentially valuable directions for further research.

First, a multi-setting perspective would be useful in examining links between behavior settings cultivated by children. The external environment as a context for development is not simply an array of separate and isolated behavior settings. Children move from behavior setting to behavior setting, and it is likely that their experiences in one behavior setting will influence their cultivation in another.

Second, interesting questions arise concerning the impact that rapid societal and environmental change has on how the availability of behavior settings in certain towns, regions, or countries is altered. For example, the concept of developmental phases, one growing to some extent upon another, implies that there are progressions from, say, more-restricted to less-restricted behavior settings. There could also be progressions in the other direction. That is it could be that children and youths in cities of rapid sociophysical transformations such as those occurring in countries of Eastern Europe are increasingly and rapidly cut off from transacting with their "old" behavior settings in a self-related manner. The question arises of how these rapid alterations of children's outdoor environments either facilitate or inhibit their cultivation (see Fuhrer 1995).

Third, despite the emerging interest in an ecological view of child development, less than five per cent of the studies were empirically based (Moore 1987) and no general theory had emerged that presented child-environment links in a sociophysical context. All major developmental theories such as those of Stern, Piaget, Vygotsky, and Bronfenbrenner, point to the need that children have to act in an environment rich in resources, to explore, or test, and to learn from feedback on their entire actions. Thus, to facilitate personal growth, the opportunity to explore rich, varied, and open behavior settings appears related to cognitive, social, and motor development. Unfortunately, existing behavior settings for children are totally inadequate in many cases, often consisting of physically fixed milieus and behavior-setting programs that do not accommodate the self-specific needs of children's transactions with them. The question is what the consequences are for the developing child when the physical environment in which he/she grows up does not fit his/her need for cultivation.

Fourth, some evidence is available to support the suggestion of a link between specific environmental experiences and intellectual abilities (Webley 1981). Aside from the differences between the sexes in their territorial range (cf. Wohlwill & Heft 1987), the present study also revealed differences between girls and boys with regard to their opportunities to transact with behavior settings differing in both variability and openness. I hypothesize that transactions with behavior settings may be one of several unintended learning experiences that contribute to the differential development of some intellectual abilities and even of independence and self-certainty in males and females. Along these lines of theorizing, it is, therefore, not surprising to find males so disproportionately represented in such fields as the physical sciences, engineering, and architecture, where, for example, spatial ability is an important element in successful performance (see Quaiser-Pohl & Lehmann 2002).

Fifth, there seem to be only a few published findings on historical, intergenerational change of behavior settings for children (Gaster 1991). However, relating Bronfenbrenner's (1979) ideas on the significance of chronosystem models for developmental research with Wicker's work on the life-cycle of behavior settings would open a highly promising avenue for future research on culture and human development (see Wicker 1987). Along these lines of reasoning, development may best be described as the sum of self-specific transactions that people, from childhood to adulthood, undertake over relatively long periods of time and across multiple behavior settings as means for cultivating the self.

Last, I hope that the perspective emerging from the thinking behind the cultivation-as-development paradigm has begun to demonstrate significant features of person–environment transactions that help one to better understand children's development-in-their-contexts. In fact, there is much to learn on how behavior settings and children make each other up.

Chapter 8

The writing on the wall

Cultural piracy to struggle with the self

What is it about an empty wall that causes people to feel the need to cultivate themselves or the compulsion to express on it their frustrations, fantasies, desires, wisdom, their innermost secrets, things they would not ordinarily reveal to their closest friends or loved ones? One answer is that graffiti are a form of communication that is "beyond" everyday social restraints that normally prevent people from giving uninhibited reign to their thoughts and feelings. As such, these sometimes crude inscriptions as well as the process of producing them offer some intriguing insights into how people create developmental possibilities "beyond" the sociocultural maze to cultivate their culture to cultivate themselves. Case-study data come primarily from interviews with graffiti artists which are accessible on the Internet. Later in the chapter, I want to analyze more extensively a short autobiographical text of a graffiti artist. The story of graffiti artist Flint-707 is a nice example to illustrate the process of cultivation—as a meaning-making practice—towards the formation of Flint-707's personal identity.

Graffiti to establish themselves "beyond" the norm

The study of graffiti is not only amusing and interesting, but it may have a great deal of psychological relevance in that it gives us (as psychologists) something to think about as we try to relate the cultivation of graffiti to identity formation. This is the intriguing side of graffiti as a medium of cultivation, since what seem to be a trivial or coarse banality to one person may take on special significance for developmental psychologists as they come to realize that graffiti are written by people who find their walls or subway trains the only confessional with which they can struggle with their evolving self. Indeed, graffiti are announcements of one's identity, a kind of testimonial to one's existence in a world of anonymity: "I write, therefore I am." Thus, every public graffito can be seen and or read as a fragment of someone's identity or even as a miniature autobiography of a member of a society in the sense that the graffiti reveals a part of him/herself and his/her society in all that he/she writes.

Today graffiti artists have pushed the spray can's technical possibilities to the point where they parallel those of the paintbrush. Thus, with its creative possibilities limitless, graffiti now has much more important questions to answer with regard to its mediational meaning for the cultivation of the growth of both the self and its culture. Why do some people take the trouble to paint? Why do some of these people put the rest of their life in second place to an art form and its perfection?

From a Simmelian view, the most obvious answer to these questions is that humans need to express themselves. For the graffiti purposes, however, that is not a good enough answer. Painters, dancers, authors, and photographers all express themselves. "I need to express myself" explains away all the arts, graphic or otherwise, but does not address graffiti specifically (Sonik 1998).

Instead, people paint graffiti because it is a means of expressing themselves and establishing themselves well outside the norm. As an artistic work, even when created legally, any graffiti will have a certain renegade edge which has been bolstered by years of illegal work. In creating these public art works, graffiti writers experience a level of risk and adventure, artistic and otherwise, that anyone outside the graffiti community would have great difficulty comprehending. This thrill that graffiti people experience becomes evident when we look at an excerpt from an interview where a graffiti writer from the Netherlands (his name is "Sign") was asked to, "Tell us about one of your bombing nights"

> One night I was preparing to make a huge piece on the local train station together with my friend Cabin. On the way over there a black car passes by. I normally never looked inside, but this time I did, it was a policeman in uniform, with an undercover car. This was giving me the creeps, when the car passed us again we were on the spot. The car makes a huge turn and drove it on the train platform, all his lights were on the spot where we were hiding. We climbed over a little fence and lower ourselfs into the grass. Then we saw the car moving back again. We talked to each other about what to do? We decided to go to another place to make our burner. Half way down there I heard a spinning motor, but I didn't see any moving cars. There was our little black friend waiting for us to come this way. As quick as we can we moved to a building and kept ourselves hidden on a spot where we could see the black car. Suddenly he turned on his lights and moved towards the building. We ran like hell in the other direction but we did find a spot on that night. After we finished it, it became a little lighter in the sky. My feet were killing me. But it is the biggest thrill when the cops don't know how to beat me and my friends.
>
> (http://www.hifiart.com/index/talk.html)

Thus, graffiti is also one hell of a lot of fun. But this hardly scratches the surface of what graffiti is to any moderately serious graffiti writer. Usually, people start to practice graffiti because in doing so they are different. However, if and when they decide to commit seriously to graffiti as more than a teenage weekend diversion, they will realize that they are hardly alone in doing so.

Today, there are thousands of very dedicated graffiti writers worldwide. Being the local graffiti writer may create a rebellious artist image for you along the way, but in the global graffiti community, that "cool" is standard issue. There is nothing special about being a graffiti writer in a room full of graffiti writers! How, then, can one truly maintain the true original attractions of graffiti: to be different and to be yourself? On the one side, the answer lies in graffiti people's motivation to expand or create possibilities as media for re/forming their identities by acting "beyond" the prescribed social rules and/or the pre-designed physical-spatial structures. In doing so, these people create a kind of "difference" or even a form of "deviance" and they become self-conscious about their difference which guides the cultivation of themselves. That is, the distinctiveness of a person's identity to some extent hinges on deviations from the normative pattern, or, more generally, on the ways in which the conflicting tasks of enculturation and individualization are negotiated (Boesch 1991).

That is one of a graffiti artist's main motivations has traditionally been the kick of doing something illegal. A sprayer's pride in evading the law is often evident, with prominent messages such as "You can't catch us!" LOOMIT, an artist based in Munich since 1983 who has achieved international commissions and recognition for his work, explains the motives behind his hobby-turned-career: "It has nothing to do with fame and fortune, just the urge to do something forbidden and creative" (http://www.munichfound.de/issues/1996/7/articles/LOOMIT.html).

From here, it is obvious that trains are very important in the graffiti scene. Trains allow for the total and ultimate freedom of expression. Reading the excerpt of an interview with ATOMEONE (AT), one of the most famous Australian writers, illuminates the importance of trains.

I: What's up with trains there?

AT: Trains always be the jewels in the chest. Everywhere. Regardless of time and conditions. I think they have been, and to an extent will always hold the true essence of writing. . . . To be in a yard surrounded by steel, painting in the darkness with a thousand emotions running through your body is an experience in itself.

I: How important are trains now?

AT: My answer to all of that is a very general one: The trains are the sacrifice. . . . The trains allow for total and ultimate freedom of expression. . . . Personally, I see the painting of trains as being the test, the educator, and the experience within the experience. . . . In many ways the trains are where you put your skills to the test, break society's rules and laws, and reach an understanding of what it is really like to be a writer.

(http://www./hifiart.com)

Thus, graffiti tends to be anti-establishment. It is often used as a form of public protest by otherwise silent members of a community who lack legitimate, or more convenient means of expressing their grievances. Graffiti writers become self-conscious about their difference and uniqueness through a kind of identificatory collision or cultivation in the Simmelian sense.

This process indicates both cultural production (transformation, creation) and cultural reproduction (appropriation, assimilation), where contradictory relations imply a renewed cycle of cultivation to resolve the underlying conflicts between the internal mind and the external mind or culture. Other examples of actions "against" the official line of behavior setting, such as hanging out at shopping centers or roughhousing at swimming pools are extensively described in the work of Martha Muchow (see Wohlwill 1985) and, later, by Silbereisen *et al.* (1986b). On the other side, the answer lies in a comprehension of style (Sonik 1998). In an effort to promote a better understanding of "style" as a meaning-making activity to express oneself, an understanding of the term is needed.

Aestheticization as a meaning-making practice

Of course, for most of its participants, graffiti is, at least in part, a quest for identity. Psychologically, this is rather obvious, for the act of leaving one's mark has been associated with self-affirmation since the dawn of time. However, since there are currently so many people out there doing graffiti, each participant strives to have something special about the way they write their name in order to stand out. Indeed, the great challenge of graffiti is to create a design framework for the letters in one's name which is so personally tailored that it allows for the expression of attitudes, opinions, emotions, and the self. Since the set of letters in the name that one paints does not change, the way they are painted is what conveys meaning. For example, one writer paints an S, an O, an N, an I, and a K, in that order, but in each painting he has different messages which he hopes to convey. In order for anything personal to show through in his paintings, he must paint them with a style that is every bit as personal. If he paints in a way that is truly his own, he will have a voice that is truly his own. He will paint with a voice that is entirely personal. Thus, he can convey messages which are every bit as personal without losing any of their meaning.

However, style alone will not impart serious meaning upon a graffiti piece, but it is only a tool or a meaning-making activity with which meaning can be effectively conveyed via lettering (Sonik 1998). Style is how one presents one's ideas. It is the way one creates, the framework and the foundation for all of one's work. Beyond that, it is the one true voice that exists within each of us, the voice that has often been buried by years of acting like other people. The framework of style is the framework of yourself. Style means fully knowing one's self. Thus, once one's style is firmly established, letters develop for the graffiti writer in a way that is meaningful. The design and shape of the letters means something beyond looking pretty, all the arrows and connections used have a purpose (compare the *causa finalis* in Simmel's cultivation principle). With a strong personal style, one can experiment and learn new methods of painting without rendering the work trivial.

Thus, in contrast to technique, style is something which must be discovered within one's self (Sonik 1998). Technique is universal, style is personal. However, many graffiti writers make the mistake of learning the technique first, in order to make their pieces pretty, and think that style can somehow wait until they have the means to express it in a way that is technically pretty. This is a great mistake, as Sonik (1998) says, "The first thing any writer must do is develop his/her own style."

However, style has to be distinguished from art as we follow Simmel's (1908b) ideas on the functions of aesthetic objects for individuality which he outlined in his essay on *The Problem of Style*. In his sociological analyses, Simmel implicitly uses a normative concept of individuality, which he derives from the social norms with which modern man is confronted. Wherever human beings interact with each other, they are guided by a double and contradictory normative requirement to develop a unique and differentiated personality *and* to find the social recognition for this uniqueness. From here, Simmel conceptualizes the relationship between the self and the elements of the cultural environment in terms of "difference in distance." Cultural objects such as graffiti, however, do not have a given distance to the individual, but they can be brought at different distances from him/her by using social strategies of taking distance. Among those strategies style is one of the most important ones by which the distance between the cultural artifact and the self can be manipulated. And it is the very tension between generality, on the one hand, and individuality, on the other, that gives human identity formation its specific sociocultural character (see Nedelmann 1991).

According to Simmel's (1908b) dualistic worlds of aesthetics, the ambivalence between generality and individuality manifests itself in two contrasting principles of aesthetic perception; the principle of style and art. Whereas the principle of generality is expressed in style, the principle of individuality is expressed in art. To perceive a graffito according to the principle of style means that the observer is oriented towards common laws of form and design. He/she is only attracted by those elements of the artistic object which it has in common with other objects belonging to the same category. Thus, we can speak of stylization as a social technique of aesthetic perception with the help of which the individual manages to put a distance between him/herself and the artistic objects under observation.

According to Simmel (1908b), to perceive or to create an object according to the principle of art means to focus our attention on the singularity of the artistic work, on its uniqueness and individuality. A graffito does not appeal to us because it represents a specific style, but because it is something unique. To perceive aesthetic objects of art means creating an intimate relationship between the art consumer and the object of the aesthetic sphere. We can, therefore, speak of aestheticization as a special technique with the help of which individuals can structure an intimate relationship with the objects of the aesthetic sphere and him/herself. However, to say of some things that they are unique, and of others that they are one individual thing out of many, often has only a symbolic meaning (Simmel 1908b). In that we refer to a certain quality which is characteristic of the thing and gives its existence the meaning of singularity or repetitiveness. In fact, through the meaning-making activity of aestheticizing objects the cultural consumer can realize the personal pole of his/her ambivalent action orientation and the principle of individuality, i.e. cultivation. Thus, art supports the development of the unique aspects of the individuality, whereas style supports the development of its sociocultural aspects. For cultivation, both art and style are necessary to develop a unique and differentiated personality and to find social recognition for this uniqueness which, in turn, is so important for the evolving self. To illustrate this tension between the need to be unique and the necessity of being recognized by others I draw on an interview excerpt, with Thomas Evert a Swedish graffiti artist, which was published in 1998 on the Internet.

I: How long have you been into graff?
TE: I did my first piece in the Winter '92. It consisted of the word "wart." It was a bubble style text in silver, and it had warts all over. It had no meaning other than I wanted to be seen. I still got the sketch from it.
I: How has your style changed over the years?
TE: First I started out doing the original graff and later on I got stuck to characters. I could express more with them so I continued. I have gotten more perverted in my sketches, don't know why. It just feels right. It shocks people more than I like. Before I was afraid of what people would think of my sketches but now I don't care any more.
I: Why did you start doing graffiti?
TE: I have always been drawing and stuff. When I was a little kid I collected these stickers with graffiti you got from bubblegum packs, and that I think woke my interest for graffiti. The motivation to do my first piece came from my sister's old boyfriend who was a graffiti artist. I liked the idea to shock people with my art and I wanted to be seen. And the size of the paintings appealed to me. So after I did my first piece I was caught with it and couldn't stop.

(http://www.hifiart.com)

Many great graffiti writers got their start by basing their work on the style of their local heroes, but then, initial lessons learned, they moved on to establish their own. It is indeed a beautiful sight, as Sonik (1998) mentions, to see individual writers make leaps and bounds as they develop their own voice and build on the work of their elders. Thus, the best way to repay culture is to contribute something individual and unique back to it.

The case of Flint-707

Flint-707 is a graffiti writer's pseudonym. Flint-707 started out as a graffiti artist, who during his early teenage years was a pioneer in the art of the real American graffiti from Brooklyn, New York (see http://www.hifiart.com.index.talk.html for the complete story of Flint-707). Flint-707 started to use spray paint to make his name more permanent and everyone could see it written in all the most popular places like 42nd Street and Times Square, Central Park at the fountain or in Coney Island. Eventually all bridges and grand locations fell victim. He challenged the other artists by painting styles that were more intricate and defined using multiple fat caps and variations of colors that eventually separated the writers into categories of writers or stylemasters. The latter will be more significant during the course of these ever-evolving levels of transitions (see Fuhrer 2000).

Next, I will quote the first part of the story of Flint-707 which illustrates the subtle changes in the meaning-making practice of a graffiti artist's cultivation:

> Growing up in the early 1970s in the Bushwick section of Brooklyn, New York, I was a pure daredevil daring to challenge anything that was exciting and different and full of enchanting experience. Experiences that could heal the social scars and wounds found deep within cities' clusters of ethnic neighborhoods. Everywhere that a young man would look for as far as direction or support, there would always be despair and hope embedded into our minds by the older people from the previous generations. They would give to the youth large promises and little achievement or commitment to satisfy all of our dreams. I would look for extracurricular activities to keep me out of trouble and keep my mind on the right track. Things like playing skellies, or spinning tops, or even dancing to salsa and disco music. But there was always the extra urge to do more, do dare mighty things and to achieve great conquests. In my neighborhood the most aggressive basketball, stick ball and football jocks combes the streets for competition. . . . Everyone had hotshot nicknames to depict their attitude and aggressiveness. . . . I was called Hotstuff back then . . . I later found myself searching for a unique identity. One day I was drawing with chalk on the asphalt when I noticed the letter F in script was not only very outstanding but full of beauty and style. Then I started practicing that letter with different names until I came up with this name and number; the name and number I came up with was Flint-707. Soon afterwards the legacy begins and the rest is history.
>
> (http://www.hifiart.com.index.talk.html)

The excerpt of Flint-707 shows that to "liberate" the people, especially our kids, is not just to set them free of the already determined sociocultural meanings but to impose on them the choice to discover the cultural (objective) opportunities in activities, artifacts or behavior settings and the freedom to create or to cultivate action possibilities to cultivate themselves (Fuhrer & Josephs 1998). Along this line of reasoning, the empirical ethnographic evidence of mundane human activity such as graffiti presented in this section challenges once more conceptions of successful identity formation as a process which necessarily ends in an acceptance of and conformity to the prefabricated sociocultural maze. Through a careful tracing of a graffiti artist's autobiography, we see him entering a sociocultural world, acquiring and applying social skills and practical knowledge, to redefine and achieve his personal goals and his identity within and outside the society's norms.

What is relevant here for becoming socialized into the sociocultural world is that Flint-707 will take some goals or activities in the course of socialization to form his own style. In fact, that is where we might begin to acknowledge, as already the early pragmatists like Peirce, James, or Dewey postulated that we are not born with complex identities, but rather that we form our personal identities through ongoing social activities. With this as the conceptual background, a detailed tracing of Flint-707's activities illustrates the steps that take place when he enters a community of graffiti writers, learns and then masters the community's cultural rules and expectations. Usual treatments of socialization or enculturation assume an internalization of the (sub)group's knowledge and values, transforming the identity of the participant in successful cases such that those individuals who have mastered the system will personally value the framework and continue to desire working within it (see Figure 8.1, p. 142).

Yet contrary to that perspective, once a participant understands the rules, he/she can use the skills and cultural resources learned in that community to increase his/her capacities and challenge the community's structure itself. Socialization in this model is not so much bringing the young writer into line with the social and institutional goals of the particular community, but rather providing access to the tools to make informed choices and master the community in one's own terms or meanings for self-cultivation. Thus, Flint-707 is an active subject defining his social world and his place within it, empowered to act on his own informed goals.

From here, I hypothesize that much of what gives Flint-707 a distinct "identity" are the meanings he "cultivates" through transactions between himself and the community.

> Soon writing your name in popular places showed that you really got around and led to people writing their names everywhere, in hallways, in schools on the desks, on the buses. I decided that there had to be something more daring, more challenging and more impressive. What if I could paint on the side of the trains just like many of the other writers but with mad flavors? This feat would set me apart from the others as being a greater artist. So it was I set out to paint the iron horses that were there for the taking. As I conquered the underworld with ever growing and advanced strategies, I would often be found lurking into the purple hazes of New Yorks's depths deep into the wee hours of the morning looking to find myself and my purpose here in life.
>
> (http://www.hifiart. com.index.talk.html)

Indeed, graffiti is one medium by which youth can cultivate the sociocultural world as individuals and as members of their communities, creating the potential for strong commitment and attachment. With regard to the case of Flint-707, I argue that these skills contribute to young people's development of personal and social identities. On the more social side, Flint-707 learns how to cooperate with others, learns what skills are valued by their group, learns how to interact, and so on, by watching and interacting with them. On the more personal side, Flint-707 has cultural opportunities to hone and test his skills and learn about competition and how to handle winning and losing. Graffiti communities allow graffiti writers to manage transitions, changing identities, and changing social relationships.

In applying Boesch's (1991) concept of the "mediation object," graffiti with its artistic play structure might be of relevance here in phases of changing I–world-orientations. The subjectivity of the transactional person can be characterized as an active web of cognitive/affective meanings, intentions and desires, along with graffiti as artifacts that serve expressive-constitutive and pragmatic-communicative functions. Boesch's I–world relation here is, in fact, a double relation. "I" and "world" constitute a differentiation of consciousness into subjective world and objective world. This is the "I–world" that forms the center of inquiry for the investigator building a theory about the relationship of person and perceived culture; I call this the intrapsychic. From the external point of view, "I" and "world" entail two entities: person and culture. This is the "I–world" that is the center of inquiry for the investigator concerned with communication and culture; I call this the interpersonal. In each case, action, which is in fact co-action, constitutes the fundamental change mechanism that explains the development of person–culture transactions.

Moreover, Flint-707 also experiments at the boundaries of the physical environment, where he provides a demonstration of the limits of the material structure, and how one can acceptably gain access to illegitimate painting activities. Here is where Simmel's cultivation principle slightly elaborates the sociocultural approach accounting the quest for individuality along the epigenetic line of reasoning. For Simmel (1990), cultivation means the maximum development of a person's potential from its natural stage, following the "authentic intrinsic direction" of the particular personality while necessitating the "teleological intervention" or mediation to guide his "energies", i.e. the purposive element of cultivation processes. Remember Simmel's famous quote:

> The unity of an object is realized for us by projecting our self into the object in order to shape it according to our image, so that the diversity of determinations grows into the unity of the ego . . . In refining objects, man creates them in his own image.
>
> (Simmel 1990: 454)

Moreover, Simmel (1990) postulates that whenever an individual's energies do not produce something whole as a reflection of the total personality, then the proper relationship between subject and object is missing. That is the internal nature of an individual's achievement is bound up with parts of achievements accomplished by others which are a necessary part of the totality, but it does not refer back to the producer.

As a result, the inadequacy that develops between the child's self and that of his/her product because of greater specialization easily serves to completely divorce the product from the child. The significance of the artifact is then to be found only in the objective achievement that leads away from the subject. Thus, the more completely a graffito is composed of subjective components, and the more the character of each part serves only as a part of the whole, then the more objective is that whole and the more its life is independent of the subjects who created it. That is by cultivating a wall with graffiti, that is by increasing their "value" beyond the performance of their natural constitution, people cultivate themselves.

> One time I went bombing with my crew all night. And we got up on a wall that had been buffed and hadn't been hit in weeks and we killed it. We also got up on a billboard of Interstate 95 one of the biggest highways on the East Coast. Cops chased us and we walked about two miles to get away. And we chewed all the paint off of our fingers in case they caught up with us. A few days later our pieces were on the news on a graffiti story.
>
> (http://www. hifiart.com.index.talk.html)

If, then, the development of the subjective culture or the internal mind does not involve any objective artifact or external mind as a means and stage of its progress back to itself, then even values of the highest order are created, within the internal mind or in the external mind. All these "spheres of the inner and outer world" (*sensu* Simmel) are developed teleologically beyond their "natural" limitations. They thus, of course, become capable of functioning as "cultural values."

That is, individuals are not cultivated simply because they have formed this or that individual item of knowledge or ability within themselves, but only if all those things serve the development of that psychological centrality which is connected to culture but does not coincide with it. In Flint-707's terms the above mentioned Simmel quote reads as follows:

> I pretty much have expressed to you what this is all about, it's about growing up in the greatest city in the world, it's about being an adolescent that wants to see and make a change, it's about having this incredible inner feeling of uncontrolled energy and finally discovering a channel in which to funnel this sensational urge. Growing up in the large metropolises of this world form a different type of person because of these combined superimposed elements of lights, glass, peoples, and buildings all interconnected by this huge subway system and a unique diversity which enables us all to see life from many extreme perspectives. I take this concept and add the realities of an over-shadowed urban ghetto mixed with the most talented kids and the freshest music and there you go you now have the formula for the Flint-707 experience.
>
> (http://www.hifiart.com.index.talk.html)

Here, Simmel's key presupposition is the assumption of the fundamental inter-relatedness (*Wesenszusammengehörigkeit*) of phenomena such as self, identity, or personality. In fact, he points to the culture-inclusiveness of self and self-development. Thus, for Simmel (1911/12), the specific meaning of culture is fulfilled only when the person adds something external to that development, where the path of the soul leads through values and scales that are not themselves subjectively psychological.

The closeness of this general perspective to Pierre Janet's (1929) or Lev Vygotsky's (1929) general genetic law of cultural development is obvious. That is, people act and "think through artifacts" (Cole 1990: 287) and the shape of this acting and thinking is constrained by the way the particular set of artifacts such as graffiti is put together as part of a sociohistorical stream of human activity.

Painting graffiti as cultivation

Perhaps the most important evident goal of the Flint-707 case is the one refering to culturally mediated meaning transactions. With regard to the close subject–object-interpenetration (cf. Boesch 1991), identity-formation corresponds precisely to the individual's effort to distinguish him/herself from his/her environment. The I necessarily defines him/herself in relation to the surrounding. Thus, Flint-707's deviances can also be developmentally supportive. For adolescent graffiti writers painting on walls, bridges, buildings, and subway trains is a private area that gives a great freedom of control over activities and objects than other spaces and this is an activity system where autonomy itself can be cultivated through meaning transactions with the paintings, sometimes co-constructively with other kids. Although Vygotsky's notion of the zone of proximal development or Stern's concept of the proximal environment have the advantage of envisioning active agents, constructed and empowered in and through social interactions, it still includes a trajectory of greater involvement—gradually increasing expertise and the taking on of a larger role within the graffiti community. Following Simmelian cultivation, as the creative end of the spectrum, young people like Flint-707 reinterpret the official meanings of a society's artifacts to produce new meanings intrinsically attached to feeling, to energy, to excitement and psychic movement. At the other end of the spectrum, many stylistic features of their self-expressions presuppose identification with, and loyalty to, local moral worlds and circumscribed status domains.

In the end, the graffiti community thus serves an identity-forming function, not simply by providing "templates" or models as media through which young people co-produce or co-express themselves as persons in a shared sociocultural community, but also by positioning selves in distinct status domains to cultivate their graffiti culture as sociocultural artifacts. Both functions of identity systems are evident when identity is viewed from a cultivational perspective, and both contribute to the full communication and subsequent interpretation of a person's intentions, abilities, and goals. Such an orientation to self and identity, as it is developed out of both Vygotskian semiotic mediation and Simmelian cultivation is necessary if we are to understand identity as functioning not only for individuals, but also for the sociocultural community, especially in their capacity to maintain a transactional relationship between person and culture.

From the perspective of the *cultivating minds* paradigm, we must somehow learn how to use symbolic energy before all the sociocultural resources are burned out. The sociocultural world contains artifacts that can make us grow and change our natures—change our needs. Objects can have meanings that may transform the very sociocultural world in which we live. But by themselves objects alone cannot help us; only in the way we (intentionally) relate to them is their symbolic energy released. That is the primordial concepts of self and personal development gradually emerge from processes of cultivation, i.e. intentional self-development through culture (Fuhrer & Josephs 1998).

Cultivation as a culturally-mediated co-production (transformation, creation) towards the growth of the self is an essential precondition to identity formation and enjoyment, to learning, to growth, to freedom, and hence to the qualities of experience that transform people from totally determined entities into open systems of self-cultivating personalities (see Fuhrer & Josephs 1998). Culture means taking differences seriously. Graffiti artists like Atomeone, Sonik, or Flint-707 became self-conscious about their difference. Culture gives value to life by making each activity a unique, objective experience. Activities which are intended as cultivation are framed as adventuresome as they are symbolically transformed into developmental possibilities. In other words, cultivation is symbolically induced, as in the case of painting names on walls. In the end, the process of cultivation is motivated by belief of possibilities held to be ultimate by individuals. This does not mean that these beliefs are necessarily ultimate but only that they provide a provisional sense of purpose around which to shape one's life course. Any ultimate beliefs, however, are still open to cultivation and so are only provisionally ultimate for any given individual. In the words of the English psychoanalyst Donald Winnicott, "It is creative apperception more than anything else that makes the individual feel that life is worth living" (Winnicott 1971: 65). Or to put it in Flint-707's words:

> This very essence that letters, words, and symbols could be my building blocks to build my self and define my desperate, rebellious need to express myself. Graffiti spoke to me all this time line and said that these writings are more than threatening words of defiance, but a path, a spirit of voice, a true voyage to seeking my own identity.
>
> (http://www.hifiart. com.index.talk.html)

In the present culturally-mediated constructions of Flint-707 graffiti, owing as much to their ease of manipulation as to their symbolism, allow the building of bridges between him and his society (see Figure 8.1).

At first, the letters mediate in a conservative sense Flint-707's identity as he paints on the asphalt of his neighborhood. He started his graffiti career as a tag guy. However, he was very soon able to personalize his letters to a degree; had he remained home, he might not have dared to do this. The letters chosen mirror his perceived identity, and thus guarantee and preserve it across the boundaries of his neighborhood. However, the graffiti letters also mediate in an innovative way. Flint-707 also chooses from the letters and names offered by the graffiti community, selecting from these, to the extent that his means permit, first those which appear immediately useful, but also those which appeal to his interests, his readiness to identify with himself. In other words, he will again, by choosing objects, define

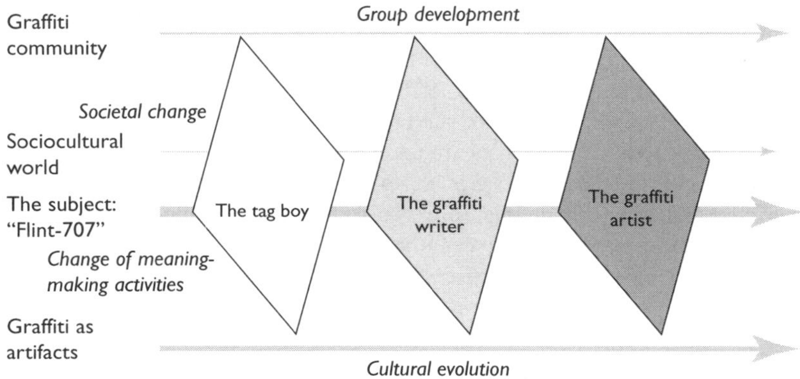

Figure 8.1 The example of Flint-707's identity formation as cultivating meaning-making transactions in tetradic semioses

his identity, but this time with an orientation towards becoming, towards an intended future. Such objects may also be those which are officially not allowed within the society, such as painting on bridges and on subway trains. However, they play an important symbolic role in the graffiti community. In fact, they offer new amenities, and symbolize the kind of personal agency desired. More precisely, the chosen objects as well as the activities which deviate from the sociocultural maze appear to mediate between an "is-reality" and a "should-reality" of Flint-707's self. In transactional terms, the community of graffiti writers' identities are enhanced as the individual graffiti writer participates in events and contributes to the graffiti culture; and individual identities are enhanced when Flint-707 makes decisions and receives recognition for particular contributions, even when he goes beyond the norm.

> If you ever do the very best in whatever you strive for in this life then eventually you will be recognized by someone who will help lead you into another level that you never thought possible. In my case this other level came in the form of gallery shows, television shows, books, video, and other media exposures. And in some cases I have found people who were just so bewildered by life's unfair crossroads to the point of vast dismay and disarray until they perished or eventually led themselves into a derelict lifestyle, so yes if it weren't for graffiti, many more crimes, would have resulted from the further neglect of artistic yet poor kids.
>
> (http://www.hifiart.com.index.talk.html)

The excerpt illustrates that Flint-707 made the switch from the underground world to the corporate one. He worked in various advertising companies, and then owned a store which did speciality painting on motorcycles. The transition has been successful. Instead of spending their nights running from transit cops, Flint-707's crew now loses sleep trying to meet the expectations and deadlines of paying customers.

However, the transition to legal art from the adolescent underground thrill of running from police dies hard for some subway writers. *The New Yorker* recently recorded the escapades of one 28-year-old Bronx man named Cope who, in an almost nostalgic effort, continues to spray paint the trains in the subway tunnels. Cope is an old friend of Flint-707, who read the article with a smile before his graff class started. "This is funny," Flint-707 said quietly. He looked up from the article: "You look back sometimes and you miss things in your childhood" (http://www.hifiart. com.index.talk.html).

The teenage kids Flint-707 and his partners teach these days, however, admire Flint-707's professionalism. At one class, an interviewer from a German news crew asked 17-year-old Julio "Shea" Oliveras what he wanted to do when he grew up. "To be like them," Oliveras said without looking up from an intricate pen drawing of his name, motioning towards Flint-707. "I just want to be like Shea," Flint said, "young again."

Overall, and following Figure 8.1, the Flint-707 story illustrates how culture shapes individual development and how individuals shape their cultures. Others, within the sociocultural field, also use this argument, and, in my view, they fall short of really showing how individuals shape their cultures. The graffiti example, however, really shows how graffiti artists cultivate their sociocultural environment. It is there, where the cultivation model is different from other claims regarding this issue and where cultivation expands sociocultural approaches.

Cultivation goes beyond the socialization model

The ethnographic evidence presented in this chapter challenges conceptions of successful self formation as a process which necessarily ends in an acceptance of, and conformity to, the prefabricated cultural norms. Through a careful tracing of a graffiti artist's autobiography, we see him entering a world, acquiring and applying cultural skills and practical knowledge, to redefine and achieve his own self within and outside the norms, and ultimately increases his independence to evolve out of the structure altogether. Socialization in this model, as it is described in Figure 8.1, is not so much bringing the writer into line with the norms of the community, but rather providing access to the tools to make informed choices and master the community in one's own meanings for self-cultivation. Flint-707 is an active subject defining his culture within it, empowered to act on his own informed goals. From here, I would hypothesize that much of what gives Flint-707 a distinct self are the meanings he cultivates to negotiate between himself and his community as medium through which he defines his self or identity. On one side, he learns how to cooperate with others, learns what skills are valued by their group, learns how to interact by watching and interacting with them. On the other side, he has cultural opportunities to hone and test his skills and learn how to handle winning and losing.

That is Flint-707 experiments at the boundaries of the given cultural opportunities, where he provides a demonstration of the limits of the material structure, and how one can acceptably gain access to illegitimate painting activities. However, the more completely a graffito is composed of subjective components, and the more the character of each part serves only as a part of the whole, then the more objective is that whole and the more is its life independent of the subjects who created it. That is, by cultivating a wall with graffiti, that is—following Simmelian cultivation—by increasing their value beyond the performance of their natural constitution, people cultivate themselves.

With regard to identity formation, perhaps the most important evident goal of the Flint-707 case is the one refering to mediated meaning transactions. With regard to the close subject–object-interpenetration, self-formation corresponds to the individual's effort to distinguish him/herself from his/her cultural norms (see for a similar view Goffman 1963). The "I" necessarily defines him/herself in relation to the surrounding. Thus, Flint-707's difference can also be developmentally supportive. Following Simmelian cultivation, young people like Flint-707 reinterpret the official meanings of a society's artifacts (as cultural opportunities) to produce new meaning (i.e. new action possibilities) intrinsically attached to feeling, to energy, to excitement and psychic movement towards the growth of their self.

In the end, the graffiti community thus serves a self-forming function, not simply by providing cultural opportunities as media through which young people co-construct themselves as persons in a shared sociocultural community, but also by positioning selves in distinct status domains to cultivate their own graffiti as artifacts. Both functions of self systems are evident when the self is viewed from the perspective of cultivation, and both contribute to the full communication and subsequent interpretation of a person's intentions, abilities, and goals. Such an orientation to the self, as it is developed out of the concept of cultivation, is necessary if we are to understand the self as functioning not only for individuals, but also for the cultural community, especially in their capacity to maintain a transactional relationship between person and culture.

In contrast to socialization, cultivation is not limited to adapting and training individuals to behave and successfully perform within the cultural norms, with people internalizing and identifying with the given cultural norms. That socialization model can only describe a culture of conforming members. Deviance in that view must then be assumed to arise from ineffective socialization or unusual individual psychological incapacity. In this socialization model, non-conformity is only negative. Nonetheless, this out-dated perspective still continues to operate in the background in our theories and assumptions about socialization, education, learning, and, of course, human development.

Yet deviant roles like Flint-707's activities can also be positive. A similar case is found in the "alternative scripts" used by adolescents who inhabit adult spaces or behavior settings but for reasons different from those of adult users. Interestingly enough, a telling example was already observed and described almost 70 years ago (see Wohlwill 1985). In their landmark study, Martha Muchow—a student of William Stern at Hamburg University—showed how kids and adolescents utilized props like escalators in a shopping mall not for actual purpose but rather as a way to make sure of their agency as well as to show off to their imagined or real audience. To attract girls' attention, for example, boys walked the escalator against the intended direction—a little step that makes a big difference.

Along this line of reasoning, the cultivation model challenges the model of socialization as a model of cultural transmission and cultural adaptation. Once we accept the subjects as cultivators of both their culture and themselves "through culture," we need more consciously to rethink our assumptions about socialization, learning, and human development as necessarily resulting in conformity to and persistence within existing norms. Cultivation clearly involves more than simply learning the given norms and internalizing a valuation of the given cultural structure to conform to collective expectations. Both Piaget's (1970) assimilation-accommodation model and Vygotsky's (1981) zone of proximal development have the advantage of envisioning active agents, constructed and empowered in and through social interactions. However, they still include a trajectory of greater involvement—gradually increasing expertise within the given environment.

In contrast, the cultivation model challenges this rather conservative scenario of development and learning involving a willing child who wants to take on the adult's role as ignoring the reality of both resistance and identification. In fact, I would argue that children and adolescents' desire to move beyond the cultural norms is in itself an act of resistance, a resistance to being dependent and controlled by another. Hence a practical and useful conception of learning, socialization, and education must take into account infinite cultures, where kids develop, modify, and cultivate their own cultures. Thus, cultivation tries to incorporate this awareness, including as a primary goal the development and empowerment of individuals within and beyond the specific cultural norms, and accepting as a successful outcome the potential movement of the independent individual beyond the immediate cultural structures or opportunities.

Along this line of arguing, I see several reasons to encourage people to cultivate themselves: (1) kids are more likely to feel a sense of personal investment if they cultivate their cultural opportunities themselves; (2) when kids cultivate their own cultural opportunities, they will quite likely find that preformed opportunities are not always well-suited to themselves; (3) self-cultivated cultural opportunities will provide a context of action possibilities for reflection, for example, a child's self-created opoortunities (out of his/her action possibilities) serve as external shadows of the child's internal mental models, providing an opportunity for children to reflect upon (and then revise and extend) their internal models of the world—and of themselves; and, finally, (4) kids with a chance to cultivate themselves through their own cultural opportunities will more likely feel what Csikszentmihalyi (1996) called the flow. The flow contributes to the cultivation by stimulating growth through the intrinsically rewarding nature of the transaction with cultural action opportunities such as artifacts. With regard to learning and education, a flow usually happens not by acting out "standard scripts" but rather "alternative scripts," when kids are actively involved in a difficult enterprise, in a task that stretches their physical and mental abilities, in cultivating their differences beyond the norm. These implications, for example, fit quite well into some of the guiding principles for creating new technologies for a lifelong Kindergarten (see Resnick 1998). Thus, cultivation of a sense of self that emphasizes special, individual uniqueness may be an adaptation to the cultural and historical changes (Baumeister 1986). Along these lines of reasoning, it is obvious that the cultivation paradigm is practical not in spite of but preciseley because of its refusal to deny the role of context and meaning in human self-development.

Taken together, cultivation as tetradic, multiple mediation towards the growth of the self is an essential precondition to enjoyment, to learning, to development, and hence to the qualities of experience that transform people from determined entities into open systems of self-cultivating personalities (Fuhrer & Josephs 1998). Cultivation means taking differences seriously. The habit of learning and education, for example, in schools must be cultivated. This is the real goal of a liberated education. That is to liberate the people, especially our kids, is not just to set them free of the already determined cultural opportunities and meanings but to impose on them the choice of discovering the given cultural action (or learning) opportunities in activities, artifacts or behavior settings and the freedom to cultivate these opportunities to (co-)construct new action possibilities to create "difference," to reflect about themselves and, in the end, to cultivate themselves.

Overall, the idea of a "cultured mind" has some far-reaching implications not only for how psychologists need to think about culture but also for how psychologists need to think about identity and, of course, about development. This is not simply the problem of thinking about culture and mind but specifically the challenge of conceptualizing "culture in mind" and—mostly overlooked by psychologists—"mind in culture." This is a developmental conception of the mind—both the internal and the external mind with far-reaching consequences for understanding the growth of the self.

Coda

Cultivating Minds presents a theoretical framework for the study of identity that is deeply rooted in the perspective of cultural psychology. The theoretical framework proposed is based on a scholarly analysis and integration of core philosophical, sociological, and psychological ideas from the intellectual traditions of pragmatism, socioculturalism, constructivism, and transactionalism. The primary contribution of the integrative theoretical framework lies in its focus on cultivation as a metaphor for the process of identity formation. Here *Cultivating Minds* extends existing perspectives, which are mainly concerned with explicating the relation between individual development and culture and delineate guided structure formation. In contrast, the cultivation model emphasizes the transactional nature of the relation and focuses on the individual's self-referenced creative activity in actively creating and cultivating identity through culture. The concept of cultivation and the tetradic mediational model (which describes the process of identity formation) draw attention to the notion that I–world transactions are mediated by artifacts and objects as well as by social partners. The elaboration of how these transactions are mediated by artifacts and objects and how an individual's cultivation of the sociocultural environment is similarly mediated through artifacts and objects is where the cultivation model expands existing sociocultural perspectives on identity formation (and human development in general).

Along this line of reasoning, the Flint-707 story, for example, shows that people somehow must learn to use symbolic energy for their cultivation before all the physical resources are burned up. The world contains artifacts that can make us grow and change our identities. Artifacts can have meanings that may transform the very world in which we live. But artifacts alone by themselves cannot help us; only in the way we transact with them is their symbolic energy released.

The meaning that releases the symbolic power of artifacts is created, first of all, by the act of perception. The primary skill one needs to unlock the magic of artifacts in the process of cultivation is seeing them objectively and subjectively at the same time, thus joining the nature of the perceiving subject with the nature of the object. This act of bringing together two entities in a transactional process that unites while preserving the distinctive characteristics of the elements is the basic symbolic act—sym-ballein, to "throw together."

The second skill to cultivate artifacts to cultivate oneself grows out of the first: the ability to enjoy one's actions. Here is where the Flint-707 story is so significant. The flow of experience, which focuses a person's attention on the task at hand, is symbolic because it brings together the psychic processes of the person and unites them with a set of objective stimuli in the environment. This is exactly the opposite from alienation, in which one feels separated from oneself and from the elements of one's environment. Motivation gives intrinsic value to whatever one is doing, even when the task is not meaningful in terms of material values.

The ability to perceive and to motivate make it possible to develop the third skill that is necessary to control the need for material rewards with regard to the growth of the self: cultivating the ultimate goals of one's existence. People who discover the cultural opportunities of artifacts through perception and/or create new possibilities through action cease to see the world strictly in terms of their own self and thus see many new things in it. If these actions or rather cultivations are enjoyed, they will gain meaning and be valued independently of the terminal material goals.

In fact, the contribution of artifacts to the development of human personality is, according to Simmel (1908a) exactly of this matter:

> However excellently they may serve our specific ends, their value for our lives as a whole, for the well-spring of our being in its struggle for development, may be very slight. Conversely, they may be imperfect and insignificant in the objective, technical perspective of their specific province, but may, for all that, offer precisely what our life needs for the harmony of its parts, for its mysterious unity.
>
> (Simmel 1908a: 43)

Here we see the essence of Simmel's (1911/12) definition of culture as cultivation. That is, individuals are not cultivated simply because they have formed this or that "individual item of knowledge or ability" (Simmel 1911/12: 56) within themselves, but only if all those things serve the development of that "psychological centrality which is connected to culture but does not coincide with it" (Simmel 1911/12: 56).

Moreover, an individual's efforts are aimed at particular biological potentialities, and this is, according to Simmel (1911/12), why the development of every person, viewed according to what can be named in them, is ". . . a bundle of lines of growth that extend in quite different directions and with quite different lenghts. However, it is not all these . . . which make a person cultivated, but only their significance for or their development of the individual's indefinable personal unity" (Simmel 1911/12: 56). Looking more closely at the feedback process from the point of view of culture, one could say that what Simmel calls objective culture functions as the intermediary station between the not-yet-cultivated subject and the cultivated subject. Cultivation is the process of developing a state of being in a creature, a state which would not come about naturally, but for which he/she has a natural propensity, by shaping, reconstructing, or creating objects external to it. As a consequence, Simmel gives a definition of culture in which these dynamic and goal-oriented mechanisms are included: "Culture is the way that leads from closed unity through the unfolding multiplicity to the unfolded unity" (Simmel 1968: 28).

Psychologists who study human development tend to agree that different sets of goals are typical at different points in the life cycle. In other words, the priorities around which people order their psychic energies to cultivate their selves change with time. Children generally start with using their immediate physical world as a medium to cultivate themselves. Later a new set of values will slowly emerge, and even take precedence, based on the need to be accepted and respected by others. At this stage a person will begin to follow the rules of his/her social partners and his/her community even when they are not to his/her immediate advantage. But if these are the only orientations one recognizes, the danger is that self-development will be reduced to thoughtless conformity, a purely social self. With time, such social orientations will in turn generate for some individuals new, antithetical orientations: the goal to be independent and autonomous. People who reach this stage are fully individualized, unique, and interesting. At the final level the person who has differentiated him/herself returns to invest attention in broader goals, and derives satisfaction from helping a cause greater than the self—not because of coercion or conformity, but because of reasoned conviction. This process of spiraling growth of forming one's identity or self has been described, more or less independently, by many scholars such as Erikson, Maslov, Kohlberg, Loevinger, Kegan, Whitbourne, or Noam who have studied how people change through the life cycle (cf. Kroger 2000).

However, part of the difficulty in moving beyond the developmental adaptionist framework is to determine what to do after we abandon the idea of identity as a thing-like phenomenon as the main explanation in favor of a process-oriented, transactional view of identity formation. The task in a culture-inclusive developmental psychology of the self is to change the logical geography of the debate by studying meaning transactions, transactional relations of holistic units among the parts to be explained. The first step is to analyze processes of cultivation as satisficing rather than optimizing or perfecting in the Simmelian sense. Second, cultivation implies a completely new kind of explanatory concept for a new understanding of adaptation as a developmental mechanism. Here the opposition between inner and outer factors will be replaced by a coactional or coimplicative relation, since the person and the cultural medium mutually coevolve with each other. The sociocultural environment or Simmel's objective culture is not a structure imposed on living beings from the outside but is in fact a creation of those beings through processes of cultivation.

With this transactional view, we approach again the coactional (or co-evolving) developmental model as it is depicted in Figure 5.1 as a bio-psycho-cultural framework to understand cultivation in its full sense. Just as there is no person without culture, so there is no culture without a person. In the end, the cultivation model's goal is no less than to show how a cultural developmental psychology can provide the bridge between biological, psychological, and cultural evolution (see Csikszentmihalyi 1996 for a similar view).

The key point, then, is that human beings bring forth and create their own culture by satisficing; this culture does not exist "out there" in an environment that acts as a landing pad for organisms that somehow drop or parachute into the sociocultural world. Instead, human beings and their sociocultural environment stand in transaction to each other through transaction or coaction. Thus what we describe as sociocultural structures are not external features that have been internalized, as cognitive representationism or biological adaptationism both assume. Sociocultural structures are the result of a conjoint history, a congruence that unfolds from a long history of coaction. Indeed, the person is both the subject and the object of evolution. And nature and nurture stand in a coaction to each other as product and process.

Thus, if we are to make progress in cultural developmental psychology, we must focus on the question of what motivates people to externalize their internal minds into external structures, and we must seek to understand the transactional constitution of the self between internal and external structures, i.e. cultivation. Here, it is important to mention, as a general heuristic, that both intra-individual and extra-individual structures of a given individual make each other up (Fuhrer 1993a) which is due to the high degree of their phylogenetic, ontogenetic, and culture-genetic co-development (cf. Shweder 1991, Valsiner 2000).

Following the cultivation principle, of central importance for cultural developmental psychology is to understand, for example, why children shape or create for themselves—and for others as well—the possibilities that they do and why other children or adults sometimes transform these possibilities in such a way that they become a part of their own developmental efforts. Thus, for cultural developmental psychology we have to focus more thoroughly on those cultural mediational means that not only set the limits but rather open up possibilities for individual development beyond the norm. The favorite personal objects and territories, for example, to which children, adolescents, and adults are attached are exactly those kinds of externalizations that structure future developmental processes. In fact, all physical environments for children or adolescents should serve certain common functions with respect to their development (cf. Fuhrer & Josephs 1998): to foster personal identities; to encourage the development of competence; to provide possibilities for growth; to allow social interaction; and so on. Analyzing processes of how individuals of various age groups shape, reconstruct, or create their artifacts would lead to more insights into the phenomenon we call the cultivated mind.

Although it is considered a form of happiness, cultivation extends beyond hedonic (pure) enjoyment in that it involves a sense of purpose, direction, and fulfillment. Cultivation involves not only happiness and enjoyment but also an intense sense of personal meaning and direction within one's life. Unlike Maslow's (1968) concept of self-actualization, cultivation is not a personal trait. It is a process of meaning-making activities associated with being an "I" in a particular cultural community. That is, a person may be thought of as personally cultivating him/herself if he/she has identified one or more meaning-making activities that promote feelings of progress and happiness when he/she engages in them. It can, therefore, be argued that cultivation is a characteristic shared by the combination of the person and the meaning-making activity or practice.

As such, cultivation may be a step on the path to self-actualization. Identifying one's best potentials, as well as engaging regularly in meaning-making practices that draw on those potentials, is a necessary ingredient in becoming self-actualized. For example, Michael Jordan (1998) documented in his autobiography that, as a teenager, he often shot free throws from sunrise until sunset, barely noticing the day as it went by. This example illustrates the intense involvement and the resulting tendency to lose track of time that accompany cultivating practices.

Finally, the life-long person-culture transactions that allow us to be active agents in both our own development and the development of our cultural environment appear to have been involved also in human cultivation. In accord with Lerner's (1989) assumption that individuals produce their own development, following the cultivation principle, individuals also produce (or cultivate) their own artifacts. Simmel's theory stresses that individuals shape, reconstruct or create their own artifacts toward shaping, reconstructing or creating their own mind. That is individuals and their artifacts reciprocally constitute each other or co-develop with each other (Fuhrer 1993a). Consequently, people develop co-developmental competency across their life span.

However, one puzzle we still face today is how to conceptualize the individual. It would appear that there is little room for a serious exploration of the nature of individuation once we accept the importance of culture. Yet Simmel (1990) suggests another possibility. He opens up for us the question of how to conceptualize both individuation and culture by his persistence in alerting us to the problem of developing identity within modern culture. And he shows us by his own example that we need not abandon our interest in culture in pursuing the nature of individuation.

However, Simmel leaves us with a problem more than a solution, yet an awareness of this problem may be exactly what we need. In the present book, I focus at the interface where person and culture interpenetrate each other. Meaning transactions are purposely cultivated in which the person experiences his/her identity, i.e. continuity, consistency, subjectivity, and agency. Identity is, therefore, neither within nor outside the person, but rather is a meaning transaction, i.e. person and culture co-create meaning transactionally. Cultivating personally relevant meaning transactions take place through signs and symbols, i.e. tetradic semiosis. It is in these meanings that people like graffiti artists ultimately co-create their identities. Reflection and transformation of symbolic meanings are made possible through production and self-expression as modes of meaning transactions. It is exactly this tension between the need to be unique and the necessity of being recognized by others which is highly significant for cultivation; between symbol and reflection are the central processes where identity is "trans-acted" (Boesch 1991).

Following this line of theorizing, identity formation through culture does not, as viewed in some psychoanalytic accounts, end in a stable ego-formation. Rather, identity as the cultivation of meaning transaction is life-long transaction. That is identity is never something complete or finished that one can possess the way one owns an object. Identity redefines, reproduces, or recreates itself constantly anew in meaning transactions within I–world relationships. Michel Foucault (1967) expressed this insight in radical form in his own unique way:

> Man has never ceased to construct himself, that is to constantly shift his subjectivity; this series of new shifts in subjectivity will never end and never confront us with that which is man.

Bibliography

Allport, G. (1949) *Becoming*, New Haven, CT: Yale University Press.

Altman, I. and Rogoff, B. (1987) "World views in psychology: trait, interactional, organismic, and transactional perspectives," in D. Stokols and I. Altman (eds) *Handbook of environmental psychology*, New York: Wiley.

Ash, M. G. (1995) *Gestalt psychology in German culture 1890–1967: holism and the quest for objectivity*, New York: Cambridge University Press.

Bandura, A. (1997) *Self-efficacy: The exercise of control*, New York: Freeman.

Barker, R. G. (1968) *Ecological psychology*, Stanford, CA: Stanford University Press.

Barker, R. G. and Wright, H. F. (1955) *Midwest and its children*, New York: Harper & Row.

Barker, R. G. and Schoggen, P. (1973) *Qualities of community life*, San Francisco, CA: Jossey-Bass.

Baumeister, R. F. (1986) *Identity. Cultural change and the struggle for self*, New York: Oxford University Press.

Belk, R. W. (1992) "Attachment to possessions," in I. Altman and S. M. Low (eds) *Place attachment*, New York: Plenum.

Belke, I. (1971) *Moritz Lazarus and Heyman Steinthal*, Tübingen: Mohr.

Bergson, H. (1911) *Creative evolution*, New York: Henry Holt.

Berlyne, D. E. (1960) *Conflict, arousal, and curiosity*, New York: McGraw-Hill.

Bernstein, R. (1966) *John Dewey*, New York: Washington Square Press.

Boesch, E. E. (1991*) Symbolic action theory and cultural psychology*, New York: Springer.

Boring, E. G. (1950) *A history of experimental psychology*, New York: Appleton-Century-Crofts.

Bosma, H. A. (1995) "Identity and identity processes: what are we talking about?" in A. Osterwegel and R. A. Wicklund (eds) *The self in European and North American culture: development and processes*, Amsterdam: Kluwer.

Briggs, C. L. (1992) "Mazes of meaning: how a child and a culture create each other," in W. A. Corsaro and P. J. Miller (eds) *Interpretive approaches to childhood socialization*, San Francisco, CA: Jossey-Bass.

Bronfenbrenner, U. (1979) *The ecology of human development*, Cambridge, MA: Harvard University Press.

Bronfenbrenner, U. and Ceci, S. J. (1993) "Heredity, environment, and the question 'how?'—a first approximation," in R. Plomin and G. E. McClearn (eds) *Nature, nurture, and psychology*, Washington, DC: APA.

Bruner, J. S. (1990) *Acts of meaning*, Cambridge, MA: Harvard University Press.

Cairns, R. B., Elder, G. H. and Costello, E. J. (eds) (1996) *Developmental science*, New York: Cambridge University Press.
Cassirer, E. (1944) *An essay on man*, New Haven, CT: Yale University Press.
Chawla, L. (1992) "Childhood place attachment," in I. Altman and S. M. Low (eds) *Place attachment*, New York: Plenum, pp. 63–86.
Cicero, M. T. (1960) *Tusculanum disputations*, trans. J. E. King, London, Methuen.
Cole, M. (1990) "Cultural psychology: a once and future discipline?" in J. J. Berman (ed.) *Cross-cultural perspectives. Nebraska Symposium on motivation 1989*, Lincoln: University of Nebraska Press.
—— (1996) *Cultural psychology*, Cambridge, MA: Harvard University Press.
Cooley, C. H. (1902) *Human nature and the social order*, New York: Scribner.
Cooper Marcus, C. (1992) "Environmental memories," in I. Altman and S. M. Low (eds) *Place attachment*, New York: Plenum.
Coser, L. (1965) *The stranger in the academy*, Englewood Cliffs, NJ: Prentice-Hall.
Cotterell, J. L. (1998) "Behavior settings in macroenvironments: implications for the design and analysis of places," in D. Görlitz, H. J. Harloff, G. Mey and J. Valsiner (eds) *Children, cities, and psychological theories: developing relationship*, Berlin: de Gruyter.
Csikszentmihalyi, M. (1996) *The evolving self*, New York: Harper.
Csikszentmihalyi, M. and Rochberg-Halton, E. (1981) *The meaning of things*, Chicago, IL: University of Chicago Press.
Dahme, H.-J. (1990) "On the current rediscovery of Georg Simmel's sociology—a European point of view," in M. Kearn, B. S. Phillips and R. S. Cohen (eds) *Georg Simmel and contemporary sociology*, Boston: Kluwer.
Damon, W. and Hart, D. (1988) *Self-understanding in childhood and adolescence*, New York: Cambridge University Press.
Daniels, D. (1996) *An introduction to Vygotsky*, London and New York: Routledge.
Danziger, K. (1983) "Origins and basic principles of Wundt's Völkerpsychologie," *British Journal of Social Psychology*, 22: 303–13.
Dewey, J. (1896) "The reflex arc concept in psychology," *Psychological Review*, 3: 357–70.
—— (1934) *Art as experience*, New York: Capricorn Books.
—— (1938) *Experience and education*, New York: Macmillan.
Dewey, J. and Bentley, A. F. (1949) *Knowing and the known*, Westport, CT: Greenwood.
Dilthey, W. (1897) *Einleitung in die Geisteswissenschaften*, Vol.1, Berlin, Leipzig: Barth.
Dittmar, H. (1992) *The social psychology of material possessions*, New York: St. Martin's Press.
Eckensberger, L. H. (1995) "Activity or action: two different roads towards an integration of culture into psychology?" *Culture & Psychology*, 1: 67–80.
Engeström, Y. (1996) "Interobjectivity, ideality, and dialectics," *Mind, Culture, and Activity*, 3: 259–65.
Erikson, E. H. (1968) *Identity, youth, and crisis*, New York: Norton.
Ford, D. H. and Lerner, R. M. (1992) *Developmental systems theory*, London: Sage.
Foucault, M. (1967) *Madness and civilization*, London: Tavistock.
Frisby, D. (1985) "Georg Simmel: first sociologist of modernity," *Theory, Culture, and Society*, 2(3): 49–67.
—— (1992) *Simmel and since*, London: Routledge.
—— (1994) *Georg Simmel. Critical assessments*, vols 1–3, London: Routledge.

Frisby, D. and Featherstone, M. (1997) *Simmel on culture*, London: Sage.

Fromm, E. (1976) *To have or to be?* New York: Harper & Row.

Fuhrer, U. (1990) "Bridging the ecological-psychological gap: behavior settings as interfaces," *Environment and Behavior*, 22: 518–37.

—— (1993a) "Living in our footprints—and in those of others: cultivation as transaction," *Swiss Journal of Psychology*, 52: 130–7.

—— (1993b) "Behavior setting analysis of situated learning: the case of newcomers," in J. Lave and S. Chaiklin (eds) *Situated learning*, New York: Cambridge University Press.

—— (1995) "Stadt als Entwicklungsrahmen," *Magdeburger Wissenschaftsjournal*, 1: 35–41.

—— (1998) "Behavior settings as vehicles of children's cultivation," in D. Görlitz, H. J. Harloff, G. Mey and J. Valsiner (eds) *Children, cities, and psychological theories: developing relationship*, Berlin: de Gruyter.

—— (2000) "Individuierung durch Kulturbildung—das Beispiel Graffiti," in N. Knolle (ed.) *Kultureller Wandel und Musikpädagogik*, Essen: Blaue Eule.

Fuhrer, U. and Laser, S. (1997) "Wie Jugendliche sich über ihre soziale und materielle Umwelt definieren: eine Analyse von Selbst-Fotografien," *Zeitschrift für Pädagogische Psychologie und Entwicklungspsychologie*, 74: 183–96.

Fuhrer, U. and Josephs, I. E. (1998) "The cultivated mind: from mental mediation to cultivation," *Developmental Review*, 18(2): 279–312.

Fuhrer, U. and Josephs, I. E. (eds) (1999) *Persönliche Objekte, Identität und Entwicklung*, Göttingen: Vandenhoeck & Rupprecht.

Fuhrer, U. and Quaiser-Pohl, C. (1999) "Wie sich Kinder und Jugendliche ihre Lebensräume aneignen: Aktionsräume in einer ländlichen Kleinstadt," *Psychologie in Erziehung und Unterricht*, 46: 96–109.

Furby, L. and Wilke, M. (1982) "Some characteristics of infants' preferred toys," *Journal of Genetic Psychology*, 140: 207–19.

Gallagher, S. (2000) "Philosophical conceptions of the self," *Trends in Cognitive Sciences*, 4: 14–21.

Gal'perin, P. (1967) "On the notion of internalisation," *Soviet Psychology*, 5(3): 28–33.

Galliker, M. (1993) "Die Verkörperung des Gedankens im Gegenstande: zur kontroversen Begründung der Völkerpsychologie," *Psychologische Rundschau*, 44: 11–24.

Gardner, H. (1985) *The mind's new science*, New York: Basic Books.

Gaster, S. (1991) "Urban children's access to their neighboorhood. Changes over three generations," *Environment and Behavior*, 23: 70–85.

Gergen, K. (1991) *The saturated self*, New York: Basic Books.

Goffman, E. (1963) *The presentation of self in everyday life*, New York: Doubleday-Anchor.

Görlitz, D. and Wohlwill, J. F. (eds) (1987) *Curiosity, imagination, and play*, Hillsdale, NJ: Erlbaum.

Görlitz, D., Harloff, H. J., Mey, G. and Valsiner, J. (eds) (1998) *Children, cities, and psychological theories: developing relationship*, Berlin: de Gruyter.

Gottlieb, G. (1996) "Developmental psychobiological theory," in R. B. Cairns, G. H. Elder and E. J. Costello (eds) *Developmental science*, New York: Cambridge University Press.

Gulerce, A. (1991) "Transitional objects; a reconsideration of the phenomenon," *Journal of Social Behavior and Personality*, 6: 187–208.

Gump, P. V. and Adelberg, B. (1978) "Urbanism from the perspective of ecological psychologists," *Environment and Behavior*, 10: 171–91.

Habermas, T. (1996) *Geliebte Objekte. Symbole und Instrumente der Identitätsbildung*, Berlin: de Gruyter.

Hall, G. (1898) "Some aspects of the early sense of self," *American Journal of Psychology*, 9: 151–95.

Hart, R. (1979) *Children's experience of place*, New York: Irvington.

—— (1987) "Children's participation in planning and design: theory, research, and practice," in C. S. Weinstein and T. G. David (eds) *Spaces for children*, London: Plenum Press.

Havighurst, R. J. (1948) *Developmental tasks and education*, New York: McKay.

Hayward, D. G., Rothenberg, M. and Beasley, R. R. (1974) "Children's play and urban playground environments," *Environment and Behavior*, 6: 131–68.

Herder, J. G. (1778) "Vom Erkennen und Empfinden der menschlichen Seele," in B. Suphan (ed.) *Herder's sämtliche Werke*, vol. 8, reprinted Hildesheim: Olms, 1967.

Hickman, L. A. (ed.) (1998) *Reading Dewey. Interpretation for a postmodern generation*, Bloomington, IN, Indiana University Press.

Hilgard, E. (1980) "The trilogy of mind: cognition, affection, and conation," *Journal of the History of the Behavioral Sciences*, 16: 107–17.

Hoeber, F. (1918) "Georg Simmel: Der kulturphilosophi unsererzeit," *Neue fahrbücher für das Klassische Altertum*, 21: 475–77.

Hormuth, S. E. (1990) *The ecology of the self*, New York: Cambridge University Press.

Jahoda, G. (1982) *Psychology and anthropology*, New York: Academic Press.

James, W. (1890) *The principles of psychology*, vol. 1, New York: Holt.

Janet, P. (1929) *L'évolution psychologique de la personnalité*, Paris: Chahine.

Jaworski, G. D. (1989) "The fate of Georg Simmel in functionalist sociology, 1937–1961," unpublished doctoral dissertation, New School for Social Research, Columbia University.

—— (1997) *Georg Simmel and the American prospect*, Albany, NY: State University of New York Press.

Jordan, M. (1998) *For the love of the game: my story*, New York: Crown.

Josephs, I. E. (1998) "Constructing one's self in the city of the silent: dialogue, symbols, and the role of 'as-if' in self-development,' *Human Development*, 41: 180–95.

Kaminski, G. (ed.) (1986) Orduung und variabilität im alltagsgeschehen, Göttingen: Hogrete.

Kearn, M. (1985) "Georg Simmel's sociology of Als-ob," unpublished doctoral dissertation, University of Pittsburgh.

Kearn, M., Phillips, B. S. and Cohen, R. S. (eds) (1990) *Georg Simmel and contemporary psychology*, Boston: Kluwer.

Kegan, R. (1982) *The evolving self*, Cambridge, MA: Harvard University Press.

Koch, W. A. (ed.) (1989) *The nature of culture*, Bochum: Brockmeyer.

Koehnke, K. C. (1990) "Four concepts of social science at Berlin University: Dilthey, Lazarus, Smoller, and Simmel," in M. Kearn, B. S. Phillips and R. S. Cohen (eds) *Georg Simmel and contemporary sociology*, Boston: Kluwer.

—— (1996) *Der junge Simmel in Theoriebeziehungen und sozialen Bewegungen* [*The young Simmel in theories and social movements*], Frankfurt a.M: Suhrkamp.

Kohut, H. (1977) *The restoration of the self*, New York: International Universities Press.

Kreppner, K. (1992) "William L. Stern, (1871–1938): a neglected founder of developmental psychology," *Developmental Psychology*, 28: 539–47.

Krewer, B. and Jahoda, G. (1990) "On the scope of Lazarus and Steinthal's Völkerpsychologie as reflected in the *Zeitschrift für Völkerpsychologie* and *Sprachwissenschaft* (1860–1890)," *The Quarterly Newsletter of the Laboratory of Comparative Human Cognition*, 12: 4–12.

Kroger, J. (2000) *Identity development*, Thousand Oaks, CA: Sage.

Lang, A. (1988) "Die kopernikanische Wende steht in der Psychologie noch aus! Hinweise auf eine ökologische Entwicklungspsychologie," *Schweizerische Zeitschrift für Psychologie*, 47: 93–108.

Lapsley, D. K. and Powers, D. C. (eds) (1988) *Self, ego, and identity*, New York: Springer.

Lave, J. and Wenger, E. (1991) *Situated learning: legitimate peripheral participation*, New York: Cambridge University Press.

Lawrence, J. and Valsiner, J. (1993) "Conceptual roots of internalization. From transmission to transformation," *Human Development*, 36: 150–67.

Lazarus, M. (1851) "Heber den Begriff und die Moeglichkeit einer Völkerpsychologie," *Deutsches Museum*, 1(2): 112–26.

—— (1865) "Einige synthetische Gedanken zur Völkerpsychologie und Sprachwissenschaft," *Zeitschrift für Völkerpsychologie*, 3: 1–94.

Lazarus, M. and Steinthal, H. (1860) "Einleitende Gedanken über Völkerpsychologie," *Zeitschrift für Völkerpsychologie und Sprachwissenschaft*, 1: 1–73.

Lerner, R. M. (1989) "Developmental contextualism and the life-span view of person–context interaction," in M. Bornstein and J. S. Bruner (eds) *Interaction in human development*, Hillsdale, NJ: Erlbaum.

Lerner, R. M. and Busch-Rossnagel, N. A. (eds) (1981) *Individuals as producers of their development. A life-span perspective*, New York: Academic Press.

Levine, D. N. (ed.) (1971) *Georg Simmel on sociability and social forms*, Chicago: Chicago University Press.

Lévi-Strauss, C. (1967) *Structural anthropology*, Garden City, NY: Anchor Books.

Lewin, K. (1943) "Defining the field at a given time," *Psychological Review*, 50: 292–310.

Lohmann, G. (1993) "The ambivalence of indifference in modern society. Marx and Simmel," in L. Widding and M. Waerness (eds) *Individuality and modernity. Georg Simmel and modern culture*, Bergen: Sociology Press Bergen.

Lukács, G. (1991) "Georg Simmel," *Theory, Culture, and Society*, 8: 145–50.

Marcia, J. E. (1989) "Identity diffussion differentiated," in M. A. Luszez and T. Netterbeck (eds) *Psychological development across the life-span*, North-Holland: Elsevier.

Marcia, J. E., Waterman, A. S., Matteson, D. R., Archer, S. L. and Orlofsky, J. L. (eds) (1993) *Ego identity: a handbook for psychosocial research*, New York: Springer.

Markus, H. R. and Kitayama, S. (1991) "Culture and the self: implications for cognition, emotion, and motivation," *Psychological Review*, 98: 224–53.

Maslow, A. H. (1968) *Toward a psychology of being*, Princeton, NJ: Van Nostarnd.

Mead, G. H. (1934) *Mind, self, and society*, Chicago, Ill: University of Chicago Press.

Miles, S. (1996) "The cultural capital of consumption: understanding "postmodern' identities in a cultural context," *Culture & Psychology*, 2: 139–58.

Mitscherlich, M. (1984) "Die Bedeutung des Übergangsobjektes für die Entfaltung des Kindes," in C. Eggers (ed.) *Bindungen und Besitzdenken beim Kleinkind*, Munich: Urban and Schwarzenberg.

Moore, G. (1987) "Environment and behavior research in North America: History, developments, and unresolved issues," in D. Stokols and I. Altman (eds) *Handbook of environmental psychology*, New York: Wiley.

Muchow, M. and Muchow, H. (1935) *Der Lebensraum des Großstadtkindes*, Hamburg: Martin Riegel.

Munroe, R. L. and Munroe, R. H. (1971) "Effect of environmental experience on spatial ability in an east African society," *Journal of Social Psychology*, 83: 15–22.

Nedelmann, B. (1990) "On the concept of 'Erleben' in Georg Simmel's sociology," in M. Kearn, B. S. Phillips and R. S. Cohen (eds), *Georg Simmel and contemporary sociology*, Boston: Kluwer.

—— (1991) "Individualization, exaggeration and paralyzation: Simmel's three problems of culture," *Theory, Culture & Society*, 8: 169–93.

Nuttin, J. M. (1987) "Affective consequences of mere ownership: the name letter effect in twelve European countries," *European Journal of Social Psychology*, 17: 381–402.

Oerter, R. (1991) "Self–object relation as a basis of human development," in L. Oppenheimer and J. Valsiner (eds), *The origins of action*, New York: Springer.

—— (1998) "Transactionalism," in D. Goerlitz, H. J. Harloff, G. Mey and J. Valsiner (eds) *Children, cities, and psychological theories: developing relationships*, Berlin: de Gruyter.

Orlofsky, J. L., Marcia, J. E. and Lesser, I. M. (1973) "Ego identity status and the intimacy versus isolation crisis of young adulthood," *Journal of Personality and Social Psychology*, 27: 211–19.

Osgood, C. E. (1964) "Semantic differential technique in the contemporary study of cultures," *American Anthropology*, 66: 171–200.

Overton, W. F. (1998) "Relational-developmental theory: a psychological perspective," in D. Goerlitz, H. J. Harloff, G. Mey and J. Valsiner (eds) *Children, cities, and psychological theories: developing relationships*, Berlin: de Gruyter.

Paetzold, H. (1997) "Die symbolische Ordnung der Kultur," in D. Frede and R. Schmücker (eds) *Ernst Cassirers Werk and Wirkung*, Darmstadt: Wissenschaftliche Buchgesellschaft.

Peirce, C. S. (1931–1935) *The collected works of Charles Sanders Peirce*, vols 1–6, C. Harthshorne and P. Weiss (eds), Cambridge, MA: Harvard University Press.

Penuel, W. R. and Wertsch, J. V. (1995) "Dynamics of negotiation in the identity politics of cultural other and cultural self," *Culture & Psychology*, 1: 343–59.

Piaget, J. (1970) "Piaget's theory," in P. H. Mussen (ed.), *Carmichael's manual of child psychology*, vol. 1, 3rd edn, New York: Wiley.

Plomin, R. and McClearn, G. E. (eds) (1993) *Nature, nurture, and psychology*, Washington, DC: APA.

Posner, R. (1989) "What is culture? Toward a semiotic explication of anthropological concepts," in W. A. Koch (ed.), *The nature of culture*, Bochum: Brockmeyer.

Proshansky, H. M., Fabian, A. K. and Kaminoff, R. (1983) "Place-identity: physical world socialization of the self," *Journal of Environmental Psychology*, 3: 57–83.

Quaiser-Pohl, C. and Lehmann, W. (2002) "Girls' spatial abilities—charting the contributions of experience and attitudes in different academic groups," *British Journal of Educational Psychology*, 72: 245–60.

Ramsey, P. G. (1987) "Possession disputes in preschool classrooms," *Child Study Journal*, 16: 173–81.

Rapaport, A. (1968) "A philosophical view," in J. H. Milsum (ed.) *Positive feedback*, Oxford: Pergamon Press.

Resnick, M. (1998) "Technologies for the lifelong kindergarten," *Educational Technology Research and Development*, 46: 43–55.

Rochberg-Halton, E. (1984) "Object relations, role models, and cultivation of the self," *Environment and Behavior*, 16: 335–68.

—— (1986) *Meaning and modernity*, Chicago: University of Chicago Press.

Rogoff, B. (1993) "Children's guided participation and participatory appropriation in sociocultural activity," in R. H. Wozniak and K. W. Fischer (eds) *Development in context*, Hillsdale, NJ: Erlbaum.

Salomon, A. (1943) "Simmel Georg," in I. Landman (ed.) *Universal Jewish Encyclopedia*, New York: Universal Jewish Encyclopedia.

Sameroff, A. (1983) "Developmental systems: contexts and evolution," in P. H. Mussen (ed.), *Handbook of child psychology*, New York: Wiley.

Sameroff, A. J. and Suomi, S. J. (1996) "Primates and persons: a comparative developmental understanding of social organization," in R. B. Cairns, G. H. Elder and E. J. Costello (eds) *Developmental science*, New York: Cambridge University Press.

Sartre, J.-P. (1956) *Being and nothingness*, New York: Philosophical Library.

Schoggen, P. (1989) *Behavior settings: a revision of Barker's ecological psychology*, Stanford, CA: Stanford University Press.

Sennett, R. (1990) *The consciousness of the eye*, New York: Knopf.

Shore, B. (1996) *Culture in mind. Cognition, culture, and the problem of meaning*, New York: Oxford University Press.

Shweder, R. A. (1991) *Thinking through cultures*, Cambridge, MA: Harvard University Press.

Shweder, R. A., Goodnow, J., Hatano, G., LeVine, R. A., Markus, H. and Miller, P. (1998) "The cultural psychology of development: one mind, many mentalities," in R. M. Lerner (ed.), *Handbook of child psychology*, vol. 1, New York: Wiley.

Shweder, R. A. and Sullivan, M. A. (1990) "The semiotic subject of cultural psychology," in L. Pervin (ed.) *Handbook of personality: theory and research*, New York: Guilford.

Silbereisen, R. K., Eyferth, K. and Rudinger, G. (eds) (1986a) *Development as action in context*, New York, Berlin: Springer.

Silbereisen, R. K., Noack, P. and Eyferth, K. (1986b) "Places for development: adolescents, leisure settings, and developmental tasks," in R. K. Silbereisen, K. Eyferth and G. Rudinger (eds) *Development as action in context*, New York, Berlin: Springer.

Simmel, G. (1890) "Über social Differenzierung," *Staats- und Socialwissenschaftliche Forschungen*, 10, whole issue.

—— (1893) *Einleitung in die Moralwissenschaft*, Berlin: Göschen.

—— (1895) "The problem of sociology," *Annals of the American Academy of Political and Social Science*, 6: 52–63.

—— (1903) "Die Grossstädte und das Geistesleben," in G. Simmel (ed.) *Das Individuum und die Freiheit, Essays*, Berlin: Wagenbach.

—— (1908a) "Vom Wesen der Kultur," *Oesterreichische Rundschau*, 15: 36–42.

—— (1908b) Das Problem des Stiles. *Dekorative Kunst*, 16: 307–16, trans. M. Ritter as "The problem of style," *Theory, Culture & Society*, 8: 63–71.

—— (1911) *Philosophische Kultur*, Leipzig: Kröner.

—— (1911/12) "Der Begriff und die Tragödie der Kultur," *Logos*, 2: 1–25.

—— (1918) *Der Konflikt der modernen Kultur*, Leipzig: Duncker & Humblodt.

—— (1918) *Lebensanschauungen*, Leipzig: Barth.

—— (1950) "The metropolis and mental life," in K. M. Wolff (ed.) *The sociology of Georg Simmel*, Glencoe, IL: Free Press.

—— (1968) *The conflict in modern culture and other essays*, trans. K. P. Etzkovu, New York: Teacher's College Press.

Simmel, G. (1971) *On individuality and social forms*, Donald N. Levine (ed.), Chicago, IL: The University of Chicago Press.

—— (1990) *The philosophy of money*, 2nd edn, London: Routledge,

Simon, H. (1957) *Models of man*, New York: Wiley.

Smith, W. D. (1991) *Politics and sciences of culture in Germany, 1840–1920*, Oxford, New York: Oxford University Press.

Spykman, N. J. (1964) *The social theory of Georg Simmel*, New York: Russell & Russell.

Sonik (1998) "Style, technique, and cultural piracy: never bite the hand that feeds," http://www.graffiti.org./faq/sonik.html (accessed November 1998).

Stanjek, K. (1980) *Die Entwicklung des menschlichen Besitzverhaltens*, Berlin: MPI.

Stern, W. (1938) *General psychology: from a personalistic standpoint*, New York: Macmillan.

Stetsenko, A. and Arievitch, I. (1997) "Constructing and deconstructing the self: comparing post-Vygotskian and discourse-based versions of social constructivism," *Mind, Culture, and Activity*, 4: 159–72.

Stokols, D. and Shumaker, S. A. (1981) "People in places: a transactional view of settings," in J. H. Harvey (ed.) *Cognition, social behavior, and the environment*, Hillsdale, NJ: Erlbaum.

Sykes, J. B. (ed.) (1982) *The Concise Oxford Dictionary*, 7th edn. Oxford: Oxford University Press.

Sztompka, P. (1986) *Robert K. Merton: an intellectual profile*, London: Macmillan.

Turkle, S. (1984) *The second self*, New York: Simon & Schuster.

—— (1995) *Life on the screen: identity in the age of the internet*, London: Weidenfeld & Nicolson.

Vaihinger, H. (1911) *Die Philosphie des Als-Ob*, Leipzig: Meiner, English version, *The philosophy of "As-If,"* New York: Barnes and Noble, 1935.

Valsiner, J. (1997) *Culture and the development of children's action: a theory of human development*, New York: Wiley.

—— (1998) *The guided mind*, Cambridge, MA: Harvard University Press.

—— (2000) *Culture and human development*, London: Sage.

—— (2001) "Process structure of semiotic mediation in human development," *Human Development*, 44: 84–97.

Valsiner, J. and Winegar, L. T. (1992) "Introduction: a cultural-historical context for social context," in L. T. Winegar and J. Valsiner (eds) *Children's development within social context*, vol. 1, Hillsdale, NJ: Lawrence Erlbaum.

Van der Veer, R. (1996) "The concept of culture in Vygotsky's thinking," *Culture & Psychology*, 2: 247–63.

Van der Veer, R. and Valsiner, J. (1991) *Understanding Vygotsky. A quest for synthesis*, Oxford: Blackwell.

Vygotsky, L. S. (1929) "The problem of the cultural development of the child," *Journal of Genetic Psychology*, 36: 415–34.

—— (1978) *Mind in society: the development of higher psychological processes*, Cambridge, MA: Harvard University Press.

—— (1981) "The genesis of higher mental functions," in J. V. Wertsch (ed.) *The concept of activity in Soviet psychology*, Armonk, NY: Sharpe.

—— (1986) *Thought and language*, 2nd edn, Cambridge, MA: MIT Press.

Wagner, H. R. (ed.) (1970) *Alfred Schuetz: on phenomenology and social relations*, Chicago, IL: University of Chicago Press.

Wapner, S. (1998) "A holistic, developmental, system-oriented perspective: child-environment relations," in D. Goerlitz, H. J. Harloff, G. Mey and J. Valsiner (eds) *Children, cities, and psychological theories: developing relationships*, Berlin: de Gruyter.

Waterman, A. S. (1990) "Personal expressiveness: philosophical and psychological functioning," in G. R. Adams, T. P. Gullotta and R. Montemayor (eds) *Adolescent identity formation: advances in adolescent development*, Newbury Park, CA: Sage.

Webley, P. (1981) "Sex differences in home range and cognitive maps in eight-year-old children," *Journal of Environmental Psychology*, 1: 293–302.

Weinstein, C. S. and David, T. G. (eds) (1987) *Spaces for children*, London: Plenum.

Werner, C. and Altman, I. (1998) "A dialectical/transactional framework of social relations: children in secondary territories," in D. Goerlitz, H. J. Harloff, G. Mey and J. Valsiner (eds) *Children, cities, and psychological theories: developing relationships*, Berlin: de Gruyter.

Werner, H. (1957) "The concept of development from a comparative and organismic point of view," in D. B. Harris (ed.) *The concept of development*, Minneapolis, MI: University of Minnesota Press.

Wertsch, J. V. (1991) *Voices of the mind: a sociocultural approach to mediated action*, London: Harvester Wheatsheaf.

—— (1998) *Mind as action*, New York: Oxford University Press.

Wicker, A. W. (1987) "Behavior settings reconsidered: temporal stages, resources, internal dynamics, context," in D. Stokols and I. Altman (eds) *Handbook of environmental psychology*, New York: Wiley.

Wicker, A. W. and King, J. C. (1988) "Life cycles of behavior settings," in J. McGrath (ed.) *The social psychology of time*, Beverly Hills, CA: Sage.

Wicklund, R. A. and Gollwitzer, P. M. (1982) *Symbolic self-completion*, Hillsdale, NJ: Erlbaum.

Winnicott, D. W. (1953) "Transitional objects and transitional phenomena: a study of the first not-me possession," *International Journal of Psycho-Analysis*, 24: 89–97.

—— (1971) *Playing and reality*, London: Tavistock.

Wohlwill, J. F. (1985) "Martha Muchow, 1892–1933: her life, work, and contribution to developmental and ecological psychology," *Human Development*, 28: 198–224.

Wohlwill, J. F. and Heft, H. (1987) "The physical environment and the development of the child," in D. Stokols and I. Altman (eds) *Handbook of environmental psychology*, New York: Wiley.

Wolff, K. (1950) *The sociology of Georg Simmel*, Glencoe, IL: Free Press.

Wölfing, S. (1996) "The use of identity-relevant functions of things and places in the context of migration," *Swiss Journal of Psychology*, 55: 241–48.

Worthman, C. M. (1993) "Bio-cultural interactions in human development," in M. E. Pereira and L. A. Fairbanks (eds) *Juvenile primates: life history, development and behavior*, New York: Oxford University Press.

Wright, H. F. (1967) *Recording and analyzing child behavior*, New York: Harper & Row.

Wundt, W. (1886) "Ueber Ziele und Wege der Völkerpsychologie," *Philosophische Studien*, 4: 1–27.

—— (1912) *Elements of folk pschology: outlines of a psychological history of the development of mankind*, London: Allen.

Zinchenko, V. P. (2000) "The thought and world of Gustav Shep (return from exile)," *Journal of Russian and East European Psychology*, 38: 4 and 5.

Index